My Sister's Veil

My Sister's Veil

K.C. Marshall

Library of Congress Control Number: 2008901815
ISBN: Hardcover 978-1-4363-2569-1
Softcover 978-1-4363-2568-4

This book was printed in the United States of America.

To order additional copies of this book, contact:
Xlibris Corporation
1-888-795-4274
www.Xlibris.com
Orders@Xlibris.com
47407

Contents

Whittenhall's Story

It was the year of our Lord, eighteen hundred and forty seven. Deep in the bush of Quidad, Africa; myself, Lord Quinton Gale Whittenhall, and my crew of men caught sight of what would turn out to be a most gruesome ritual.

I was a vibrant healthy forty three year old man with a crew of thirty five brazen, healthy comrades. Their health and ravenous attitude was all that mattered to me, for it was a great feat to survive this voyage. They ranged in age from sixteen to thirty something years old. Fortunately, many of them had survived this trip, and I counted it a success.

I learned the hardships of slave trading through torturous trials and errors. This was my fourth venture to West Africa, and only the second to land at my destination. Each trip had cost more money, desire, and lives than I had bargained for. The ocean itself was an unforgiving opponent. Storms, shifting tides, and unpaid Gods of the sea, exacted the highest toll. More than two dozen of my men were lost to it alone on this trip. Lack of water, food stuffs and jungle diseases claimed another dozen or so. On my second venture, four of my remaining men dropped with raging fever, within fifty kilometers of shore, and later died. I had to pay dearly for that journey, for neither did most of my slaves survive, but the youngest son of my brother also succumbed. That loss cost me my awaited inheritance. I had however, acquired on my own, through unlawful, backroom dealings, enough wealth to substantially indulge all of my perverted whelms.

Many ones tell me, that I am not at all the mannerly British Lord one would suppose, considering my lineage. I've been referred to as a hostile, brut, swearing atheist. I wouldn't solidly deny that description, however, I simply had love for neither heaven nor hell. I'd allowed nothing or no one ever dear enough to my heart, to break it, at least up to that point.

I set out to explore and conquer the Dark Continent. I had acquired three hundred native Benin slaves, on this journey, and sent them packed and sailing on their way with what I believed to be the weaker half of my men. For now the others and I remained in the bush, solely for collecting and adventure. Even though we were quite unfamiliar with this land, I wanted to claim on this journey a personal victory.

Plowing through the marsh and swamp was a test in itself, but tales of riches unappraised, drove us deeper than we had realized. We decided it would be cleaver to mark our trail, and synchronize our time pieces, even though we were in arms reach of one another. We backpacked ropes, poison darts, guns, and gallons of water, which had now dwindled to a precious few, due to the scorching heat of high noon. I knew that one wrong turn or the cloak of night would likely cost us our lives. We did however, risk it all peering through the thick bush. We watched with palpitating chest, and parched mouths. Sweat rolled constantly from our brows. The stench and the heat rose with the deafening beating of the drums. We were so completely spellbound by the precision and dedication of the sight before us, that we were totally oblivious to our own impending seize and capture.

We knew little of the ritual we were about to witness. It appeared some tribal rite of passage, from girlhood into Amazon Warrior. I'd say it was an austere, rigid commitment to say the least. I felt myself groan as I examined the fine specimen of women. They looked like giants, each one of them well over six feet tall. Actually the fact that they were heathenly bare to their waist, was the only clue, that they were women. With one dangling breast at the top of their chests, the legend was that these women cut off their right breast in order to better butt their guns up against them. It was a perfectly amusing auspices. They stood perfectly erect on stilt-like muscular legs. Their faces were as chiseled of stone and they were single-minded. They were black as midnight, with eyes fierce like hungry beast.

Each of them was bare to the waist which skirted only a small loin cloth. Attached to their cloth, they wore a thin metal belt, from which hung remnants of vicious battles. Bear's claws and lion's teeth, not to mention human skulls; probably those of males, since there hadn't been one spotted for at least a hundred kilometers, all adorned their hipbone. Humph just think what a hefty price we'd get per head for one of those I sneered. Probably more than for two Benin male slaves, my companion quipped.

There seemed the strangest phenomenon about these women. Somehow their nudity was almost invisible, after the first glance or two. There was either some kind of force field or their commanding blackness that cloaked them. Our curiosity grew as the women suddenly began to yelp like wild dogs, and the thunderous drums sent vibrations to the center of the earth. The women marched, and skipped around a campfire, encircling a woman that stood out from the rest. She was fully draped in purple and scarlet cloth. She wore a three-tiered beaded collar around her neck, and headdress that ended in tall spikes of some sort. Had I not known better; I would have sworn she was actually standing in the fire. Apparently the chief priestess, she danced separately from the others as they adorned her with oils and a wealth of medicinal leaves from nearby greenery. Her movements were almost balletic, with a certain spiritual overture. Suddenly, things grew still, and quiet. With the leaves on the trees and bushes still trembling; the quiet compelled creatures of every sense and size, to peek. Then the chief priestess flung open her robe to reveal a girdle full of arsenal. Huge, shiny knives, razors and well-fashioned stabbing spears hung ornately around her waist. She fell to her knees, with her face raised to the fleeting sun, and her arms stretched over her head. She chanted something, then rose to her feet again. Walking over to the fire, she poured an accelerant on it, and it shot violently up to the treetops. She selected a huge machete from her arsenal and pitched it into the fire. Ushered forth was a young girl, whose years numbered no more than fourteen. She too was bare-chested. From the waist down she was wrapped like a mermaid, barely able to walk. Her arms were wrapped behind her from the elbow to the wrist in the same gauzy white cloth, inmate style. The chief priestess poured oils upon her head and danced around her ceremoniously. She then saturated her right breast with a variety of the oils she had been presented. Ah ha ranted Allenmeir, my companion, they're bloody dikes. We laughed and quickly turned our attention back to the women. The chief priestess then snatched the machete out of the fire with her bare hand, while the other tightly cupped the young woman's breast. In the blink of an eye she struck the child with the scorching hot machete. The child let out a blood curdling scream that was joined unanimously by the yelping and hollering of the other women. Me and my companions gasped simultaneously, and stretched our eyes in disbelief. The noise was temporarily blinding as well as paralyzing. The other women rushed to her, padding her with the medicinal leaves and wrapping her breast with cloth. Surprisingly, there was precious little bloodshed. The high priestess continued the ceremony by yelping some sort of song and dance. She then discarded the breast, pitching it into the fire. She then carefully selected some of the arsenal from her girdle, including the bloody machete and approached the victim. "Now what, her head" quipped Allenmier suspiciously. The men snickered under their breath. The young woman was now robbed and seated upright. With some copper bands around her arms and feet which had been loosed, a gold band around her head, the priestess presented the arsenal to the young woman. Upon receiving the arsenal the young woman bowed to the priestess and forced a grimaced smile. The ceremony concluded with a showering of flowers and leaves upon the young woman's head, and the tribe dancing around her, gleefully presenting their individual gifts of arsenal and food.

Darkness fell from nowhere. My partners and I scurried to shake off our mesmerized states. We had totally lost track of the time. We knew we were in eminent danger. As we stumbled through the night we wrestled back our swelling fears. The bush was merciless at night. We had cleverly left an embedded rock trail, but there was not even a glimmer of light. Even the light of the moon forsook this thick, deep bush and jungle. Every untamed beast was lurking about. The dung in the ditches were said to have anaconda twice as long as the nearby trees. I felt my chest pounding, and was afraid it could be heard, if not by the nearby Amazon tribe, then by beast. Was there any difference; I took a moment to humor myself. Our flashlights barely cast enough light to see the ground under our feet, which we watched desperately. We were frantic. There was no way we could have expected those tall black structures which suddenly appeared before us. We first thought we had simply all bumped into the same Poisonwood tree. Hardly such luck! Looking up at the structures caused us all to freeze in our tracks, and grapple for breath. There were tall thin figures moving about us. At first glance, we thought they to be demons or some sort of apparitions, since they were so perfectly silent. I stood paralyzed and awestruck watching the movement of the black figures until I realized, it's them! The same retched heathen winches! The women worked quickly, and thoroughly. It was clear they were tactically trained. They had seized and restrained each of us before we could put up any worthwhile resistance. They worked in complete silence, but never as much as tugged in opposite directions. They had stripped us down to our drawers. Our legs were bound together from the hipbone to the knee. The rope was then wrapped around our arms, from the elbow to the wrist, forming a loop. We were then dragged by the loop face down. They could have just as easily carried us like luggage, which is what we felt like when we were thrown into a tiny shanty like structure.

The shanty must have been an outhouse. In fact there was a loose board on the floor that was hollow underneath. The four of us barley fit. The blackness inside the narrow shanty bought on bitter weeping and howling. We were certain the heat would kill us by day break since we were stripped of all our belongings including water canteens. I was more miserable than I had ever been in my life. But I privately vowed to survive whatever those black witches dished out; and for good measure, to take a couple of them home with me, alive. But the night was more than an equitable challenge. I would have sworn, there were a number of wild beast surrounding us at any time, all smelling a foreign entrée.

As dawn squeezed through the small gaps in the rickety shack, we could for the first time in hours see one another. At first glance I knew that Allenmier, and some of the others, didn't survive. So focused as we were on our survival, we never spoke of their death among the remaining ones of us. The heat began to rise again. That was our only measure of time. The women either ignored or forgot us, as they went about their normal routines. I'd frequently catch glimpses or shadows as they passed by the little hut. I estimated it must have been around four o'clock the following evening, when the door was snatched open. We were pulled out face down, and dragged approximately ten meters or so. The mud and the dung from the murky soil splattered in our faces and mouths. They stood us upright in the center of them. There must have been upwards of a hundred of them, and now only three of us. We were equally bare, as we stood next to their heathen black bodies, in only our drawers.

One Amazon stepped forward and spoke to us in a rough snappy voice. She towered over us by at least a foot or so. We stood completely silent, but not still. We had not the strength to stand still. Our weariness caused us to sway and fidget unintentionally. She repeated herself in a louder, rougher yelping squeal, stepping even closer to us. Her small yellowish eyes roved around between the three of us, waiting impatiently for a response, to her completely untranslated words. Again we said nothing. She raised her long powerful arm and back-handed Dracenkal across the face. Blood flung from the side of his head, which immediately ballooned outward to twice its' size. You stinkin' bitch, he screamed in a raging, trembling voice stumbling to his feet. She proceeded to abuse him in the worst way. The other women looked on casually and even slightly bored. He was completely unrecognizable when she drug him away. We didn't know if he was dead or alive. We never saw Dracenkal again. The rest of the women stood glaring at us. Hemmithorne fell to the ground involuntarily. What do you want? What do you want? My God what do you want, he asked whimpering and pleading like a child. A woman stepped forward with a quizzical expression on her face. She watched Hemmithorne's mouth move as if to read his lips. She snapped instructions in a harsh tone. In disbelief I stumbled forward. She was speaking a broken dialect of French and Portuguese that I had learned trading in Morocco. A reply rolled off my lips. She stepped right in front of me, looking down on me almost sympathetically. She spoke slowly and deliberately, without blinking. Yes, yes I frothed quickly, my mouth dry and hard to move. She barked rapidly. I took a single step back, and threw my head back, looking up to her towering face. Her dialect was impressive but not impeccable. I didn't believe my ears. I studied her expression. She was solid as a rock. The strangest of thoughts occurred to me as I struggled with the right response. The legend said that these Amazon sisters were born with a transparent veil over their eyes. The closest translation stated that this meant that these women were able to see all things, including those of an invisible realm. I wondered as I tried to hurry my response, if she could see straight through my plotting thoughts. I agree squeezed through my buckled throat. She unequivocally had asked me for guns and vessels. This request sent chills up my spine. A hundred questions raced through my head as I stood there contemplating how to bargain with her. This warrior regiment was in no way trustworthy. If I gave them my guns and transportation what the hell would they do to me. I tried to think quickly, but my bones shuttered. I despised the racing fear these warrior sluts commanded in me. I will cooperate with you, if you spare our lives, I rambled off, thanking my undying wit even as I spoke. She stepped back, turned on one foot and walked away from my remaining army of two. The women huddled for several minutes reverting to their choppy, yelping, native tongue. Afterward the same woman returned with a plate of food, and a jug of water. They loosed us rapidly, and placed a guard over us. I drank savagely. The water was lukewarm, but Hemmithorne and I fought over it. The food didn't resemble anything I had ever seen before in my life. The village people of Dahomey frequently ate chicken, goat and swine. But they were somewhat civilized, I reasoned silently. This group of heathens could probably stomach anything I imagined studying the plate. In any case, I forced myself to eat the horrid slop, with hopes of gaining strength to work through this deal I proposed. The women continued to huddle all while we ate. They had moved somewhat out of sight. Later, two of them returned, rebound us and threw us back into the shanty. I was totally flabbergasted. I was livid, cursing the retched whores under my breath. I didn't dare holler out loud, but I trembled at their betrayal.

It turned out to be another two days, almost to the exact hour, before we saw daylight again. But we had been served food and water twice a day, this time. Hemmithorne had become ill over this two day enslavement. He puked his living guts out all day long. He was raqing with fever, and it looked as if his life was slipping away. The stench from the puke wrung my stomach in knots. I pasted my face up against a small crack in the rotting wall boards. Gasping in short wisps of fresh air had been my only means of survival. And I was dammed determined to survive, someway, somehow. I explained the deal I had made to Hemmithorne. I couldn't imagine what had gone wrong. I didn't have a clue how long we would have to suffer this enslavement.

As I was plotting a fantastical escape, the door was yanked open. It was two different women this time, who drug us out of the hut face down, to the same spot. It wasn't easy to tell the women apart. They certainly all looked alike. I could identify a couple of distinguishing marks, starting with their head crowns. They did vary in height. They also arranged their arsenal differently, suggesting some type of order or perhaps hierarchy. I was about to speak up, when she nudged her way through the crowd. I cried out before I realized it. I actually was crying and reached out to grab her hand. I pulled her toward me and pressed her hand to my heart. In loss, I fell to my knees sobbing. My translator, where have you been, I repeated in my best translation of the tongue. She easily pulled me to my feet. She explained politely that she and some of her sisters had to go to the village to make deals with the king of that village. This king apparently owned their land and they had a covenant with him to protect it. In return they provided enforcement for him, and were quite dedicated to him. Her voice had an unexpected softness to it. She stood over me placing my face directly level with her one good, firm, rounded tit. I laid my head against her chest, like a child in need of nurturing. I've no idea what made me do such a fool hearty thing. Either she was affecting me in a strange way, or this imprisonment had gotten the better of me. I jumped back and quickly begged her pardon as best I could. She looked deeply into my eyes. Her eyes were light and soft, and clear. For a split second, the veil lifted from her eyes, and I could see the misty shadow of a majestic, regal, yet fragile woman. It was as if we were the only two standing there. The other women had disappeared. I wanted to say, you're beautiful, please come home with me, but I didn't dare challenge her integrity to the sisterhood. I was about to express a somewhat vaguer version of these sentiments, when another woman stepped up and whispered something in her ear. To my regret, the spell was broken. She instantly restructured into her warrior status. She instructed me to draw a map showing where we had banked our vessels. Her voice remained somewhat softer than usual, but the veil was again covering her, body and soul. She explained to me that they were going to take us to the river and we were to turn over our trades at that time. She called a command to the other women, and someone promptly returned with our clothing. They cut off our bounds and watched us dress. I breathed a sigh of relief, just to separate my limbs and see my own clothes. Hemmithorne felt better but was still very weak. He dressed himself very slowly, and guzzled all of his water when we were handed our canteens. There were approximately a dozen of the armed women escorting us out of the village. I knew this would be our only chance of escape. I was able to chat with the translator as we walked. She questioned me about my vessels and arsenal. I was careful about what I said. Again I had to thank my gifted wit. I drew the map approximately a kilometer east of the third and smallest vessel. There was plenty of room in that vessel for the two of us, but we had greedily bought three vessels to carry back all of the treasures we had planned to obscure. As we neared the banks of the Aboney River, the women instructed Hemmithorne and I to walk single file and hold hands. This was a fortunate turn of events, since it allowed us to speak to one another through hand signals. When we arrived at the banks, there sat the two larger vessels. I directed the translator to the second larger vessel, a few yards west of our spot. I informed her of its' secret compartments hiding guns and ammunition. The bulk of them headed for the other vessel. We were left outside the smaller vessel with one guard. The other women called to her frequently, and held the guns up in the air for her to see. They were so excited and impressed they for the first time lost their focus. Hemmithorne and I agreed to make a break for it and run toward the southern end of the bank where we had stashed the smallest vessel. When one of her sisters called her away for a moment, it was the perfect time. She was totally engulfed with the weapons.

We first started in tiny side steps, then larger ones. Then we broke all out into our fleet. We darted back into the bush and trees. Only one of the women spotted us and only caught a glimpse of our dash. She hollered to the others and immediately the forces were launched after us. They scrambled to load the guns. We had only a few seconds jump ahead of them, and we knew they were athletically superior to us. We somehow beat them to the south bank and jumped into the river. I swam to the third vessel. Hemmithorne, who was still back on the shore, broke and ran toward the south end of the bank. I heard them loading the guns and shooting into the water. It was impossible to see through that muddy stink hole of a river. I didn't come up for air the four feet I had to swim. I was able to drag the dingy from under the brush with fairly little trouble. I paddled in the opposite direction of the women. I got a chance to break while they were trying to push the vessels, and run down the river banks after Hemmithorne. I was just beginning to glide, when someone grabbed the edge of the boat. I gasped. It was Hemmithorne. With one of the women holding on to his leg, he scrambled to pull himself onto the boat. It was her, my translator, hanging on to Hemmithorne with all her might. She was pulling with all her strength and was able to slow the vessel. She began to pull herself on board. I scooted toward the back of the boat and anchored myself. I felt a surge of rage and energy as deep as the river, well up in me. I swung my leg to kick her in the head. I never knew what hit me. I only recall seeing a shiny flash of light thundering downward. It was as swift as lightning, and I to this day believe I saw a strike of lightning at the same time. She had drawn her machete, and took off my leg. I let out a scream that pierced straight through the heavens.

The current shifted and caused the boat to tip. She fell backward pulling Hemmithorne in the water with her. She panicked as if she were drowning. I then realized the others were afraid of the water as well. I pulled the orrs with all my might, with the current on my side. From the distance of three miles and dimming light, the screams and howls of Hemmithorne blurred my vision. I wouldn't let myself imagine what they were doing to him.

Sheer determination got me through the trip home. I fell unconscious many times, waking up drifting in the middle of nowhere. I was pulled from my vessel semi-conscious, by a group of slave traders west of the coast of the British Isles. They procured my safe return home.

A long recuperation ensued. Six weeks hospitalization, and eighteen months in-home convalescence put me through all levels of recovery. That is everything except my heart. It took another year to rebuild a working fragment of my manhood. I had a myriad of nurses and aides at my disposal. I'd only allow them to stay an hour at a time. My family had disowned me by this time and took no bother to see after me. All the better. I sorely feared that anyone witnessing my sudden bursts of anger, trembling and wailing; would presume me fit only for institutional life.

I spent my whole recuperation preoccupied with seeing Africa and her riches again. I studied maps of Dahomey and its' surrounding villages continually. As much as I tried to deny it, I couldn't rest until I saw the ruthless tribune once more, especially the translator. I was certainly a changed man, but I couldn't live with this damming defeat hanging over my head.

It took three full years and better, but mustering the courage to face my fears, I gathered a crew of men and vessels. I gathered a group of the most immoral racists I could find on short notice. They were a wreckless, debased, heinous klan. Overpowering in stature, all of them stood upwards of six feet five inches. They were dirty and unkept, hellish and hungry. I lorded it over them by enticing their greed, the only moral sense they claimed. I told continual tales of gold nuggets as big as their clad fists, all while we travelled. Diamonds as brilliant and plentiful as the glassy waters of the Nelvilla Sea, lay just beneath the thick soil. They yearned to get their hands on the guardsmen of their soon to be fortunes. Take your fill I commanded so long as you bring me the head of the chief priestess on a slab of marble. I'd roar with laughter on the outside, but shuttered faintly on the inside. I went on with tales of guardsmen so fierce they'd butt their heads against trees for sport. One brawny brut got so anxious, he commenced punching the side of the vessel. No no no I pleaded, save your strength for them. Damned idiot. Besides, I sadly enough had to explain, a hole in the vessel would cause it to sink. We'd have to leave so much of our fortune behind. Of brains, they were lacking.

When we reached the Ivory Coast, we docked three miles west of the village. That gave us enough distance to enter at the western-most back end of the village. Each morning at the break of dawn, we entered the village in small groups. We slept and ate in shifts. Heavily camouflaged and heavily armed we'd track further inward, familiarizing and routing trails for ourselves. It was clear these were not well travelled paths, yet they lay open to any ferocious man-eating beast. By the end of the eighth day, we had all but stepped foot in the mouth of the beast, and still no treasures. Though they tried not to show it, the men flinched at the smallest creak or crack. They'd flex their muscles to stiffen their confidence, but it was not a convincing show. On the ninth day, the men set out at dawn as routine as it had become. We used our south central route and reached its' end quickly. Instructing them to add an eastern sub-route to it; we stumbled upon an ambiguous clearing. There was a strange air about it, yet it was irresistibly inviting. Although the back end was wooded, there was a narrow trail heading into it. There was a dim glow from within the woods. The front of the landing seemed to offer a primitive lounge, with purposely placed boulders for resting. I snickered to myself. This damned jungle has completely distorted my vision. I was apparently longing for the comforts of home. We were unwisely drawn to investigate.

As we entered into the lounge, we could see a cemetery in the distance. We were undaunted. We had no respect for their dead. The closer we got to the graveyard, the more curious we became. I had to stop and study the decorative black veils which hung over each tomb. As I reached to touch the veil, portions of the legend came to my mind. It is believed, by these heathens, that each time a veil is lifted, and Amazon Warrior is awakened from her sleep. She then either blesses or curses, at her own discretion, the one that disturbed her eternal rest. I tore off the veil in my hand, out of sheer repulsion, and immediately felt a freezing wind blow on me from behind. Without realizing it I jumped and turned to see no one there. While my face was sweating profusely, from the scorching heat, the back of my neck had goose bumps. Ridiculous I mumbled to myself and forced a brave face with a long shaky breath.

I motioned my men to continue onward. Before we had traced six feet inward, we stumbled upon the treasure of the Gods sitting openly in a chest. It was surrounded by what appeared to be a sacred altar. It was adorned with the finest of the finest gold, silver, and copper, which we now knew had created the warm, inviting glow. Four statuesque figures stood post at each corner of the chest. The figures were absolutely exquisite. They had to have stood at least twenty feet tall. They were solid granite with the most brilliant marquise-shaped, diamond eyes. The diamond eyes could actually blind one if he stared too long. Their bodies were strangely enough those of male gender. Their arms lie crossed, gently bracing a warning in large black print. "ENOKTA PAUKE." It certainly wasn't French or any other language I had ever seen in print. It struck me, that there must have been other natives around here. Surely those dike women wouldn't have a male God. They hated men.

Three layers of trees; each layer approximately a yard apart, and a yard in circumference, surrounded the statuesque figures. Though I had no respect for their fine deities, just observing the premises left me breathless.

Before I could pronounce any warnings of restraints, three of my comrades sprinted mindlessly forward. The strongest and most brutal of all my men, Mendelike was the first to die. I had so hoped he'd be one of my few survivors. I'd presumed to return with a scant one tenth of my army. Now by all sensibility, I knew that was far too optimistic.

The treasure looked as if it were there for the taking. All three men had stepped on a trap without ever getting to touch the treasures. The ground simply opened up and they dropped straight down. I could hear the rattles of many snakes. They were evidently sparred death by snake bites, however. The jagged edged boulders which tore them to pieces, and killed them instantly, making it easier for the snakes to swallow them. A gruesome site I tisked, to myself. Though I was determined to have my fill of the treasures, I thought it best to return to camp immediately. The next morning we set out for the treasure landing using extreme caution. Although I had mapped a different route to the site, I felt an erie eye watching us. Knowing what I knew from my previous encounters; I for the first time in my life prayed, it was the eye of God.

I had men over head in trees with binoculars, which was the only reason I continued forward. We approached the site at the south entrance this time. The site was undisturbed. The hole in the ground was still there where the men had recently fallen. I felt a sigh of relief. I had sternly instructed my men to wait for my signal before entering the tabernacle. I had planned some test to determine the best way to break and enter. I had to keep noises at a minimum, so I was limited to rolling marbles and pitching rocks around the diameter of the chest. I had to marvel. Those black winches had situated the altar so that one foot on the east perimeter of their holy ground, you'd drop into the pit. Once we investigated the circuitry closer we realized that it was a very intricate yet somehow, still crude system. If thieves were to enter from the western perimeter, they would have been caught by their feet and swung back and forth repeatedly into two triangular shaped knives, protruding shrewdly from opposite trees, holding them about mid-chest. They cleverly, used the circumference of the trees to create a tension and pulley system. If they entered from the northern perimeter, they would be roped at the midsection, lifted around three feet into the air and dropped head first onto a sixty inch cleaver. The average man would be split in half. If they entered from the southern perimeter; God forbid they'd survive the confrontation with those juno leagues, and their torturous games, they would be chained by the feet and arms, and slowly torn apart limb by limb. I morbidly contemplated which death I'd prefer, and decided the eastern perimeter would be my choice. Those ruthless sluts, I mumbled with awe and begrudging twinge of admiration. What was most astonishing was the fact that the whole altar would drop into the ground with as much as a raindrop from overhead. It somehow rested perfectly centered on the tip of a boulder hung in mid-air. It took considerable examination and curiosity to come to the conclusion that these savage witches understood the ancient secret of Egyptian pyramid construction.

We returned again to our camp without a jewel. It would take some study to accomplish this seizure. I knew I could out smart those savages with a little simple geometry. The circumference of each circle was one yard. The distance between each circle was one yard. The distance between the edge of the altar and the chest was . . . I worked on and on into the night. I finally figured I could use their own system against them. My heart grew weaker as dawn approached. By now they had to know who and where we were.

We made two unsuccessful attempts over the next two days. The plan called for tricking their existing pulley system, and gently lifting the treasure while air-borne. It was a smooth plan but not quite exact. It took tedious adjustment, but what worthwhile treasure is easily laid bare, I reckoned. Oddly enough, no attack or threat was made on us. I found it futile to try to reason in the mind of a beast. I simply told my men to stay on guard at all times.

On the sixth attempt, the system began working for us. I had opted to lift as many treasures as we could carry and flee. The men had grown weary, feeble and irritable. I had lost two more to jungle illnesses. I had decided to avoid confronting the Amazon women, since my manpower had dwindled so hopelessly. I would have called it a total loss but the remaining men wouldn't hear of it. We had to lift the pieces one at a time. O but they were precious! Jewels, gems, stones of the greatest brilliance, and sparkle were eased out of the chest. We used the pulley in all three directions; north, south and west, but it was a slow process. As dusk approached, I sternly ordered the men to stop the lift, and pack up for camp. We had already lifted more than half of the jewels. For thirty minutes, the men argued with me. I had to convince them that what they had in their hands was worth a lifetime of riches.

We exited by the northwest route, a new twisting obscure path, I had mapped. As we reached the perimeter of the holy campground, we were met with a ghastly surprise. From nowhere, the mighty towering structures surrounded us. Had I not known who they were, I too would have thought it an apparition. They were so black, it was but a trick of the eye to bring them into focus, even in the dusk's light. They had to be demons, I scuffed quietly. Their small, blank eyes lay recessed behind a thin grayish veil, that hid the evil running through their veins. I scanned the look on my army's faces. I apparently hadn't given a thorough enough description of our foes. Their shock couldn't be registered. We were as defenseless as babes. They had trapped us while our arms and hands were tangled with jewels. These rarities were not easily dropped, and I was more than certain these mindless bruts would rather die than relinquish them anyway. I shuttered to my bones as they moved in on us boldly. It looked like hundreds of them. By the time the men broke their arms free, it was too late. They commenced to strip us down to our bare drawers, all without saying a word. One of the stronger remaining men chose not to accept the cruelty. He swung his fist with all his might. He hit one of the women square in the jaw. As I had noted from the beginning, these women never shied away from a good fight. It reinforced their stature and sharpened their skill. She took the punch like a man. Remaining erect, she did not even take one step backward. She hit him with such force that his eyes crossed. I pitied Nathoff's foolishness as he went round after round with this monster. The brawl lasted for all of two minutes. I had never witnessed a match such as this before in my life. The only injustice was that at the end of the brawl, which I would have called shamefully uneven, the Amazon had the strength to hurl him into the pit. A few of the other men had foolishly decided to fight also. These women were meticulous death machines. They even toyed with the men to see which death would be most suitable to each one. It was sport to them.

The remaining three of us were beaten mercilessly. Apparently since we didn't fight back our lives were spared. We were tied together chain gang style, and led off down a northern trial. I, on my one good and other pegged leg, especially had difficulty walking. My eyes were swollen shut. My vision was blurred and doubled. I was partially delirious. It felt like we had walked for miles, when we were sat on a tree stump. I felt a presence in front of me, breathing down on me. I recognized the voice immediately. It was her. The chief priestess stepped up to me. She peered deep into my eyes for several minutes. I could feel the scored being tallied, as her eyes beamed down on me. Her face was angry. Her voice was harsh. She began by waving he finger in my face. She stumped her foot each time she said the words "ENOKTA PAUPE," in her savage yiddish. I felt as if she was lecturing me for some naughty deed. I paid close attention however. When she stopped, I sighed relief. I felt fortunate to have gotten off with just a stern scolding. The fear had obstructed my senses. She stepped back, crossed her arms, and rattled off some instructions. We were led off down another path. We again walked for several miles. I could hear several voices surrounding us, but not that of the priestess. We walked all through the night. It was near dawn when we reached our destination. We were apparently in another village. I had been beaten so senseless, that my keen sense of direction was useless to me. I couldn't make hide or hair of it. My vision was so slight. We were bought water then tied to a tree. Two women stood guard over us. They of course were more than sufficient to control our weak and mangled bodies.

After a few hours, we were dragged before a wide marble throne. There were ten steps ascending to it. It sat beautifully adorned but empty. I would have rather committed suicide than face one of their ceremonial deaths. Somehow, there was a strange familiarity about it, but I couldn't trust my senses in this state. We stood at the bottom of the stairs, in total dismay. A few minutes later a short heavy man entered the throne and sat on it. The chief priestess sat on the throne next to him. I gasped. I couldn't believe my eyes. King Jeppa I called interrupting his conversation with the priestess. He leaned forward, and twisted his ugly black face. He was a horrid looking man. He was grayish-black in color. No facial features stood out against that purplish skin tone. His eyes were small and yellow. His teeth were yellowish brown with dirt and food caked between them. He was dressed in high fashioned, heavily jeweled garb. King Jeppa, I repeated and collapsed to my knees with folded hands. Whittenhall, he exclaimed, wagging his finger. What the hell you doing here you white fool, he said with a sinister laugh.

Jeppa was hard to look at, and even harder to deal with. I again thanked my imperial wit, that I had had the good sense to treat him well when I purchased that large batch of slaves from him. Actually, that was my second deal with Jeppa, but we had established a good relationship. He was certainly no fool. His kingdom was very strong and very wealthy. He had gotten the better of both of our deals, but I had chalked it all up to future business promotions. Jeppa instructed the guards to escort me before the throne. They picked me up by the arms and carried me easily up the stairs. Jeppa and I conversed for several minutes. I explained what had happened to me. He informed me that these women were his wives. The high priestess was his first and main wife. The Warriors were fiercely loyal to both of them. He found it quite amusing that the women had captured them with their hands full of his treasures. They had sparred my life by order of Jeppa with orders to bring us to him. I offered him more money and guns than he had ever been offered in one single deal, if he'd let me go home with his high priestess. Shamefully that stinkin' bastard seriously considered it.

After long debate and persuasion, she agreed to his command. He explained that I couldn't take her home, but I could have my way with her or any of the other women I wanted. I was taken aback. I was afraid to turn down his generous offer for fear of offending him. I spent the next hour trying to convince him that I only wanted her for novelty purposes, not a lover. He laughed sinisterly. He wouldn't hear of it. As usual, his offer was non-negotiable. I was to sleep with her and any of the others I wanted, plus give him tens of pounds of ammunition and money. After all it was most generous of him to spare my life when I was caught red-handed with his treasures. I obliged.

I was immediately escorted to a fine hut in his village. Running water, bed linens and a basket of fresh fruit were waiting. I cleaned up and laid down for a nap. A knock at the door startled me. I had forgotten in my weariness about the women. The priestess entered proceeded by servants bearing more towels and clothing for her. When they left she reluctantly undressed looking at the floor the whole time. To my surprise, her naked, deformed body excited me, and I swelled to my fullness.

The complexity of the situation made talking awkward. We didn't speak. We tangled and humped our bodies on one another repeatedly. As she dressed to leave, I asked her if she would come home with me. She declined. She explained that she loved Jeppa to the death. Studying my eyes carefully, she informed me that for some reason, she cared for me as well, right from the beginning. It was she that had taken care to convince Jeppa to spare me to this point. Then placing my hand on her belly she said, that now I had given her a prize, she would make sure I was kept safe. I was too stunned to reply or react. She left quickly.

The next morning I was escorted, with the remaining two men of my crew, to a small unsophisticated vessel on the Aboney River. I left all three of my vessels and tons of armor with King Jeppa. King Jeppa had arranged for the male escorts, seemingly business partners from hell, to escort me to the Ivory Coast. I was to have my assistants meet us there with the remaining monies.

We spent an additional week on the raged boat waiting for my assistants to reach the Ivory Coast. I gave no thought to a coup of any kind. We were guarded by six of the ugliest, nastiest patrollers I'd ever seen.

Once we gave them the monies, we were loosed and they returned or proposed to return to Dahomey. My assistants jetted me back to Brittan. I was overly joyful to see the mainland. Madsen my companion died within weeks of our return, and Deboise simply went mad.

With no one to share my memories, I left my beloved Brittan, and moved to the United States. It was the year nineteen hundred and four. There my fame or insanity would be of no account to anyone. There I soon became smitten by the plight of the African American descendants of slaves. I became interested in their culture though I didn't care much for them.

My own health had declined constantly from the day I returned home. I sat alone night after night with a strange longing and disdain for Dahomey or perhaps for the Priestess. I no longer knew whether I loved or despised her. My every thought remained captive to that journey. Africa's long arms had me in an unshakeable grip. I had never been so wholly defeated and humiliated. I concluded it must be one in the same whole defeat and humiliation the black American man must feel. I carefully studied their carriage of humility and rage. To be so put asunder, I figured, with no way out, and no one to even hear or care was maddening. I studied them from my library and visits to certain areas of town. I understood and even epitomized their rage as I never thought I would. I concluded that the black woman then must feel completely defenseless, with their male partners emotionally, mentally and physically (when necessary) emasculated.

I had gotten word shortly before my move to the Americas, from neighboring and even rival slave traders, that King Jeppa was still alive with a white heir to his throne. I finally realized that the Amazon women were unconquerable. The only way to beat her was to break her heart. Alas, she was still just a woman.

As I grew feeble and senility began to set in, I added to my parting wishes, the building of a three unit housing complex for wretched and poor women. For my own assurance I had the plans and blue prints drawn up immediately. On sheer determination, at one hundred and six years old, I lived to the inauguration of the Whittenhall Complex, April 12, 1912.

I knew I could never sustain a return to Africa, but her images and people would haunt me till the day I expired.

Forever,

Lord Quinton Gale Whittenhall
April 15, 1912

TONI'S STORY

Chapter One

The Whittenhall Wall

Toni Patterson was born into the world behind the wall Friday April 12, 1952. A hodge podge of crumbling brick and mortar, the Whittenhall Projects were the oldest in the city. Donated to the city by a white patron, whose picture hung in the lobby, the Whittenhall Projects were once a refuge, with the esteemed reputation of protector of poor and widowed women.

Situated in the southwest corner of the city, at the edge of the industrial district, atop a long crooked hill; the Whittenhall Projects, consisted of three five story buildings in an attempted octagonal shaped project. In actuality, it looked like the top half of a broken star. That appearance was quite appropriate, in its later day commission.

The Whittenhall Projects were surrounded by the noises of steel manufacturing, and the smells of a whiskey distillery. A dilapidated eight foot tall brick wall surrounded the front and sides of the projects, framing the steep slopes of the prized creation. Though it was not a part of the original architecture, the wall was constructed in 1962. That year, the projects were legislated to become "*lower-class*" housing.

The wall created a world within itself. From the outside the wall was an obvious signal of danger and despair. From the inside, the wall signaled hopelessness and entrapment. The residents of the upper floors of the five story buildings, were privy to an exquisite view of the murky grim river, and the lower west-end parts of the city sprawling underneath them. Quite often residents sat on the fire escape smoking reefer, and watching the riverboats transport riches they'd never attain.

The wall itself had procured the history and brutality of the projects within its mud-covered bricks. Both of which were gradually buried in the falling slopes of the uneven wall. Oddly somehow the wall became a peculiar comfort to the ones trapped behind it. It had always been the gathering place and a recreational area of the projects. It had been scaled so often that a path had been worn completely through it, down to the dirt. It had been jumped off so many times, it had created Olympic trial athletes. One of the favorite tales of the projects was that a resident from previous years had won an Olympic gold medal in the high jump event. He acquired his skill by jumping on and off the wall as a daily practice routine.

Toni always glanced at the picture in the lobby. In fact it never escaped her notice, no matter how quickly she rushed through the door. It was such an oddity, but just like the others (oddities in the projects), one glanced and only assumed whatever. Still, it often peaked her curiosity to gaze at the deformed African woman with one tit standing next to the peg-legged white man. She wondered if anyone ever knew who he was and what he was doing with the African sister. Rumor had it that he was Lord Whittenhall, a slave trader that captured African queens and cut off their tits to dewomanize them. In any case, there wasn't enough time to dive into such irrelevant pursuits. It took every ounce of strength to survive life in this hellhole. Besides, Toni figured, whoever this "*Mr. Whittenhall*" was; he must have orchestrated this slow, torturous demise of black people.

There were hundreds of strict unwritten codes that ruled the Whittenhall Projects. It often took years to learn them all, and experience to apply them properly. That basic fact accounted for the numerous altercations and bloodshed day after day. One could, however, survive by skillfully applying the basic codes. The first and most important was, you **must** rise above or appear oblivious to the living conditions. The towering garbage and broken glass, the gut wrenching stench, the dilapidated buildings, the roaches, and the mice, all appeared to escape notice of skilled residents. Damned be the one that pointed out a roach crossing the wall. In fact, unless it was discussed in the form of a joke, it was never discussed. Look at this raggedy place, one of the Master tenants would occasionally say. They were the only ones that could press the matter without penalty. Is this how you think you should live, they'd ask. Everyone would look around, as if for the first time, and surprisingly agree that it is quite ragged, but no one knew how to definitively respond. They knew that they were stuck there for some time to come and didn't want to take a close, or real look at their captivity. The subject never lingered for long. Everyone would replace their blinders and someone would subtly change the subject. There was nothing more embarrassing in the Whittenhall Projects, or any other projects for that matter, than to let the conditions drive you insane. That was the highest survival code in the proud nation of project dwellers everywhere. One who lost mental faculties simply because of the ragged living conditions would totally disgrace his family and lose all respect permanently. Basic code number two was, you had to claim your position or the level on which you would exist. This claim had to be made immediately. The class hierarchy of the projects was as solid as cement. On the peek level, of the hierarchial pyrmid, were the Masters. Descending one level were the Warriors. On the third level were the Pros. Next to the bottom level were the Stars and on the very bottom level were the Dons. It took lots of power or force to move upward from one level to the next. However; a quick fall from grace was quite common. There were more complexities and fine shades of each of these codes and classes than stars in the sky.

The largest and busiest class by far, were the Stars. The Stars were the ghetto publishers. They kept the latest rumors and gossip circulating. They made sure all slanders were publicized and reached the intended parties. In fact, they would personally deliver any insulting message for free. It was just one of the perks of their class. Another of their primary duties reached beyond the wall. It was also their duty to introduce the latest fashion trends into the projects. This was usually done with such finesse and style that; little did Paris know, the ghetto runway was a formidable co-author. This group usually fell between the ages of fifteen to twenty five years old, and were predominantly female. The Pros were the project hustlers. They always had a scheme, a game, a trick, or a treat to offer the tenants. A pack of cigarettes for thirty five cents, a thirty inch television for fifty dollars, or maybe twenty pounds of sliced bacon for five bucks; the Pros were entrepreneurs at heart. Their hustle kept them outside the wall most of the time. You could even place orders with the real Pros. Yeah, T.C. would you get me one of those cameras with the reel to reel tape built in? No problem bud, that'll be forty dollars. It was just their hustle to beat the system. Somehow they often ended up two steps behind the system, and they never seemed to move up from this hustle. Poor management skills, lack of venture capital, something always kept them behind the system. This group usually ranged in age from eighteen to forty eight years old. These were usually only part-time residents and were predominantly male.

Ah, the Warriors. The Warriors were the second largest class of residents. They were the real "*tired and poor*," people of this country. These were the battled scared women of the civil wrongs wars. They had been "*working mothers*" since before the catch phrase appeared. They had also been the Atlas of the black community ever since there was a black community. Homeless, manless, penniless, and defenseless, these women bore the weight of the black and colored communities. Then, as if not enough, they also bore the blame of their men, who accused them of being overpowering, and unfeminine. That was the blame that wedged black men and women apart, and remained a bone of contention for generations. Only the HIGHEST MASTER understood these women, and what it took, to be everything to everyone. This class ranged between the ages of thirty to sixty years old and was female.

The Project Masters were the true educators and diplomats of the community and the projects. They always had a heightened awareness of "*the system*," and a solution for the conditions of their people. They would explain the plot of the system to railroad the people. For example they might be aware of foreign agreements on the part of corporations, or social invasions on the part of the government and monetary tactics on the part of the United States Treasury, all aimed at keeping the poor poorer and the rich richer. It was typical conversation, to hear them lament something like, IBM just announced a special stock class to increase the monetary value of the Japanese yen. Then he would gladly relate how these things affected the Whittenhall dwellers. Their specialty, was relating how to rise above "*the plot*" as knowledgeable strong African Kings and Queens. Simply brilliant! They didn't waste words, however. They imparted this special knowledge only to those who were genuinely interested. These conversations could take hours. It would seem that these would be the primary candidates for rage against the system. Yet, somehow they twisted this knowledge of injustice into an advocacy for higher education and self awareness. Above all, their message was non-violence among brothers. Unfortunately these ones were few and far between. As quiet as it was kept, they were highly valued stabilizers, in the projects. They kept self-esteem and social awareness at a premium. Everyone respected them, a hard won advantage in the projects. But these were the quickest to move on. They were like missionaries that had to spread their message as far as possible. Therefore the Master's class was always a small one.

The third basic code was, never invade anyone's personal space. If there ever was a golden rule, in the Whittenhal Projects, this was it. Yet, this was the rule that was most often violated, and the one that exacted the highest penalty. Everyone had a God-given right to a minimum twelve inch diameter around them. It was justly considered rude to enter that space, or "get up in someone's face", unless of course you were invited.

This was the only world Toni had ever known. This was the world behind the wall in the Whittenhall Projects. As retched as it was, Toni realized she was afraid to leave it, and challenge the world on the other side of the wall, regardless of its' luring promises.

Chapter Two

Past Haunting

Toni turned eighteen in the spring. On the third Saturday in May she graduated from high school. Her freedom was fretful and ackward for her. She had nowhere to go or no one to turn to. Unlike her best friend and cousin, Linda, she had no children. She didn't even have a boyfriend at the time.

She hadn't reached for the stars or sky in high school. She hadn't acquired any accolades or recognition. College was just a fancy thought. She completed the requirements by going through the motions, with a grade average of "C". She was normally the only one in the house up and going to school because she had promised her mother she'd finish.

Her mother had been her whole life support system. She had taught Toni the pride and glory that a poor woman could have. Her mother was a non-conformist. She refused to fall into the pre-cut pattern of ghetto life. She made her own rules. She constantly spoke of a wonderful life beyond the wall, and how they were soon to be out of the ghetto trap. Anna Sue Patterson was a courageous woman. She had no fear.

Toni could remember even at the age of five, her mother's brisk, soulful stride. It commanded everyone's attention for at least the time it took for her to pass by. Chin up, shoulders square, and toes pointed. It was as if she were walking the runways of Paris. The cat calls and gossip of the Stars all skillfully escaped her notice.

Anna Sue was a very attractive woman, and had vigorously pursued a modeling career. That was a dream without much hope in those days. Black women were just beginning to get noticed, but more for their body form than what was considered beauty. Their larger breast and rounded buttocks were suddenly "en vogue". Anna followed her dream courageously until she met Toni's father. Toni only remembered that Aunt Sue had said his name was Frank, and he was an extremely handsome con artist. But Anna fell for him. She broke all of her rules for him. He never appreciated her. Even though she had to put her goals on hold for him, she never lost sight of her dream, and remained confident. Once he left her, baby in bundle, Aunt Sue said Anna pulled herself up by the bootstraps and continued where she had left off. Anna imparted the assumption that any day now they'd be on easy street. Everything would soon work out she'd assure Toni. With her unwavering confidence and calm determination, Anna Sue Patterson was a Master, a surprising exception to the rules. Toni lived a happy fearless life with her mother. When her mother passed away suddenly all of the rules changed for Toni.

Her mother had become ill with pneumonia when Toni was ten years old. At thirty nine years of age, she died. Devastated and frightened, Toni lost herself in sorrow. She was taken in by her mother's only sister. Her Aunt Sue had five kids of her own and also was a Whittenhall resident. Toni was already close to her cousins and was flooded with extra love and kindness during her bereavement. In spite of that, the emptiness and shock from the loss caused her to withdraw into the infantile recesses of herself. She found a black hole within herself and spiraled down through it. She lost all sense of time and for the most part awareness. Aunt Sue cradled and nursed her. Sue ignored all the talk about "putting her away." She refused to give up on Toni. Sue knew Toni's condition was fragile, so she extended special patience. Mainly since Toni was born "*that way*" Sue took extra precaution.

Toni was born with the veil over her eyes. Just a clear piece of skin that lay over the eyes, but it allowed the person to "see things." These were the sort of things ordinary people couldn't see with the naked eye. The veil provided high definition visions. Its' owner is given the privilege of seeing and understanding the root and cause of realities unclear to others. It was a gift. This gift was bestowed upon the chosen recipients by the Ancient Sisterhood of Warrior Queens.

Having been a nurse's aide and a dietician at various stages in her life, Sue paid special attention to Toni's diet. She would literally spoon feed Toni, then rock her to sleep in her arms like a newborn child. When she wasn't sleeping, Toni sat motionless where ever placed, with a blank stare on her face. Her life was a eat and sleep existence. Her cousins, most of them close in age range, played all around her. They offered her candy and treats. They talked to her as if she were part of the game. From her black hole, she could feel the vibrations of their far away voices. She never bothered to reply since she knew she was much too far away for them to hear her. She couldn't see them either, only the blackness of her dark path, spiraling to nowhere. Time had seemed to take its toll on Aunt Sue. She was beginning to wonder if she was actually helping Toni. As a last resort, she tried reading the bible and singing gospel hymns to her along with her regular routine. Still Toni didn't respond. By all appearances she seemed to be getting worse. She began wetting her pants more regularly. Sue kept her clean, but was losing sight of the goal. With five other kids, Sue was graying faster than her vanity could catch up.

It was one regular Saturday morning around what Sue thought was the end of the road for Toni. Sue made peace with the fact that she had done all she could for Toni. She had decided that Monday she would go to the courthouse to relinquish guardianship of Toni and make her a ward of the state. Her heart ached sorely for her baby sister's child.

Sue sat Daryl, her youngest son on the floor next to Toni to watch cartoons, with a bag of bar-b-que potato chips. For no explainable time or reason, the smell rapidly spiraled through the black hole. The familiar scent hooked Toni's nostril like a fish hook and reeled her rapidly into the present place and time. Gimme a potato chip Daryl. Her voice was scratchy and hoarse. The young fella stared at her for a long time with his mouth open. Being the youngest of the tribe he couldn't remember ever having heard her speak. Daryl stumbled to his feet terrified, and ran away screaming, leaving the chips behind. All of her cousins, along with Aunt Sue hurried into the room and stared at her wide eyed. Linda handed her one chip all the while her mouth hanging open. They all moved in closer as she chewed and swallowed the chip. She handed her another. Everyone held their breath while she took it and again chewed it and swallowed. One by one they took turns handing her chips until the bag was finished. Afterward everyone was silent. Toni's eyes scanned the faces in front of her then roved about the room. In sudden confusion Linda blurted out, was you mad at us all this time cause we didn't have no bar-b-que potato chips? Everyone started hugging and kissing Toni and cheering her forward. Little Daryl climbed up in her lap and picked up the empty potato chip bag. He looked inside the empty bag and began to wail like a thunderstorm. From that day forward Toni was addicted to bar-b-que potatoe chips. She ate a bag daily. It reminded her of the dark journey from which she had been called back. It also confirmed her resolve not to fall into that black hole again. There was some freedom in her life now. She could remember her mother without sobbing to exhaustion. She now celebrated the glorious woman Anna Sue Patterson had been.

Now though, her destiny was up in the air, as far as she was concerned. She had applied to a couple of colleges because it was the obvious next step. Staying with Aunt Sue wasn't a comfortable option, since everyone expected her to move forward with her life. In reality though, she didn't want to struggle through another four years of school. The academics weren't the worst part. The local universities were predominantly white. She could never imagine herself fitting in with the "*college crowd*". They would never understand her ghetto style. They spoke different. They acted different. They were from homes with both mothers and fathers that had cushy jobs, and bought them ponies and tennis lessons. She'd be the laughing stock of the university. At least in the Whittenhall Projects, she was accepted. To this point she had not received any letters of acceptance or rejection. This aptly captured her life-hanging in thin air.

Toni feared leaving the only family she had left. She had seen what had happened and was said about others who had left the projects for the fancy life. Connections were severed, or strained at best, and many families were split into the ghetto half and the up-idy half. Though they hoods and thieves, they were the only family Toni had in this world.

Aunt Sue's family structure was different than her mother's had been, and Toni stood out among them. Aunt Sue had one daughter and four sons. They all accepted Toni, and treated her like a sibling, but with extra tenderness. Toni was a mild mannered, soft hearted girl. She had keen delicate features that she had inherited from her mother. Her hair was what was called "*good hair*" by the ones with the prejudicial eye. Her hair was jet black with deep set waves, which she always believed she inherited from her father. Aunt Sue always called him a black Indian. In any case, her hair was gorgeous cascading over the tops of her shoulders, silhouetting her thin face and frame. Her silky cinnamon brown skin appeared to be pampered. She didn't resemble her Aunt or her cousins at all.

Even though the surroundings were familiar, the lifestyle was totally different. Aunt Sue was a caring person with the ruggedness of a sideline military commander. She was blunt and loud. Her voice was deep and foul. She spoke in angry repetitive curses. She was uneducated and grammatically incorrect. She barked orders and threats all day, but rarely left her stool in the kitchen corner. She had all the battle scars of the civil wrongs war. A hard-edged face with dents and scars, dull, dim eyes stretched in anger, thick, dry, wrinkled skin, and short thinning hair cut to eight different lengths all less than four inches long.

On sight everyone knew the system had beaten her. She had been beaten by the order of society beyond and behind the wall. This society called her a lazy woman good for nothing but sensual pleasures. Sue tried and wanted to be like the sister she had lost. She secretly envied her sister's optimism and quick wit. Sue died a little with regret for not telling her that.

Society beyond the wall was not as good to Sue as it was to Anna. Sue resigned under all the snide remarks, class labeling, and office politics. But her sister Anna seemed to take it with a grain of salt. Sue refused to ignore them and would swiftly cuss out anyone that thought they could get away with even the subtlest of injustices, in her face. Eventually the battles exhausted her. With one swift kick of the societal boot, Sue resigned to her kitchen corner behind the wall.

She had also been played by man after man, who had no other game, but to control women more beaten down than themselves. She finally came to believe what she heard and felt, that she had no control in her life.

Sue hardly ever left the projects. She had been taken in by one bad hustle after another, putting her faith in everything and everyone but God. She spoke her mind freely, but only within her realm of security of the projects. In her own insidious, obnoxious way, Sue longed for a prince charming to come and take her away from all the war and pain. She, like all other Warriors, needed a man mighty enough to fight the battle of being black and in poverty, as well as tender enough to kiss their scars away.

Sue's only reservoir of hope was her children. She loved her children, but was far too jaded. In many ways, she stole their hope and strength with her pessimism. She did not stress education and goals. She stressed hustling and getting over on the system. Every good man needs a good hustle she would say. He need to know how to make money without relying on whitey. She knew of which she spoke. She had seen more than her share of degreed black men reduced to hamburger hell, unable to find any other job. The B.S. college degree, was strictly B.S. in Sue's eyes. In any case she overindulged her kids with clothes and toys, insisting that they were proof of her love and her success. She was determined that her kids would have all that their little hearts desired, even if she had to spend her government check to see to it. Instant gratification was the rule of the house. Unlike her sister Anna, who spent all her time and money on preparation and never lived to enjoy any rewards.

Sue only feared the repeated heartbreak and loneliness of her desperate search to find a man to love her. It caused her to be reliantly needy for the love of her own children. She continually begged for their love. A new doll equaled a months' worth of loving guilt. Kiss me if you love me, she'd beam. A new outfit equaled a months' worth of, if you love me, favors. It was sickening but it was a way of life in Sue's house. Sue's children truly did love her, but the love favors began to challenge their personal space and needs, as they grew older. So one by one they left the nest at their first chance of freedom in order to pursue their own hustle.

Sue's sixteen year old son, Terrell, had found his way to the Don level. It was a comfortable level for boys between the ages of ten and twenty four years old. They could strike the cool pose, while covering up the rage and anxiety over their decomposing manhood. The order was slightly different for boys in the projects. They basically had only two levels of existence-Dons and Masters. It was unheard of for a mere boy to be a Master. Therefore all the boys in the projects were Dons. Rage and anxiety ruled this class. The Dons often took their anger and frustration out on each other. As hard as the Masters tried to educate them about non-violence, the energy and foolishness of youth, overwhelmed them.

The Dons also tended to venture beyond the wall often. Everyday around noon, a continual stream of boys trekked their way to the wall. To the Warriors, who often sat in their kitchen windows and watched, they looked like a clan of penguins, waddling to the ocean's edge. Their destination, was the nearest street corner.

During the day the projects were predominantly female, but at night the genders somehow evened out. All in all Sue McRay's children had blazed a trail in the projects. Each one of them had a reputation of fortitude and roughness. No one had challenged it for quite some time. It was by this reputation that Toni had survived, and her cousins protected her fiercely.

Toni was especially close to her cousin Linda. Linda was quite a daring and threatening girl. By now it appeared that Linda was not going to graduate from high school or the projects. She and Toni were the same age, and Linda was pregnant with her second child. Though outgoing and daring, Linda had resigned herself to project living and sadly, the same search for a man's love her mother had pursued.

Toni on the other hand, had resolved not to have children at all. She feared that her life would be short like her mother's. In any case, Aunt Sue's house was still crowded. There were still three children under the age of eighteen along with Linda and her child. Sue's oldest son occasionally needed lodging as well. Toni knew Aunt Sue would never ask her to leave, but she felt college would gracefully eliminate the awkwardness for them both.

The heat of August was tipping the mercury toward blazing. Toni received the letter which began, Congratulations, you've been accepted. She let out a long sigh. Fate had decided her destiny. She immediately began to worry. She hadn't planned a major, and had no idea what she wanted to study. Feelings of uncertainty, and incompleteness had conditioned her all these years. But now she had to use her own discretion. She tried to hide them as much as possible, and had managed to fool quite a few people. She had fooled many friends and family who felt she belonged in college. She knew better, but there was no one to share her true feelings with.

Generally, she went along with whatever the crowd or Linda planned. Now she had to use her own judgment. She called a close friend for encouragement. Tehfariah had moved away to another housing project downtown with her family, but they had been fast friends most of her life. They had discussed college casually, like any other fleeting dream . . . a big house, a fancy sports car, a college degree. Yet Tehfariah was convinced that college was the right step for her. She was going miles away to Washington D.C. to attend college. But she had always been adventurous and fearless. For Toni, attending the local city college was her greatest test thus far.

She was forced by time and circumstances to move to the college campus. She moved all of her earthly possessions, which fit into one suitcase and one brown paper bag. The other students had huge trunks and several suitcases of clothes and sentimental treasures. She watched as they parted the arms of crying mothers and fathers. She felt sick to her stomach. She was sure this life would not work out for her at all.

The proverbial class bell rang and her classes took off like a rocket. Toni made it a point to come home every weekend to hang with her old friends and family. Besides she didn't want them to think she'd changed or became to "up-idy" to deal with them.

Chapter Three

Love Changes Everything

David had come into her life at a most embarrassing moment. Although the more she thought about it, the more she felt it was all by design.

It was a plain ole Tuesday in January, right after the holidays, that Toni decided to skip her classes for the day and hang out with the home crew. Her cousin Linda had decided she wanted to see the holiday lights on the mansions, on the other side of town. Linda never shied away from exploring all sides of the city. She coaxed Charles into chauffeuring the group over to the other side of town.

Charles was a well known street hustler, a Pro and an occasional resident at the Whittenhall. He rarely did favors like that. He was all business. Actually he was a mercenary, but Linda was persistent that day, and Charles finally gave in.

They drove around the city from late afternoon until late evening. It was nearing dusk when they entered Wellesly Court. The Wellesly Township lied next to the richest section of town, in the north east corner of the city. It boasted several wealthy residents of its' own, but only the nouvea riche' (the new rich) and not the old wrinkled blue blood money.

Charles pulled into the court driving at a slow creep. The car group was silent. Their mouths hung open, their eyes stretched, as they viewed the unbelievable architecture. The houses were so large it made their hearts faint. Linda broke the silence, as usual, with a tragic question. Have you ever noticed you never see anybody home in these neighborhoods? I believe there's really no one alive in these neighborhoods they're all buried in the backyard she continued trying to salvage some sense of dignity. Yeah that's why they got so many apple trees Charles piped in. They all laughed in unison fighting hard not to show their pain. As they were leaving the court via Wellesly Circle, they surprisingly did spot a family in the yard. It was a father and two daughters throwing snowballs at each other.

When Charles caught sight of one of the girls he began salivating. He pasted his face to the window and stopped the car to pant. He hadn't noticed that he had bumped the parked car in front of them. Actually none of them had. They were all mesmerized. Linda again broke the silence with a sharp squeal. By then the Wellesly Township police department had arrived to point out the situation. After the officer checked the driver's license and the passengers in the car, he spoke very sharply. Just suck up Charles Toni mumbled through her teeth. Don't give this trigger happy cowboy an excuse to shoot you. Charles listened to Toni's advice. He remained calm in spite of the officer's attempt to rall him into a confrontation. His mildness proved to be wise. The officer let him off with a stern warning never to be caught in Wellesly Township again. Charles sped out of the Township.

Linda was livid. She ranted and raved bullishly as Charles careened down the city blocks. They just have to stop you if you got a raggedy piece of junk like this right she asked sarcastically. They act like you ain't even human if you don't drive a Mercedes or Jaguar. Stop the car Charles, Linda demanded. No drive us to the nearest Bay Burgers. I want to get away from here. Charles tried to reason with her. Linda was again overpowering in her threatening kind way. I'm starving boy, if you don't stop this car . . . They stopped in the Blue Rock section of town just on the lower half of Wellesly but out of Wellesly Township.

They all had very little money. Actually it was just change and lint, filling their pockets. As fate would have it Linda was a nickel short of her total bill. The clerk refused to give her the food. Toni and Charles searched desperately for more change. Charles clutched his pockets, and Toni emptied her purse but, could not come up with a nickel between the two of them. Alright Linda courageously conceded, just take off the cheese. Um, I'm sorry, you ordered the Bay burger, and that comes with cheese, the clerk snarled. Besides cheese is an extra dime, she quipped smugly. Linda handled it the only way she knew how. She was hungry and frustrated and couldn't take another systematic hassle from anyone. First the police, now the little hamburger girl, Linda growled. They hassle you over even the smallest thing she went on. It's just their way of showing their hatred, she said still pulling at her pockets. Her frustration turned into an explosion. She began yelling. Yaw'll got twenty billion stinkin' hamburgers in this place. I don't see why I can't have one little stinkin' hamburger. I don't even want no cheese. We don't have **TWENTY BILLION HAMBURGERS MA'AM**, the clerk snapped, raising her voice to match Linda's, and with her smug grin still in place. Can't you read ho, Linda growled back. The clerk looked confused. Linda squinted her cold threatening eyes. The sign outside says over twenty billion sold. Linda nodded her head to let the clerk know she had won. Then she continued. If you don't have over **TWENTY BILLION HAMBURGERS; THAT'S FALSE ADVERTISEMENT** and I'm suing you stank slut. Linda was screaming at the top of her voice by now. The clerk knew there was no reasoning with Linda.

She snorted and mumbled then called the manager. The situation escalated, and harsh words were exchanged. The manager threatened to call the police if she didn't either pay or leave. Toni turned to Charles to tell him to bring the car. He was nowhere in sight. Out of nowhere a calm handsome gentleman appeared and handed the clerk a quarter. Will this take care of it, he asked quietly. He then pulled a twenty dollar bill out of his wallet. He turned to Toni and said, what would you like? Toni stood paralyzed with shock. Their eyes locked and captured them both in a trance. It was Linda who slid the twenty dollar bill out of the man's hand and ordered for Toni, herself and Charles. She spotted Charles in a back corner, claiming no part of the incident. When the order came it was Linda who took it back to the table, leaving Toni and the stranger still standing at the counter staring into each other's eyes.

Toni felt surrounded with warmth. His eyes had a brilliant sparkle. His grin was soft and slight, still his pearly white teeth shown through it brightly. Toni felt herself in melt down. After a blissful eternity, he introduced himself. My name is David Spears, what's yours? They suddenly realized that they were still standing at the counter and a line had formed behind them. Everyone at the counter seemed to be caught up in their trance as well. The clerk that waited on them was lost in a romantic daydream of her own. David stepped toward the counter, and leaned forward as if he was going to order. Instead he snapped his fingers right in front of the clerk's face and belted, snap out of it Callie. She was rudely startled by the loud snap, and began tugging at her uniform. She had no idea where or how long she had been lost in her little fantasy. Angry voices from both lines snarled, yeah snap out of it Callie. Hurry up we're hungry, they grumbled. Callie looked around inconspicuously, then checked her name tag. May I help you, she snarled with her usual agitation. They laughed, then went to David's car to talk privately while their friends finished their meals.

They'd been together ever since. They often looked back on that day and laughed. David always recanted that he never got any food or change back from his twenty dollar bill. It was still an embarrassing moment for Toni. Linda's loudness always did embarrass her, but she was used to it. Besides she would never want Linda to know that, so she pretended to be as upset as Linda.

Toni felt David was a God-sent, well wrapped gift. He had elevated her life instantly and drastically. He was a student at the city college as well. She loved everything about him. She felt the ball of fear that resided in her chest, slowly dissolve whenever she was in his arms. The pain and emptiness of the past were like fading ghosts when he kissed her. His voice was soothing, and hypnotic chasing the Whittenhall demons away. His eyes had an unbound sparkle, sending her joy and happiness. Her scratchy throat watered with just a touch of his large hands. His skin was a smooth mocha color, with the gleam of slipper satin. He was an average height of five feet ten inches, weighing around hundred eighty five pounds. His spirit was calm, confident and happy. No one she had ever known before was so completely happy. It was fun to be around him and his spirit met and comforted hers. Her eyes were changing focus.

Right from the beginning, they had shared their naïve hopes and dreams for a future with one another. Finally, she had found someone she could share everything with including her fears. They would talk on the phone for hours night after night, imagining themselves living out their dreams. Toni's wildest dreams had always been of being a wealthy housewife. She had longed for a powerful love in her life that would fill that bottomless pit inside of her. David's future dreams were of football. It was his life's dream to play NFL football.

As star jock for the college, football took up a major portion of David's time. They'd meet after his football practice every evening, and spend the rest of the evening together. Their time together was spent laughing, playing, caressing, and loving. David always made time to hold her while he pushed away her aggressive thoughts of loneliness, with his kind and embracing words. It was only when it was time for lovemaking that all speaking ceased. All that existed then was one flesh tangled in a heated embrace reaching for rhapsody. Her freshman school year ended. For the first time Toni was glad she'd gone to college. David's junior year had ended and he was headed home for the summer also.

He was also a city resident. Toni felt fortunate that their relationship would continue over the summer months. In fact they had planned to spend more time than ever before together.

David had grown up in the city with his mother. He too was an only child. They spent most of their time at his mother's house. Toni had moved back into Sue's house for the summer. She rarely allowed David to come in her house. She was ashamed of her home. She hid that fact by saying, oh it's just too crowded there, I'll meet you outside at the wall.

She accepted a part-time job that summer as a file clerk in an attorney's office. Her weekday mornings were occupied with fast paced legal routines. She was supposed to be a file clerk, but found that she sometimes delivered the attorney's briefs, answered phones, and looked up backgrounds at the courthouse. That allowed her to get out of the office into the fresh air and sunshine of the busy downtown streets. She had always believed that people who worked downtown had good jobs and were rich, a myth dispelled that summer. She enjoyed her mornings but tirelessly awaited her evenings.

For the first time in her life, there was focus and clarity. She radiated with joy, and spoke of David Spears, a pretty well known name around the city, to anyone who listened. Sue and Linda thought she had procured the golden ticket, working for a prestigious law firm, and dating a star jock. Toni felt a continual surge of energy. Her spirit was bright and as warm as the sun. She helped her Aunt Sue with bills, and chores.

She and David managed to stretch those summer evenings into magical escapades. David was committed to football. He'd spend his days at the school gym or track, under the supervision of his friend and Coach. Even though he kept up his physical training during the day, he was wholly devoted to their physical satisfaction at night.

David's mother worked two jobs to maintain her upper-class household alone. She was a surgical nurse at a large hospital, during the day. She had gained the attention of a very prominent doctor, who hired her for evening work in his private practice. She was hardly ever home before midnight. David never questioned the legitimacy of that position.

He must pay her well, Toni thought as she walked around the townhouse for the first time. It was a beautiful townhouse in the Blue Rock section of town. David made her feel like the woman of the house, allowing her free run. He even gave her a key so that she could meet him there when he was running late. Many afternoons she went straight from work to his house, always hoping Ms. Spears would never walk in and catch her there.

The house was lavishly decorated, but had a cold erie feel to it. Pictures of Ms. Spears were spread throughout the house. Toni often felt Ms. Spears was watching her or that she could feel Toni's presence in her home from wherever she was. Sometimes when Toni was alone and the house was still, a cold muffled whisper would blow past her ear. The cold breeze would always frost her ears and make the hairs on the back of her neck stand up. She could see playful flashes of light circle the room when she stared off into space. She was always glad when David arrived. In spite of that, Toni eventually grew comfortable there.

Blue Rock was clean and quiet, with a nice sprinkling of affluent blacks. Often she'd bask in the luxury of the huge jet-stream bathtub. Ms. Spears was unmatched in her taste for elegance. Besides that she was retentively neat. Her house always looked like a magazine picture. Her kitchen cabinets were stacked so orderly, that she could immediately tell if someone had removed one single can. Toni took extra pains to leave everything as neat as she found it. She'd cook their dinner every night. David would turn down their bed, then massage her with one of his mother's luxurious, scented oils. Through laughter, and tender care, their relationship solidified that summer.

The summer moved quickly. One thing Toni had still hoped to do over the summer was contact her old friend Tehfariah. Her mother said she was expecting her any day now. She was anxious to share her new love, and secrets with her. It was mid August before she found out that Tehfariah had decided to stay in Washington D.C. for the summer. Toni tried to call her there, and never found her home. She hoped and prayed that her childhood friend hadn't abandoned her roots and she hadn't lost a friend

It was Toni's last week at the Law firm before the summer assignment ended. It was not an unusual day. Toni had worked that morning and David met her early that evening at his mother's house. David had stopped at the grocery store on his way home. When he got home he immediately went out to the patio and started a fire in the grill. The doorbell rang, and a few of David's football teammates stopped by with their girlfriends. They all had a great time. One girlfriend was a great singer. She sang while Toni and the other girlfriends pantomimed in the background. Another girlfriend was a great dancer. She showed them new dance steps. They almost laughed and danced the night away. With a curious, but abrupt stand, David turned off the music and threw everyone out. No one opposed him. No one ever did. Toni thought it was rude but kept quiet. She found it more odd when they all wished David good luck.

The curiosity soon slipped her mind as she gathered up the dishes and cleaned the mess left behind. Just as she finished the dishes David bought her a drink and escorted her back to the patio. They both lay stretched across a lounge chair staring up at the huge oak tree spread open before the moonlight like a large umbrella. The stars twinkled as if to blink at them in playful lure. David undressed first, then gently unlayered Toni. His lips gently tugged on her breasts, causing her flesh to throb. He pushed his tongue in her mouth and pulled her lips into his mouth. He rested his weight on her squarely then plunged his manhood inside her. As the pressure built, Toni clawed and clung to him like a desperate kitten afraid of being thrown off. He pumped and pummeled her insides like a power pushing jack hammer. Toni could only pant like a dog and howl. With all his strength and power, he exploded inside her like a wrecking ball crashing into a lit keg of dynamite. They both groaned in ecstasy. The intensity was breath taking. Toni loved his style of love making. David was a "power pusher". He was not the kind to swerve and rock, but the up and down pressure plunger that left a woman rubbed raw and sore. Toni was most satisfied. As she lay there naked next to David, the warm summer air circled around her. Out of nowhere David slid a gold band on her left ring finger. Toni was completely taken by surprise. She sprang up from her seat, and threw her arms around him. She managed to squeeze a barely audible thank you from her buckled throat. Tears streamed down her face, as they stood there embraced flesh to flesh. David fell asleep while they were wrapped in each other's arms on the lounge chair. Toni was too excited to sleep. She stared up at the sky. The moonlight squeezed between the branches of the oak tree, creating a beautiful silhouette on the glass door. The branches seemed to dance as they swayed in the wind. The stars playfully winked at her as she watched them shoot across the sky to spread the joyous news from one to the other. For a split second her thoughts saddened. She only wished she could share this news with her mommy. As her heart began to grow sad, a bird began to sing from somewhere in the darkness. After a sigh of relief, Toni began to dream of her wedding day.

Chapter Four

No Wonder

David was more eager than ever to start the football season. This was his fourth and last season. He was determined to make it a good one. He focused on his stats and scores. Toni had to relinquish most of their time together to his workouts and week-end camps. David promised it was all in the name of progress and assuring his draft recognition. He worked harder than ever but soon trouble found its way into their life.

During the registration process, David received some bad news. He was told that his scholarship was under review. David went immediately to the Coach, who called a million and one meetings with everyone from the registrar to the university president. When all was said and done, the scholarship was denied due to David's persistent failing grades and GPA.

Toni was nearly as devastated as David. She didn't know a lot about football, but she knew losing his last season of eligibility could destroy his career. David had bet his whole life on football, and up until now it had been a sure bet. Now as Toni sat alone in the bleachers watching the team practice, like she had done hundreds of times before; she wondered if maybe this would be for the last time. The coach was allowing David to practice with the team, faithfully hoping on the appeal. He still trained someone else for David's plays as well. Toni reflected on the many victories and the demanding work David had put in to this point. As he bulldozed across the field, she could only see what tremendous power he had. The sights before her faded to a blur as she clasped her hands and held them against her face. It seemed like just yesterday they had met there. Now after only a year they were staring both their wildest dreams and crippling fears squarely in the face, and there was no magic fix.

Until now someone had always fixed things for David. If a term paper was due, someone would give him a paper to turn in. Homework assignments never cost him his time. Someone would make him aware of it when they handed him a completed assignment with his name on it. He couldn't however get around taking his own tests. Therein was his downfall.

The school had just been taken off athletic probation three years ago for forging athlete's grades. The news was published throughout the country and cost the school millions of dollars in financial support and lost contracts. But for this one indiscretion, the university had always attracted the top athletes from around the country. Now they were desperately clawing for their athletic pinnacle once again and David Spears was taking them there. David Spears was a household name locally. He was often mentioned on the evening news and his plays were outstanding. David had brought a lot of attention and monies back to the school, but damage control, was the catch phrase. The National Athletic Commission was watching the university like a hawk. They were due for another audit this fall and couldn't risk the least indiscretion. All in all David had single-handedly turned the school's fortune around. It was sad they couldn't provide him the same check mate.

Tears slid down Toni's cheeks as she pondered what to do. David had worked too hard to lose it all. It would destroy him, she whimpered. She felt uncontrollable sobbing coming forth. At the point of collapse, it came to her in the whisper of a gentle breeze. Humph, she mumbled as she mulled it over and over again. It might work she said aloud, sitting up straight to focus.

David was starting his fourth year of classes, yet he only had total credit equaling a second quarter sophomore. His GPA (grade point average) was 1.39 on a scale of 4.0. This standing would also delay his graduation by a minimum of three quarters. But Toni was devising a plan that would pull David's GPA up quickly. She felt a surge of energy and excitement shoot through her as she ran off to meet David and the coach and tell them her plan.

Toni's plan called for David to start a rigid program of class attendance consisting of a total of eighteen credit hours. He also would have a rigid program of tutoring and study overseen by an instructor. She also proposed a series of appeals that would keep his case in litigation until the end of the season. By then the decision wouldn't matter, since he would be allowed to play until the decision was final. Toni formed a collaboration of instructors, administrators and student tutors who all signed a contract of commitment. Toni presented the signed contract to David and the Coach who were both a bit unsure. Toni convinced them to present it to the Athletic Commission at the appeal meeting the following morning and pray like hell all that night.

Prayers were answered. David's funds were reinstated on a trial basis pending he stick to the signed contract and bring his GPA up to 2.5. All this was in place until the final decision from the Commission. David again escaped his true fate. He worked to late and wee hours of the night, but not without his share of complaints. In any case, he cooperated and squeaked through.

In late November, Toni noticed a distinct change in David. He was suddenly irritable and tense. In the beginning she wrote it off as pressure to pass tests and impress the continual stream of scouts watching his athletic progress. There was no let up from either academics or athletics. The coach constantly pushed David into setting one record after another. He constantly dangled the proverbial carrot before him saying if you set this record or break this one you're going in the first round draft my son. David pressed himself beyond mortal limits, to oblige the coach. He wanted the draft with all his heart, but the work was becoming unbearable under his own strength.

Little was known about a clandestine meeting in which Coach gave David some pills to help him with his endurance. By December David had become a taut frame of muscle weighing in at two hundred thirty pounds. He looked and felt uncomfortable, but everything was for the sake of his career. He became easily annoyed. His movements were nearly robotic. He was hostile and aggressive. His easy confident spirit had been torn to pieces. It'd always take him hours to relax. His love-making was no longer the rhythmic powerful climax of strength. It was a quick cold robotic missionary task. In a nagging undertone Toni could tell that David was about to blow all of his opportunities with this deranged behavior.

It was only the end of December before the whole team was at a stand off with David. One by one he had alienated each member of his team. Because of the disjointed unorganized nature amongst them they were having a losing season. In addition, David's behavior was disturbing his instructors as well. Many of his contract signers had walked out or quit on him. The team had dwindled down to a few barely there hang-oners. Toni though was ever faithful, still urging and coaxing David to study sessions and practice test skills. Toni had dropped most of her classes and lost sight of her own reality.

It was near the end of the season when Toni accidentally found some little pills in David's pockets. Then it all became clear. His ugly attitude, and huge body were not a result of over working in the gym. It was the damned pills Toni thought. She immediately threw them against the wall. No wonder she screamed aloud. No wonder he's a completely different man. No wonder he's blowing his career and no wonder he can't make love to me like he used to. It's the damned pills. She confronted David and asked him to stop taking them. He was angry that she had found them, and explained that he had to take them to perform at a professional level.

A losing season, a poor showing in statistics, a rotten reputation all lengthened David's wait for a draft letter. In spite of this, they Toni, David, and Ms. Spears waited desperately for the call and letter. They were all glued to the television on the official draft nights. David was breathing so hard and heavy it was erratic. Toni was worried that the pills had ruined not only his athletic but his general health. Ms. Spears had no clue. It was the third night, the tenth round of the draft, and David was in tears. Toni and Ms. Spears were trying to console him. He was inconsolable. For the two weeks following the close of the official draft, David stayed isolated in his room just sobbing. Toni skipped her classes and lay next to him just holding him. She understood the dark abyss he was spiraling through. She also knew he couldn't hear but could feel her vibrations. He was like a hollow shell, distant and lethargic. His weight melted off like ice cream on a hot cone since he didn't eat for weeks. His eyes were sullen and blank. So different than the man she got engaged to, David had none of his original happy confident spirit, not even an amber of pride.

Over the next few months he even edged on suicide. He was drinking to excess, popping volume and other street drugs like candy. He began smoking cigarettes and reefer daily. Toni was beginning to feel herself sinking into the black hole along with him. Toni felt there was nothing to lose. She composed and mailed letters to all the national football teams in the country with David's stats and profile. She made an excellent three paged presentation. She prayed they would reach their targets.

Two months later, Ms. Spears walked into the room casually and handed David a letter. It looked official and important. Toni saw a quick gleam run through David's eyes. He tore it open and jumped to his feet. It was like a keg of dynamite was lit inside him. He exploded in a roar of laughter, then danced. Ms. Spears and Toni hugged one another and screamed simultaneously. It was an invitation to a training camp of a pro football team. It was not a historically winning team but a national professional team none the less. Toni cried and prayed silently.

News spread rapidly about David's draft letter. When it aired on the evening news Toni in her usual seat in Ms. Spears's den, her mouth dropped open. They all broke out in applause of David. His eyes sparkled like stars in the sky and his frosty white teeth flashed like diamonds. Their relationship was heating up to it usual blazing hot range. Toni felt the heat in David's hand and the fire in his groin once again. They were having marathon love-making sessions in fantasy locations.

In the days to follow David received more instructions regarding his invite to the camp. He also received an invitation to a draft banquet of the local professional team. It included two tickets and a free tuxedo rental for the evening. David was torn over which of his favorite ladies he should take. He decided to visit his old coach who had some media friends who so happened to be co-sponsors of the affair. For a last favor Coach was able to secure him one extra ticket. David was the proud escort of two very excited women.

They entered the ballroom through the front entrance. David was flanked by Toni on his left arm, and his mother on his right arm. That always made Toni feel like a third wheel, but she never complained. Lately it would have been a losing battle. She and Ms. Spears both pretended not to mind the close proximity. The tension told otherwise. Toni could feel that David's heart and attention were unfairly divided. She tried not to press him for either under the circumstances. It wouldn't be long before she'd have David all to herself, she thought. She took a long deep breath and straightened her posture.

She had never seen such elegance. The grand ballroom of the Rothwell Country Club, Toni said to herself as she looked around in awe. It sat due south of the eighteenth hole on the Rothwell Golf Course. A strictly private club and course, located in the Rothwell section, the richest section of town. As a matter of fact very few people knew it was there. It was a two-tiered circular room with a grand staircase in the middle of it. Dozens of three foot chandeliers hung free flowing from the mile high ceilings, and gave off a rich golden glow. Opulent statues sat in niches about every two feet around sides of the room. Long, crimson colored velvet drapes softened every corner and swaged in about the chandeliers on the ceiling.

The local press swarmed the room. David along with other draftees, from the university were stars for the evening. In a display of support, some of the local and team professional football players made an appearance. They were all kind enough to congratulate David and the other draftees. Some of the faces were familiar to Toni, others not quite so. They were all fine, well-groomed, strapping strong black gentlemen. Yet there was a secret code that told other project survivors, they also were all from ghettos and projects across the country. Toni studied each one of them as they shook hands and chatted, moving assembly line fashion down the room toward the door. She pictured all of their mothers, and how extremely proud they must have been when they were in David's shoes. They all kissed and acknowledged Ms. Spears. The connection with her was clear for them. However, they all overlooked Toni. It wasn't a cruel up the nose way, but a cool oh excuse me brush off. Toni didn't let it bother her at that point. She knew she'd be in David's shadow from now on, and she didn't mind. After all they had to spread themselves fairly thin. These were professional men, strategic thinkers, Toni reasoned. They could only spend an allotted amount of time in any one place. Toni felt proud for them all.

She was fascinated. Her eyes continually gazed up and down that side of the room where they had all lined up somehow in a row, as if in grade school. A smile started spreading across her face, when suddenly, just as if someone had pushed her, her head rocked backward. She noticed something that had totally skipped her gaze before. All of the professional players had white female escorts on their arms. They were beautifully striking women. They were all fashion model types. They were all different hair colors, but they all were wafer thin with the long flowing hair right from the salon. Their dresses were expensive, sparkly after five dresses. They stood still and quiet with smiles plastered to their faces. Underneath they seemed agitated and bored. This was no exciting occasion for them, it was an endless duty. A curious humph grazed Toni's throat.

Toni had lost track of time, and didn't know how long she had been gazing at the players and their escorts. She turned her attention to David, who to her surprise, was still gazing in that direction. His eyes were widely aglow. She could see the longing and anticipation in his eyes. One of the escorts turned and walked toward the table. His eyes were intently fixed on her. David watched her with a suspicious smirk on his face. She had never seen such light in his eyes. It seemed he had stopped breathing. Toni jabbed him. Ms. Spears gave her a mean look. David hardly noticed.

The background music stopped and the ceremony began. Toni couldn't get her mind off the players. She wondered if they too had exhausted some black woman in their questful journey. She wondered if their plunders or weaknesses had been covered or fixed by some old black woman that had been long since forgotten. She wondered what made so many black men long for Caucasian women. She wondered what these women had to offer or what they stood for that so systematically drew these black men.

Toni stared curiously at David while he pretended to focus on the speaker. Her eyes danced about from player to player, paying special attention to their facial features. With a gentle sigh and lowering of the veil, the vision quietly unfolded before her eyes. First there was total darkness. Then a blistery white bird suddenly appeared. It was a curious looking specimen, but nothing she could identify. It was sitting high atop a jagged cliff, and it was staring into her eyes as if it wanted to speak to her. Its' eyes were clear blue streams of water, with a reflective brilliance. At the foot of the cliff were thousands of African American men, all reaching for the bird. Many attempted to climb the jagged cliff and some reached high enough to grasp the bird. The bird began to fly away with much power and speed. For the ones who had a grasp on the bird, they realized they were unable to move along with the bird. Their legs were clamped to the ground with thick metal chains and stakes. Too greedy and stubborn to let the bird loose, they clenched tighter until one of their legs were torn at the knee from the chains. As they tread through the rivers of blood with one leg they keep tight grip on the prized bird. Toni squeezed her eyes tightly. She couldn't believe this bloody vision. She wanted to ignore it but it wouldn't leave her memory. Humph Toni mumbled as she shook herself. I see she said to herself, as she focused on the players once again.

Toni's heart sank slowly. It became instantly clear to her. Many of these men still defined themselves within the views of the slave masters of old. They had subconsciously accepted the continuous messages of self-hatred that the slaves masters forced on them. For many years they had been told that beauty is white skin and long silky hair. With that definition at heart the Caucasian woman became the coveted prize, not to mention the clout and envy that came along with her. That was the image they (African American men) longed to create for themselves and their children. There was no crime in desiring or mixing the races. The crime was the sub-conscious self-hatred that propelled these desires.

If there was a cost it was totally insignificant to them. Freedom could not be overpriced.

Umph, umph, umph, no wonder Toni mumbled under her breath. She squeezed her eyes as tightly as she could. She didn't want to see anymore. She tried to listen to the speaker, but she couldn't hear them as clearly as she could hear the voices in her head. She realized there was a puddle of silent tears that danced around on her dinner plate. The veil lifted and she composed herself quietly, both David and Ms. Spears were unaware of her tumultuous awakening.

Not much time was left, but for the rest of the summer, David assumed a low profile. He fell into a very pensive, contemplative mood. He worked out at the university gym and weight room daily. Other than that, he stayed close to home, with the exception of a few necessary appointments. He was cold to his old friends; well the ones that were left after his destructive personality disorder. Besides the ones that were drafted, his closest friends had graduated and moved on to other cities or states in pursuit of jobs. They had made no special effort to keep in touch with David, and that suited him fine.

Toni was his only close friend left in the city. She found her visits with him labored. She found him most days lounging in the den with soft music in the background. His eyes always greeted her with joy and love, but he seemed purposely reserved for some special occasion.

On this particular day, she stopped by home and dressed up to try to rouse him. He stretched his arms to welcome her, but didn't speak. Toni asked about his day, and only got grunts and shrugged shoulders in response. Why you so quiet and far away she asked sitting with her legs spread across his lap, and looking directly into his eyes. He hid his eyes from her and answered with brief responses. I don't know, he shrugged. What's the matter baby? I want to help she pleaded. I'm just tired, he sidestepped her offer. He knew Toni could read his eyes, so he wrapped her in his arms tightly and closed his eyes. That was his subtle way of ending the query. He didn't seem to mind her presence, but remained in his solitude. Toni could still feel him holding himself back. There was no good reason. There was no bad reason. Their love was still there, but a metamorphosis was occurring inside him, and no one knew the outcome, not even David. For now he just held her quietly.

He held her until darkness hid their faces from each other's view. The darkness in the room gave him the freedom or courage to open up. Toni wasn't sure which it was but was glad to get some response from him. David began to talk. Little did she know how confined his spirit had been until now. The long desperate wait for the draft letter had left its' scars. He began to speak in a passionate voice. I worked with all my strength toward being a pro football player, he began. There were no other options for me baby. My soul, my soul he paused for a moment and clutched his chest. Toni could hear faint sniffles. I dreamt I died baby. I died and never played football again. But before I died I got to see my whole life up 'til now. The most important people, the ones that were there for me were my mom, my aunt and you. Yaw'll were the ones that really loved me and took care of me. The coaches weren't there. The cheerleaders weren't there. The teachers weren't there. Jus' you, my momma, and my aunt were the only ones there. I learned something from that, that I'll never forget baby. I saw you work yourself ragged to get me through those classes, and I didn't even try to cooperate. I thought there was no reason without football. I realize that you gave up your classes and time for me. Your love is so strong and so true. I know that you will be a part of me forever. I will always love you for that. As soon as I make the team and get settled you will be my wife forever.

David went on and purged his soul of the sickening, cramped mysteries that had taken him to the other side of darkness. As soon as he finished speaking, the light that had been extinguished relit in his eyes. His body was limber and undaunted. Toni hoped he had learned the value of true love.

Chapter Five

One Armed Bandit

Everyone had found their freedom from Sue's house except Toni and little Daryl. The environment was completely different without Linda. It was unusually dreary with a ready blank canvas feel. It was as if it was just waiting for the fun and excitement to begin. It felt as if Sue were a visitor in her own house. Her if you love me's were entirely played out and she knew it. The thought of facing herself was completely exhausting to her, and Toni could see Sue's eyes pleading for companionship.

She rushed into the kitchen and ushered Sue straight to the living room couch. I got good news she sang. Sue bounced on the couch like a school girl. David and I are engaged, Toni waved her ring finger in the air. They both screamed and hugged each other tightly. They talked for hours discussing her wedding date and plans. While Sue was explaining her wishes for Toni's wedding, her color choices, her program format, her musical choices, Toni realized how bad she felt for Sue. Sue was living vicariously through Toni. She had little to no chance of getting married. She was sentenced to a damnation of loneliness and deprivation. A life without tongue kissing or caressing, not to mention love-making to the twelveth degree of power, was her forseeable future. Too bad, Toni thought while Sue bubbled on about the wedding. It was clear now that The Warriors were like a one armed bandits. They had to steal as many moments and gestures of love from every possible situation as they could. They always had one arm around their children which only left one arm to gather their necessities. They did it with such grace and fortitude that it actually looked easy. That's why a Warrior could live and die at the same time. It is why they (The Warriors) got fat and out of shape. Toni understood why they don't even bother to fix their hair. She could see why they don't put on make-up and high heels. Toni felt a tear well up in the corner of her eye. That's why she never leaves from behind the wall, Toni thought. It's her man. That damned wall is her only man. It is the only solid, strength, stability and protector she has. She took a deep long breath and looked at Sue again. She hadn't taken a single breath since she started talking. Toni let her continue without interrupting, but she made up her mind then and there to never become like Sue. She'd always fix her hair and step lively like her mother Anna Sue Patterson. She was determined to take care of her teeth, and stay fit and slim no matter what. She would become a Master and never the Warrior of her Aunt Sue's class. Toni raised her head high and smiled while Sue went on and on.

Toni knew she could not let the news reach Linda before she had a chance to tell her personally. After a late dinner with Sue and Daryl, she raced across the courtyard to Linda's apartment in the Whittenhall. Linda's apartment was full as usual. When she stepped in Linda shouted we heard Mrs. Spears. The Stars had intercepted the news and beat Toni to the punch. Someone probably saw the ring on Toni's finger when she arrived home that morning and started the news bulletin instantly. They all laughed and the celebration continued on into the night.

Toni stayed until everyone else had left. As she prepared to leave, Linda reached for her hand. I'm so proud of you cuz she sighed. You gon have the best out of life and I'm happy for you. Toni squeezed her hand and asked, why don't you go back to school Linda? As courageous as Linda was in the face of violence, single parenthood, and long term poverty, the challenge of a small book was more than she could bear. Linda generally laughed off any questions or anything that tested her. She could make a joke out of almost anything, no matter how tragic. This time neither of them laughed. Toni persisted with the subject and implored Linda to take one more shot at school. Linda just lowered her head and smiled. You doin' it for the both of us cuz, she responded, then went to her bedroom and closed the door. Toni felt as if a chamber in her heart had slammed shut as well.

The summer was blazing to an end. Toni had given no thought to the fall quarter, but it was time for registration again. Suddenly the realities of the past quarter came rushing back to her. She had dropped and neglected most of her classes last quarter. She was forced to kick things back into gear for the coming quarter.

She sighed relief when all of her classes were signed by the professors. Turning her completed registration over to the Bursar's office, she casually walked away. When the clerk called her back she was slightly annoyed. How do you plan to pay Ms. Patterson, the clerk huffed. With my grants Toni snapped back. I see no grant assigned to you for this quarter Ms. Patterson. As a matter of fact, let me see, she shuffled through some papers; ah yes, they've been cancelled. She pointed to the evidence. Toni's mouth dropped open and tears slid down her cheeks. The clerk swiftly advised, try the financial aid office. Next she called as if to dismiss Toni. The noises faded to a blur. She was dazed. She fumbled her way to the financial aid office. She explained her dilemma still dazed and teary. She was ushered to the director's office for assistance.

Mr. Howich was a short slim boyish looking man. His dark hair was tossled and messy. He scanned Toni with his eyes. Toni winched at his hot wild gaze over her body. He tried to smile but his mouth was dry and crusty. Have a seat he invited Toni. She struggled through her dilemma once again this time feeling sick to her stomach. His horny eyes were upsetting her as well. He stood up abruptly in the middle of her sentence. He walked to the front of his desk and sat spread eagle on the desk top directly in front of her. He laid his hand lightly on her shoulder, and said you need money don't you? I can get you all the money you want for school or anything else he assured her. He returned to his seat and made three quick phone calls. Why don't you come back later say around six o'clock, and I'll have all the paperwork drawn up and ready for you to sign. Toni could see his intentions were filthy, but she was destitute. She simply nodded her head and left.

Toni wasn't sure what she should do. She knew exactly what Howich expected in exchange for his assistance. Sleeping with him was not a desirable option for her. She quivered at the thought of tasting his dry crusty mouth. The thought of him touching her intimately was nearly unbearable, but she had no other choice if she wanted to attend school that year.

She immediately headed for the Whittenhall. She pondered what she would tell Sue and Linda who had just commended her for going to college. In the back of her mind she could hear the Star's rumors saying, I told you so. She never should have gone to college in the first place. The bus ride home unshadowed all of the demons that had haunted her in the past. By the time she reached the Whittenhall she looked like she had seen a ghost. Linda opened the door and immediately screamed what's wrong with you girl? Toni stepped inside the door, dropped onto the couch to tell the story in a distant haunted voice. Staring straight ahead, she didn't even realize when she had finished. She finally heard her silence. When her focus returned, Linda and her two guests were seated at her feet looking up into her eyes. The expressions on their faces only reminded Toni that all was hopeless. Linda stood up and flanked her arms around Toni. They both began to cry.

Tina who was still seated on the floor around the coffee table said Let's pray. Tina took the first prayer, and before long they were all singing songs of praise and telling tales of great faith.

As the afternoon drew to a close, Toni headed back to campus for her after hours meeting with Howich. With her patch work faith in tact she swallowed her fears. She eased into the dark office of financial aid. It was empty. Just the way Howich wanted it Toni thought. She could see a dim light squeezing through a cracked door at the end of the hallway. She walked quietly down the hall as if not to disturb anyone. The only noise was the whispers in her head warning her not to enter the danger zone. Toni hadn't completely decided how to handle his advances. Her thoughts flipped flopped from blowing his mind with her sexiness to cussing him out. She was terrified. Tears streamed down her face and she was shivering all over. Her heart was beating louder with every step. She was sure he could hear her approaching.

She stuck her head in the door. Howich had his head laid back on the chair and his mouth hung open. For a split second she thought he was asleep. Suddenly she noticed the flinch of his arm. His hands were both under the desk. His arms were jerking rapidly and his breathing followed rhythm. Toni couldn't believe what was happening. This wanna be pimp is in here jackin' off, she mumbled under her breath. She cleared her throat loudly and said excuse me. Howich flipped over the side of his chair. Is it six o'clock already, he asked surprised as a thief. Toni could hear him zip his pants as he scrambled to his feet. It's five forty five Toni quipped with a smirk on her face. Yes I lost track of time, he said looking over the top of his glasses shamefully. His face was beet red. Somehow he skillfully merged to the subject at hand. C'mon sit down. I have everything prepared and waiting for you to sign. He spread several papers in front of her. This oughta take care of you for the entire year he said clearing his throat. Why don't you look these over for a moment. Toni obliged. While she reviewed the work he turned in his swivel chair as if to look out the window behind him. Toni could see him wiggling in the chair to adjust his crouch. She held her burst of laughter in while she signed the expense paid checks. There you go she said as she recovered to a solemn expression. Thank you for everything Toni said finalizing the deal. Howich extended his hand to shake. Toni stared at it distastefully. Howich withdrew again ashamed. Um Ms Patterson, he hesitated to find the words. Hopefully this unfortunate coincidence won't cause either of us any problem, he uttered feebly. Please let me know if I can be of service to you in any other way. If maybe, you'd come back around five thirty tomorrow, we could get better acquainted and I can get you more assistance. Toni snapped her fingers and Linda, Tina and Terri rushed through the door. Howich was horrified. He nearly flipped over the side of his chair again. Linda and the girls looked crude and threatening. I'll be back next year Howich, Toni snickered. Yeah you betta' take care of my girl Linda growled. Oh yes ma'am Howich quivered. Toni and the girls ran out into the darkness and fell on the grass howling with laughter. All's well that ends well said Tina and they ran back to Whittenhall to celebrate.

Chapter Six

The Long Road Back

David made no formality about leaving. He insisted that he didn't want any fanfare, weepy bon voyage type of ordeals. He just wanted to get on the plane and go. Toni knew that he was just too excited to slow down for the good byes. He insisted that he needed to go down early and get used to the weather and schedule. He was also anxious to begin paving his road to stardom. He kept his departure date a secret telling only his mother and Toni.

His mother still invited a few close family members to dinner the night before he chose to leave, which was actually two weeks earlier than his true report date. Ms. Spears tried to pretend she inadvertently forgot to call Toni, but David insisted that she be there.

David was quiet throughout the meal. Toni watched him curiously. Just before they finished the meal David left the table. He returned promptly with two gifts in hand. Toni's heart swelled with tenderness. David kindly handed one gift to his mom and the other to his aunt. A ball formed in Toni's throat as she struggled to remain emotionless. She fought back her disappointment without moving a muscle. He gave a toast of thanks to his mother and aunt then finished his meal quickly.

After the guests had left, David took Toni in his bedroom and closed the door. He still said very little. He held out his arms and extended his hands to her. She laid her hands in his. He guided her to the side of his bed and knelt on both knees. He softly tugged her arms so that she would join him. He stared into her eyes quietly for a few minutes. The room was dark except for the light of the street lamp squeezing through the undrawn panes. Toni could see his eyes sparkling in the dark. She felt their heats interlocking without effort. Without indication, David reached under the bed and pulled out a box. It was gift wrapped. Toni was flabbergasted. It was too big to be a ring she realized. It was too small to be luggage she figured. So she tore into the wrapping and ripped open the box. It was a piece of sheer white sequined lace. Toni was confused, but she didn't want to show it. This is beautiful David she said as she threw it around her shoulders. No David responded quietly. He took the lace from her shoulders and gently laid it over her head veiling her face. It's a veil he continued. Without hesitation he bowed his head and began to speak. Almighty God, Jah, thank you for the blessing you've placed before me. I'm sorry I took the gifts you gave me for granted, and sometimes doubted myself and even you. From now on please help me to live my life to praise you, and please accept me to this woman with me tonight as I take her for my wife, and friend and lover, for the rest of my life. Please take care of my family when I leave . . . Toni's hearing faded as David continued to pray. Her heart was beating so loudly she couldn't tell what else he was saying. Suddenly he lifted the veil and kissed her passionately. They spent the night together making love and promises to care for one another eternally.

David bought her home around six thirty the following morning. He held her hand and asked her not to worry or cry, since they were now joined before God. He reassured her he would return shortly for his bride. As she watched him drive off, she felt cold and empty in the middle of the summer morning. She stood frozen on the steps of Whittenhall, seeing only his sweet sparkling eyes before her. When she finally jolted herself into the present, she realized her clothes were soaked with tears. She shuffled the box in her arms and headed for home.

For the first few months David called nightly from his training camp. He shared his experiences from that day with her. Even though it was very tough work, he loved training camp. After the third month his calls became spontaneous. Sometimes he'd call two days in a row. Sometimes he would call once a week or even every two weeks. In any case, he was happy and his joy saturated her heart.

The months melted away. Toni was lonely for David. She muddled through her days at school and evenings at the law firm where they had asked her to return for part-time work. She had moved off the campus back into Sue's house. She stayed with Linda frequently as well. She kept most of her things packed, expecting any day to be called to David's side. The wedding veil stayed unpacked and she wore it every evening while they spoke on the phone. After the call she hung it on her bedpost for pleasant dreams.

David enjoyed telling Toni about his maneuvers on the field and how he made the plays more exciting by altering them to fit his spur of the moment decisions. He was progressing exceptionally well by his accounts, but Toni felt trouble panting forward.

When the season started David expressed to Toni that he was disappointed that he was not a starter. He sounded as if it bothered him more than he cared to mention. By now Toni could hear both his spoken and unspoken voice. She felt helpless listening to him because he was always at one extreme or another. Some evenings he called elated hardly allowing her a word. Some evenings he called sounding as if he were at the edge of the world about to fall off, hardly allowing her a word. As the season moved forward David became more frustrated and complained to Toni and his coaches. Toni feared more than anything he'd turn to drugs. She finally convinced him to send for her so that she could help him through his trail. At his point of bewilderment, he agreed.

Her plane landed at twelve fifty, right on schedule. She was very relieved to see David waiting at the gate. He seemed surprisingly more like his old self than she expected. He rushed to her, picked her up, and carried her through the gate kissing and hugging her. Their magic was back, if only for the moment.

They stopped at a fancy hotel for lunch, then David got a room so they could share their love in a wild, untamed desperation. David felt stronger than ever. He pushed and pummeled her inside. Toni clawed and grabbed his flesh. It was pleasantly torturous. Before they could relax, he chauffeured her on a city wide tour. They stopped frequently so he could introduce her to a great number of friends he had made in such a short time, and his teammates. Some of their visits were rather lengthy, with informal parties starting up. Toni was so flattered that David wanted all of his friends to meet her. She fell in love with him all over again.

It was nearly eleven thirty that evening before they arrived at David's apartment. Toni was exhausted. David turned the lock, and peeped in the door as if he wasn't sure he had the right apartment. Toni was slightly tickled by his boyishness. He took her coat and asked her to grab him a beer out of the fridge. He headed for the bedroom with her bags. She was browsing around admiring his style when she heard his voice roar. She called to him curiously, what did you say? I'll be out in a few minutes baby he yelled back to her. She could hear him close the door and lock it. Before she could reach the door she heard loud rumbling and pounding noises, then screams. She beat on the door calling David at the top of her voice. He apparently couldn't hear her. She quickly searched the apartment for something to break through the door. She found some steps that led to a lower level. There was a den which led to a garage. In the garage Toni found an axe. She rushed back up the stairs where she could still hear screams and rumbling. The fear and adrenaline was pumping her with strength and anger. She swung the axe against the door three times before she heard David's voice screaming. Toni, Toni, Toni. He flung the door open. By then there was a large hole right in the center of it. David grabbed her by the arms and tried to restrain her. From the corner of her eye, she caught a glance of a woman getting up off the bed. She was half naked with only her bra and panties on. Her bra was crooked and one breast hung out from under it. Her straight blonde hair was tossled, clearly showing the signs of the struggle. She curled up next to the wall and glared with her icy blue eyes while she tried to straighten her bra. Toni responded with sheer rage. David couldn't contain her. She threw the axe straight between the woman's eyes. The axe anchored in the wall with three inches of blonde hair hanging from it. Toni went into the windmill frenzie. Some of her blows were hitting the unspecified mark, but most of them hitting the air. How could you do this to me she screamed at David. David couldn't get control over Toni, so he pushed her on the bed and ran for the door. Toni ran toward the woman and grabbed the axe out of the wall and ran after David. She didn't know how far she had run before she heard the sirens. The noise shook her to her senses. She realized she was out of breath and quite tired. She looked around and she was in the middle of a busy street with an axe in her hand, with people staring at her. She panted as she headed back to David's apartment. David was nowhere to be found.

When she got back to the apartment the woman was still there. She had fixed herself up and looked far more composed. Toni only had strength left to ask her who the hell she was and what the hell she was doing in David's apartment. I'd kick yo' ass if I wasn't so tired, Toni squealed breathlessly. The woman cringed into a ball and slid to the floor screaming, I didn't know. I thought he really loved me. Her words snatched the anger out of Toni. She heard herself say, so did I.

Toni questioned the woman about her relationship with David. At first they spoke in short harsh sentences to one another. Both of them were still upset, hurt, and unable to direct their feelings. The woman explained that they had been together since he got in town. Toni's anger rose again. But how can you love a black man, her tone was again razor sharp. How can you begin to love him or understand a person so different than yourself, Toni battered on. You can't be a part of his world because you can never understand it. The woman retorted, at first I didn't understand him. I didn't understand why he wanted me so much. I have never been so *wanted* in all my life. I enjoyed his relentless pursuit and courting. After we got engaged, she waved her diamond ring in Toni's face. Toni's mouth dropped. The woman continued, but after we got engaged things changed. You're right I guess I don't understand him. I never thought he'd do this to me. To you, you humph, Toni jumped to her feet. I refuse to stay here and play concubine. I know that I'm far too good Toni yelled. Toni knew in her heart she had just been sentenced to Warrior hell in the projects.

The woman went into the corner of the closet and came out with a small overnight bag and a large envelope which she handed to Toni. Toni looked inside the envelope. It contained hundreds of dollar bills and a man's gold wrist watch. That's my "mad money" she exclaimed. They both tried a sordid grin at each other. The woman then called a cab. They decided to ride to the airport together.

It was a quiet ride with occasional tears. When they arrived at the airport, the lady bought a one way ticket to Missouri. Toni examined her as she stood talking to the reservationist. She wasn't exceptionally pretty. As a matter of fact, Toni thought she looked quite plain. But why then had David wanted her as badly as she said he did. Toni felt her anger returning. She took in a long breath to suppress the anger, but tears forged down her cheeks. To her surprise when the woman turned to bid her good bye, she too was crying. Toni's pain stopped momentarily. Was it her fault she asked herself. Could she blame her for accepting the invitation into a life of luxury and excitement? The only cost to her was her blonde hair and blue eyes. With such an easy ticket for her to attain why should I blame her, Toni continued questioning herself. I'd do it too Toni thought. If that's all it cost, I'd accept too, Toni could hear herself mumbling. The woman reached for Toni's hand and shook it. By the way I'm Janah she said. They parted at the gate staring at one another suspiciously, akin in their love and pain for the same man.

When Toni reached home she had so much pent up anger that she was psychotic. She went straight to her room and let loose the fury that she had had to compose until then. Pounding and yelling and thumps and thuds, went on until late in the night. She took the veil that David had given her and tore it to shreds. Then there was dead silence. Sue who had sat patiently on the other side of the door, went in to check.

Once again Sue nurtured Toni. She didn't spiral into her black hole, but she was distraught. Sue helped her through her painful journey. This time Toni and Sue talked their way through Toni's hell. As time went by, Toni gradually saw Sue differently. She was so ashamed of her former opinion of Sue that she could barely look her in the face as Sue handed her a dinner plate. Now Toni could see the strength in the tattered survivor she called Aunt Sue. She saw the hero deep within the wounded woman that had courage to face each day boldly. She saw the tenderness pouring out of Sue's parched and torrid spirit, with a wealthy reserve of understanding. She finally saw the wisdom in Sue's uneducated, brash will. Toni was so ashamed she had blamed Sue for all the times she asked for love. She studied Sue with new eyes. What she used to see as a rough beaten hag, was now a disciplined, skillful soldier, fighting on, in spite of her crippling wounds. Now Toni knew she'd have to learn to be a Warrior too. Sue would gladly teach her all too well. Toni used to cringe when Sue opened her mouth. She used to be embarrassed by Sue's grammatically incorrect statements. Now she cherished the private lessons on life from a Master. Sue was suddenly the most sensible person she'd ever met.

All of Whittenhall's lessons up to this point had been hard. Now Toni was extremely proud and most of all, informed. She believed these beginnings had been the best lesson in preparation for life's harshness and irony. Toni felt a new strength growing inside her. She knew her life was irreversibly different. She could feel the beginning of a complete person forming within her. Sue had taught her to face life boldly on real terms. Toni never resorted to cursing and screaming or emotional fits. Ironically she looked and sounded completely different than Sue, but she was a protégé of Sue's school of hard knocks. Those weeks had been one of the most meaningful changes in her life. She had graduated from a naïve kitten to a crowned lioness with fearless pursuits of womanhood. It felt good in its' own way to be back home.

David had tried relentlessly to contact her. Toni knew she had a lot to say to him, but wasn't prepared to speak with him at the time. She still spent lots of quiet time in her room. She now understood David's pensive mood before leaving for camp. It wasn't the excitement or selfishness she thought it was. It was the realization, and weight of a huge new task ahead. She needed her space to grow into a unique strong soldier.

Toni was certain she wanted to pick her life back up and continue where she left off. With a lot of contemplation and urging from Sue and Linda she decided to return to school. She immediately made an appointment with Howich, her financial aid advisor. She went to his office the next afternoon again at the scheduled time of five forty five. She felt both a little worried and a little tickled inside at what she might find when she entered his office. To her surprise Howich wasn't there. She stood in front of his desk flabbergasted wondering why he'd stand her up. Feeling the disappointment begin to set in she said out loud, No More. I'll wait here until he gets back. Within a few minutes Howich rushed in looking as goofy and boyish as ever. Toni snickered under her breath. He apologized sincerely as he explained he had to run to the bathroom. He motioned for her to sit down.

Toni explained everything that had happened from her tutoring David to his draft to their broken engagement. He watched her lips with hot desire as she formed every word. Howich got up from his seat without saying a word. He walked to the side of his desk, and laid his hand on her shoulder. He promised her he would help her through whatever financing she would need including her old job back at the law firm. Finally his eyes were sincere and warm like a friend. He extended his hand to shake on the promise. Toni hesitated for a moment then grasped it lightly. They both laughed aloud without explanation.

She again chose to live off campus. For convenience and familiarity she chose to rent her own apartment in the Whittenhall, at least that's what she told herself. Before long her commute and work schedule became routine. But winter was setting in quickly. Chilly mornings made her pull out her cordaroy pants and long johns, as well as sweaters and gloves. When she tried on a pair she found out that they had shrunk since last winter. They wouldn't fit around her waist by several inches. Toni' couldn't believe that she had gained so much weight.

When she tried to force the button closed she only broke her fingernail. She glanced at herself in the mirror. For some strange reason she started counting. She couldn't remember when her last period was. To her closest recollection, it was in mid-summer before she visited David. Suddenly she heard herself scream. I'm pregnant. Oh no I'm pregnant. She sat on the bed in front of her mirror and stared at herself while dozens of thoughts clouded her mind. Before she realized it, it had been more than an hour. She felt a surge of strength go through her body. She stood up and faced the mirror and vowed; no more dark abyss for me. I'm going to school. I'm going to graduate. I'm going to law school and become an attorney. I am going to make a wonderful life for me and my child, she said as she rubbed her belly. She hesitated for a moment and allowed room for a doubt. When Ms. Spears came to her mind she nodded her head and confirmed, yes I can make it on my own.

She was extremely determined to make up for her poor grades the last quarter. She studied hard and was excelling in her classes. She still had refused to take David's calls and was surprised he hadn't given up. Even though she was very busy, the solitude and loneliness sometimes wore her down. While she was sitting in her apartment one Saturday afternoon, there was a knock at the door. Well, well, well, will wonders ever cease, Toni sprouted out when she opened the door. There to her surprise stood Ms. Spears. The shock clearly showed on both their faces. The proud mother superior had humbled herself, to the point of coming to the Whittehall Projects to ask Toni to return David's calls. She invited Ms. Spears in. Being ever the queen, she refused to sit, but stepped inside the door. When did this happen Ms. Spears asked smacking her lips distastefully and pointing to Toni's stomach. Toni politely dismissed her with no verbal response. You can tell him for me that he is soon to be a father, Toni lamented without any other conversation. Ms. Spears left more disgusted than she came.

Toni wanted to smooth everything out with David as if nothing had ever happened. The facts remained. Sue's lessons had taught her; if nothing else you have to respect the facts. The real fact of the matter was that Toni knew there was no true desire in David's heart for her. His taste had completely changed. What she was, and will always be, a black woman, he no longer truly desired. They had been wedged apart.

Two more months past before Toni accepted one of David's phone calls. By then she was six months pregnant. She wasn't completely oblivious to his standing. He was still of local interest, and brief segments were appearing on the local news about him. Nearing the end of the season, a big news story started running in the newspaper about David. He had been arrested on domestic violence charges for critically injuring his wife. Toni read it again. Wife she yelled out loud. Toni recognized the woman to be his live in fiancé, Janah, who was now his *wife*.

His last letter was delivered to her personally by express messenger. The message pleaded that it was urgent that he meet with her. It stated that he would be in town on tomorrow's date. He had been released from jail on twenty five thousand dollars bond, according to the newspaper. He was due in court two days from his arrival date.

Toni felt she was ready and needed to talk at this point. She agreed to meet David around noon at the university football stadium. She had finally organized her thoughts and decided on her feelings. She had practiced what she'd say to him as she watched herself in the mirror "telling him off."

She barely recognized David as he approached from the distance. Slightly staggering and mumbling, he stopped about a foot short of her presence. Toni looked into David's bloodshot eyes. They stood apart just staring for several minutes. He reeked of alcohol and reefer. His physique was weak and his posture poor. Toni knew something was terribly wrong. I love you was the first thing out of his mouth. Toni realized he was drunk. She curled and twisted her lips. It wasn't worth her time and emotions to yell at him, she thought. She remained silent.

I messed up babe, he stammered. I messed up bad. I didn't mean to hurt anybody, he paused for a long moment as if he was thinking things through. Not anybody, he used his hand to slice the air and make the statement absolute. But, but she, see she, he stammered with his words. She might die babe, she might die, and, and, and he could barely go on. And the baby's already dead he paused listening to his own words to see if they were correct. He just dropped to his knees and wept miserably. He stopped suddenly and looked around like someone had yanked his hair. He stood up slowly and tried to stand solid on his woobly legs. He couldn't. He stumbled back a few steps. Toni turned to leave. No babe no, please, please help me. He caught hold of her arm. Please, he squealed. His voice was so miserable, it was like an abandoned child. Toni's heart melted. She took a deep breath and turned slowly to face him. I I I I I just need you to help me, he whined. I can't lose my career. Toni stood solidly in front of him surveying him. What do you need she asked roughly. I just need to stay with you for a little while babe. See see I I can't can't he repeated shaking his head in disbelief; I can't go to jail. I just need to stay with you til my lawyers get this straightened out. Toni couldn't believe his audascity. Toni walked away rather than say the foul things about to burst through her lips. I love you babe he called to her. He struggled to catch her, but fell flat on his face. Toni's heart couldn't feel sorry for him anyway. I'll call yo' momma and yo' lawyer, she called back to him tasting the cold bloody words in her mouth.

Toni couldn't get David's words out of her mind. The betrayal was insufferable. She was sleepless for the next two nights. Her throat was swollen nearly shut due to the sympathy she felt for them all. On the third morning Ms. Spears called.

David had been rearrested and jailed. He had tried to hide away at his mother's house but the NFL insisted he return to Florida or forfeit his contract. When he reported to camp he was rearrested, without bail, she explained. How's Janah Toni asked defiantly. She's gonna pull through Ms. Spears squeezed through her clenched teeth.

David sent her a letter from jail. He explained, quite clearly to her surprise, that Janah had been released from the hospital recently and was recovering nicely at her parent's home in Kansas City, Missouri. She had sued him and been granted the remaining dispersements from his contract. It was a seven hundred thousand dollar settlement in her sole favor.

Toni felt sick. She knew David would have nothing to offer their child. She knew it would be a long time and a long road back for him.

Chapter Seven

A New Day

Toni valued the life growing inside her. She was excited and looking forward to motherhood. It wouldn't be long now, just around six weeks and her baby boy would be delivered to her like an unwrapped gift.

She still felt grief for David. His sentence was extreme and harsh. He was given fifteen years without parole for felonious assault. Toni knew that there was very little chance that he'd know his son, given the fact that their son would be at least fourteen before they even had a chance to meet. That meant only one thing to Toni; that she had to be the best mother she could possibly be.

David Spears Jr. was born May 18, 1975 at seven fifteen in the morning. He weighed in at a healthy eight pounds ten ounces. Toni's eyes were beaming with joy. She had barely had time to finish the spring quarter before he arrived. She decided to sit out for the summer and fall sessions of school.

It was heartbreaking for her to return to school in the winter quarter, because she hated leaving David Jr. But she had made arrangements for Linda to babysit him since Linda was hoping to start a daycare anyway. Toni trusted Linda implicitly. David Jr's eyes inspired her. He had that same sparkle in his eyes as his father and she felt indebted to them.

During the next two years of her life Toni concentrated on school, work and diapers. She gradually realized she was becoming more attracted to the practice of law everyday. She watched the attorneys wheel and deal daily, and admired their skills. On a long bus ride home it occurred to her that she too was designed for the law profession. That desire created a longing that she could not erase. She knew it would mean long hours and little time for David Jr., but she decided the sacrifice was worth it.

Toni's life had turned an unfamiliar corner. Success in the form of graduation was upon her. For the first time in her life she felt validated and powerful. All of the people in her life were so important to her. They were the love and support system that had allowed her to reach her goal, especially her two and a half year old son.

She was ecstatically surprised to receive a graduation card in the mail from Ms. Spears and David. Enclosed with the card was a one hundred dollar bill. It was nice to see the queen mother bow down to humility. The mixture of gratitude and rivalry that she felt toward Ms. Spears was sobering. Toni still felt unforgiving toward her for all the put downs and trashy get out of my house looks she had aimed at her. She also felt grateful to her for it was Ms. Spears that had been the role model she aimed for and the success story she yearned to be. For so long she never really thought it would happen, but Toni finally realized she had targeted all of her anger over David's infidelity, over society's injustices, and even over loosing her mother, toward Ms. Spears. That anger ironically, was the fuel that propelled her through her last two years of school. She wasn't quite sure how to thank Ms. Spears for that.

As a matter of fact Ms. Spears had never visited her grandson for those two years or so much as bought him a diaper. According to Toni's record of affairs, there was still plenty to be upset with Ms. Spears about. Instead she thought, a simple thank you card ought to settle matters nicely. Toni felt herself laugh out loud. I don't have to bow down to her anymore either. The freedom felt joyous.

Along with the freedom came a responsibility that Toni could not ignore. She discussed her goals and plans with Linda and Sue to attend Law School. The three of them made out a schedule that would accommodate them all. She also discussed her intentions with Howich, who was also accommodating with financial and academic aides. He assisted Toni in securing test materials as well as books.

Everyone in Toni's life was now in a different position. Toni kept her job at the law firm, but scaled back her hours. Sue and Linda were now Toni biggest supporters and motivators. Sue called her every morning before she bought over breakfast and a motivational thought for the day. She had been learning to read through her private tutoring lessons. She would barely stumble through the thought but it was like music to Toni's ears while she dressed herself and David Jr. She would then transport David Jr. to Linda's daycare for the day. At night Sue also made a nutritious dinner so that Toni had no bother with finding or preparing an evening meal for her and David Jr. Sue also continued to teach Toni lessons on becoming a Master. She counseled Toni on how to let go of the pain and hatred toward David and Ms. Spears. Sue was now more than dear to her she was like a mother. Their bond was secured forever.

Toni's love and indebtedness to Linda was also growing. Linda was like a foot soldier for Toni. She would run many of Toni's errands and handle paying her bills for her. Most importantly, she provided loving care for David Jr. It was evident to Toni that Linda loved him along with her own children the way Sue had shown love for her along with Linda and her other children.

One evening, Toni returned home early from her study group and found Linda in the middle of reading a story to the kids. When she looked up and saw Toni standing there her face filled with shame and embarrassment. She slammed the book shut and ushered the kids off to play. Toni had always known Linda was a poor reader but not to the extent she had just heard. Toni hugged Linda and said it's alright cuz. I love the way you take care of the kids. I've got a deal for you. Why don't I stop by at least three times a week and I'll tutor you in reading and writing. Linda stoically declined. Toni hushed her gently. Then I won't owe you a zillion and one dollars when I get out of Law School, for all you do for me, Toni jokingly consoled Linda. Toni was insistent with Linda who was grateful but still ashamed. Toni sat down immediately and worked out a schedule with Linda for her tutoring sessions.

The next day Toni stopped in on Linda with loads of reading and writing materials. She started the lessons right away. The lessons started off slow and awkward. Linda for the first time had nowhere to hide her vulnerability. This often made her angry so she often sabotaged the lessons by starting an argument with Toni. Fortunately, Toni recognized it for what it was-simply Psychology 101. She would comfort Linda and persist with the lesson. It wasn't always easy, especially when Toni had had a long dogged day of her own. Occasionally, Toni would give in to Linda's bitterness and resentment and they'd both argue. It took only a few minutes or a good night's sleep and everyone was back on track. After all's said and done Toni lamented to Linda, Sue built a house of love and love prevails.

As slowly as Toni was becoming a lawyer, Linda was becoming a reader. Painfully slow and difficult were both of their lessons. Added to that Toni felt guilt over the little time she could spend with David Jr. She took advantage of every opportunity, but she only wished there was more time for it. At times when she felt like less than a good mother, Sue was there to console Toni with comforting thoughts from the scriptures. Toni maintained holding those words close and dear.

Linda became more eager as she progressed in her reading lessons. As a second year law student, Toni became more accustomed to the grueling schedule and didn't hurt as much. Linda was buckling down as well. By the end of the third year, they both had sunk their teeth into their subjects like pit bulls, and both of them were ferocious. Linda had advanced so much; Toni was able to turn her studies over to advanced GED classes conducted at the Whittenhall Projects.

During her fourth year of Law School, Linda and Toni cried on each other's shoulders. Both of them were at the height of their goals, and it took time and tenacity to pull them both through. In June of that year, after four years of nerve wrecking, over demanding, hair shedding study; they both graduated, Linda from high school and Toni from Law School. During a private conversation between

Toni and Linda; Linda vowed to go to college and fulfill her dream of becoming a kindergarten teacher. Toni took her to visit Howich the very next morning.

It was another year before Toni passed her bar exam, and joined her law firm as a staff attorney. As she had watched David Jr. grow, she became more convinced that he needed a father figure in his life. She sat in her office contemplating what was best for David Jr. She decided to buy a house and settle down more like suburban families. She had cried privately to God over all the time David Jr. had spent in the Projects. She felt she owed him more than that. Now she was ready to move on.

The townhouse in the Blue Rock section of town was not far from Ms. Spears. It was very nice and roomy and most of all clean. She had acquired "the good life." She had a nice home and a fancy foreign car. She wore only designer labels and was gathering a valuable collection of fine jewels, but something was unresolved in Toni's life. After a couple of months in their new home, Toni realized she was haunted by the fear of being alone. For this she still held David responsible. She was particularly annoyed and irritated on this day as she sat in her office with a case review in front of her. She began to contemplate how many more years David Jr. would have to be without a father. She found herself angry over the unfair sentence David had received. It suddenly occurred to her, she could ask her senior officers to review and appeal David's case. She knew she had to act immediately.

She set up a meeting with her senior officers and presented a request for a law review on David's case. After several meetings she was cleared and began reviewing David's case. She was able to find several case discrepancies and incongruous case protocol. It was a long year, but at the end David's case was declared a mistrial and he was released on time served, which had been eight years. Toni realized that was her greatest victory to date. Reuniting her son with his father had really healed her wounds and made her complete. It gave her greater joy to see the wholeness David bought to her son's life. Toni knew this work needed to be done throughout the community. She initiated a program that united absentee fathers with their children. Toni knew that spreading this kind of joy would also spread the basic self love needed to face life's challenges.

Toni stared in the mirror with contentment for the first time in years. She fluffed her hair and pouted her lips. She gasped when suddenly before her eyes, in the mirror, stood an African Warrior Queen. She was strong and proud. She wore a large crown on her head and a small veil hanging from it. She beckoned to Toni. Without moving and without words Toni watched herself being crowned by the African Warrior Queen. It was some sort of ceremony when a mirror full of Queens appeared. Toni knew instinctively she had had her coronation into a unique sisterhood. She was now a proud member of the Sisters of the Veil, a royal sisterhood of queens with the ability to see the reality of this existence and heal torn communities. It was a new light and a new day.

TERRI'S STORY

Chapter One

Foreign Lands

Terri sat at the dinner table waiting impatiently for her father to speak. She glared at the newspaper spread in front of his face, while she fidgeted with her food. This standoff had seemed to last forever now, although it had only been two weeks. She was usually the victor in these kind of battles. All she had to do was wait. Why just last week the odds had seemed to turn in her favor, but her father's stubborn rejection to her pleas made the outcome undeterminable. Her mother had the strongest voice in the family, but she was split right down the middle of the issue. For both Terri and her father, there was no compromise. So the agonizing wait continued.

Terrena (Terri) McDaniels was in her senior year at Iverson's Preparatory School. She had been afforded the finer things in life, including her fine parochial education. She had been in the Wellesly private schools system all of her life. It was rated number one in academics in the entire northeastern region of the country. Terri was graduating with honors. She was well accustomed to the system and the people there. She was popular, yet not completely comfortable. She felt something was missing.

All of her friends were Caucasian. That wasn't a problem. The problem was that she found them largely judgemental of people of other cultures, especially Blacks. She had a long standing private joke that she always told herself. They (Caucasians) wore black robes and carried a gavel everywhere they went. In other words, they constantly felt it their duty to judge people of other cultures. She had been alongside these same classmates for so long, that they'd sometimes blurt out their lofty judgments of other races before they realized she was not entirely one of them.

She blended easily enough. Her upbringing had fully assimilated her into this culture. Though in appearance, she stood out slightly against the milky white surroundings. She and her sister both had inherited their mother's European features. Her hair, a sandy brown, was naturally wavy. She never minded her wavy hair, but her friends often pointed out the difference between their hair and hers after swim class.

It made them (her Caucasian friends) feel dutifully tolerant that they accepted her at all. That fact was confirmation of their non-racists convictions. They had a way of convincing themselves that any uncomfortable truths, needed to be altered slightly in their favor. They had the power to do so. It was just a perk of being Kings and Judges. Terri was one of them as long as she sounded or acted like them. Sometimes she'd stare deeply into her friend Callie's eyes and try to see the world her way. It was never clear.

Her sister Tonya, who completely denied any trace of her black heritage, despised black people. While Tonya did, Terri did not consider herself white. Their roots were firmly planted in black history. Her father was half black, and his Caucasian genes were recessed. Although light in complexion, at first glance one would consider him a black man. That was always a noose for him. He hated his wide nose and thick lips, the tell all signs of the African inside him. This was the same African that tortured him in the mirror daily. He always said he'd make sure his children did not have to suffer like that. He, however, figured with enough money and culture, he was as white as any other Caucasian. All this meant for Terri was that she was anxious to graduate and find a new crowd of friends.

Her privileged station in life, had made it easier for her to get accepted into the Ivy League colleges her father had insisted she attend. It was the natural transition her father preached.

Her father was the president of the largest university in the city-Central University. Terri adored him. She was the eldest of his two children, and she knew she held an honored position in his heart. In spite of that, her defiance and insistence on attending a black college, had challenged their blessed relationship.

Terri had secretly applied and been accepted to a private black women's college in Atlanta, Georgia. She had just recently sprang the news on her parents, and their delicate little world was in an uproar.

Whenever she tried to talk to her dad, they'd end up yelling at one another. At first her father had refused to pay for her to attend, what he called a "low-rated" school. After all, he'd invested thousands of dollars in her education. Still, Terri refused to give in.

Her mother understood Terri's need to exercise her independence. This amounted to the first major decision she had ever made in her life. But the idea was slowly gaining ground, and with her mother at the fore pushing for Terri's independence, it would all soon be settled, so Terri figured.

The university was nowhere near the little rut of a school her father thought it to be. It was a highly accredited private girl's college in Atlanta, Georgia. Terri had always accepted her father's guidance blindly, until now. The resistance seemed to be even harder for him to accept than her choice of schools. Yet, as the ground gave way under her father's refusal, his heartbreak showed ever more. Something inside him changed. Her victory was bittersweet.

Seeing his disappointment was unbearable for Terri. She offered to stay with her Grandma Rena until the waves settled. This made her father weep bitterly. Though it was never admitted directly, their black heritage was somewhat resented in their home.

Her father was the son of a bi-racial mother and a black father. The historical account of their lineage was recounted every year especially around the holiday season. Her father made sure they could trace their family through history, to affirm their Caucasian roots. Genealogy was big on their side of town.

Beginning with his great grandmother, her father would recount the story per facto time and time again. His great grandparents were rich white plantation owners in the Mississippi Delta. While Tonya listened wide-eyed, Terri always tuned out the parts of how they amassed tons of wealth and opened the first local hospital in the county. Blah, blah, Terri mouthed, and popped her fingers quietly. Instead, she would request the story about her great great Grandma Rena, the daughter of the wealthy plantation owners, who she was named after. Now, it was Tonya that was fidgety and Terri that was wide-eyed. Her father's face would twist and flinch as he told the story.

His Caucasian great grandparents had a daughter named Rena. Rena, oddly enough, happened to be smittened with the slaves on the plantation. She rarely befriended the other rich white children of her community. In fact, the nearest plantation was twenty seven miles west of their home site. Little Rena resented being sent horse and buggy all that way for an hour or two of playtime. She persistently placed herself in the company of slave children, inviting them into the main house to play like "*normal*" children. When her father beat a little slave boy nearly to death, it was a warning that no slaves should even lay eyes on her.

Little Ms. Rena, strong willed, insisted on rebuking her father. She would sneak down to the slave's quarters and play school, doctor and house with the slave children. When she was fourteen years old she was raped by a slave boy that she had befriended. Terri's father did begrudgingly admit, that by some accounts of the story it was called a seduction. She (his grandmother) persistently seduced the slave boy Ernest who was four years her senior, until she was impregnated with the slave boy's child. She hid that pregnancy until a round nosed, almond toned baby girl was born in the steel bathtub where she was bathing. The baby nearly drowned but for the quick thinking of the black mammy who happened to be bringing in clean towels. When his great grandmother came into the bathroom to see what all the commotion was about; there stood Miss Rena, buck naked holding a mulatto baby to her chest.

His great grandfather had the slave boy, Ernest, beaten them hanged to death. The baby was offered for sale to other slave owners. Miss Rena knew she couldn't live without her child. She refused to hand over the baby vowing her own death beforehand. Miss Rena's mother, the ever loving famed socialite, committed suicide to avoid the embarrassment. Her husband solidly refused to have a nigger baby in his house. He exiled his daughter and the baby.

Miss Rena, having no means of her own, lived hand to mouth as she migrated north. Her white skin afforded her permission to cross many lines that would have been denied black skin tones. She pretended that the baby was a slave baby she had been commissioned to take East to its' new owners, and she had gotten lost. In any case she finally made it to the northern east coast of Pennsylvania, where she settled. A grandiose institution for women by the name of The Whittenhall accepted and boarded her for about two years. The child, Miss Rena also named Rena was his mother. They kept the Caucasian family name, which was synonymous with medicine and medical supplies, and allowed his grandmother to eventually build her own wealth. That story, hidden by time and distance always left Terri with more curiosity about her black heritage.

Her mother's lineage was also ever present. She was the child of a Swiss mother who had married a German soldier. Her genealogy was recounted in the rows of pictures that lined the foyer walls, all of them showing war soldiers from her mother's side of the family. Some Generals, some Majors, but all of them were lily white. Her lineage dated back to the founding of the country, with proud relations to the Mayflower voyage.

With that Terri's father insisted his daughters were Caucasian, at least more than anything else. It was clear that meant if they wanted to remain in his good graces, they'd keep it that way.

They lived on the northeast side of town in a relatively new subdivision of the city. Wellesly Township was actually an extension of the Rothwell Crescent, the richest community in the city. The later (Rothwell Crescent) being the old money, and the former (Wellesly Township) being the new money. With the exception of the two other non-caucasian families in the community, who they rarely saw, it was lily white territory.

Terri of course then, saw very little of the black side of her family. It was only when they visited her Grandma Rena, on the "*lower end*" of town; as her father called it, did they even see *real* black people. Her father loved his mother dearly and did keep close contact with her. She married a black policeman, who was killed in the line of duty when her son (Terri's father) was three years old.

She'd always stayed and lived in black communities, for which Terri's father didn't understand. She had a hefty inheiritance from her mother, and a good career as a school teacher. He always felt she could afford better.

He would treat her to lunch often, careful to meet her outside her community. He spoke to her on the telephone almost daily. Grandma Rena, the third to be named Rena was a beautiful woman. It was immediately clear, that she was a biracial woman. She, however wholly considered herself a black woman. To her there was no white side of the family. She, unlike her son, gladly recounted the many trials that her mother went through to survive. They owed that survival, in her mind, to the black community. It was the black community that opened its' arms to her mother and the pretty little baby girl time and time again. Naturally why would she live anywhere but a black neighborhood, she'd proudly say. She had stressed that repeatedly to her son, but he defiantly chose to live as a non-black person. He showed the weakness of it, as she pointed out to him on many occasions. He feared both white and black men. The white man, he feared, would see his blackness, and reject his stealthy reach for riches. The black man, he feared, would see his whiteness, and punish his denial of kinship to Africa. She sighed painfully when she thought of his dilemma, knowing that she had tried so hard to make him tough and ready to stand up to this challenge. Instead, he chose to hide behind the pale ghost of assimilation. She could see a bent, twisted man, and he was teaching his daughters to assume the same position.

Terri relished their few and far between visits to her grandmother's house. It was in the part of town that they always drove really fast through. Her father insisted that they lock their car doors, and roll up the windows in *that* part of town. He took as many shortcuts as he could to avoid traffic lights. If they did get caught by a traffic light, several of which he drove through without stopping, he'd insist they look straight ahead. Then, as soon as the light changed, he'd take off on two wheels. Terri always stole as many glances as she could. The people there had always intrigued her. Their means of life, and the pride they showed in dealing with their retched surroundings often plagued her inside.

She longed to know the answers to certain unscrupulous questions. How did they (black people) live in such conditions? How did they stay so happy and prideful under such conditions? She had never contemplated how she would get these answers. She only knew the curiosity was overtaking her. Attending a black college would certainly bring her face to face with many real answers, she reasoned.

Chapter Two

New Adventures

Her Grandma Rena was thrilled that Terri had prevailed against her father's bitter judgment and disappointment. She was even more thrilled that Terri would be spending the summer with her. She was the proud keeper of not only her own black history, but that of many slave families migrating to northeastern Pennsylvania. She had always noted that, if not for the generosity of many black people, her mother would have perished. She was extremely well versed in different African cultures, tongues, geography, and history.

African art lined the walls of her house in rows. Shelves of African artifacts and ceremonial masks were scattered throughout the house. She had tons of pictures from her many safaris to Africa. She had visited several African countries and adored the Ivory Coast. Unlike her father's boring accounts, Terri found herself fascinated with Grandma Rena's stories of high adventure.

One night over coffee, which her parents had never let her drink, Grandma Rena told her a mysterious story. She told her that she had been born with a veil over her eyes. According to the old African legend that meant that these ones were selected to "*see things*" beyond this plane of reality and to "*see*" things of this reality more clearly than their counterparts. Terri was spooked and didn't question her grandma much on this story. Her grandma assured her it meant she was special. She pondered over it for many nights.

Grandma Rena also proved to be much more lenient than her father in matters of association. She took Terri to meet several of her black relatives. Grandma Rena invited her cousin Tehfariah, who lived a couple of blocks away, to spend the rest of the summer with them both. She was preparing to leave for college in a matter of weeks herself. Grandma Rena thought they'd be great roommates for one another. Tehfariah was going to attend a popular black college in Washington D.C.

Terri observed her inner city culture immediately. Her diction was poor and lazy. She dressed in seductive street style clothes. She was abrupt and ungracious in Terri's opinion. By Terri's own standards, they were a total mismatch. Terri was secretly afraid of her, but found her style intriguing.

Terri naively questioned her about everything from her social experiences to her bra size. Tehfariah was gracious throughout Terri's ignorance, and answered all of her questions. She took Terri under her wing and chaperoned her introduction to the black neighborhood. After a couple of weeks, Tehfariah had shown Terri almost every inch of the community. She didn't miss anything. On every store, movie theater, and night club in the area, she schooled Terri.

She made Terri familiar with the location, owners, and politics of the community. Terri found it hard to understand the people, but she desperately wanted to fit in. She tried to hide the ignorance and empathy she had previously felt toward them. The faults she had pinned on them and the fear they had commanded in her, she slowly relinquished. With Tehfariah as her guide, she would grow accustomed to the environment, so she thought.

Tehfariah was quite popular in the community. She had lots of friends, most of which were abrasive, and loud like herself, Terri thought. They spent most of their days hanging in the streets with her friends. Then they would talk at night in their room for hours. They began to share their intimate secrets. You got a boyfriend, Tehfariah asked Terri with her eyebrows pulled down and her mouth twisted. You a virgin, ain't you Tehfariah taunted Terri. Yeah Terri answered shyly. Are you Terri asked quickly. Naw girl, Tehfariah sounded annoyed. I got a boyfriend, she added. You ever had a boyfriend Tehfariah returned to the interrogation. No my dad won't let me date Terri continued in her shy tone. Tehfariah fell across the bed and laughed loud and wicked. I'll introduce you to some of my friends, she offered barely able to catch her breath. Tehfariah, kept her word. It seemed she knew everybody. Most of her friends lived in the projects, the Whittenhall Projects.

Terri had heard horrifying stories about the projects from both her mother and father. She had been told it was the place where only criminals lived. They were dirty, nasty, nefarious people, at the ready to devour any fragile soul that entered their domain. If the people didn't get you, the rats and roaches would. The rats were as large as kittens because that's what they ate sometimes. Terri's heart raced as they walked toward the huge encumbering maze of walls. A thousand questions raced through her mind. Would they know right away that she didn't belong there? How should she greet the people she met? She knew she only sounded stupid when she tried to talk hip. What if they rejected her right away? The bright summer daylight turned gray and dim. Her knees felt weak and she was trembling all over.

They entered the projects through the back end of the court yard. There was garbage everywhere. The stench was sickening. Terri felt as if she would hurl at any moment. She walked as fast as she could and covered her mouth and nose with her hand. Tehfariah noticed nothing. Terri turned into a small building of the courtyard to the right of the garbage dumpsters. In fact the garbage trailed almost right up to the door of the building. Terri gagged and dipped on the side of the building and threw up a little. Tehfariah shouted her name. Terri where you going girl? Terri forced down the rest of her vomit and held her breath. She hoped her terror didn't show. In order to calm herself down she pretended she was in one of the many foreign lands she had visited with her family. This would be an adventure, she told herself. In fact, she suddenly realized it was a foreign land for her. Besides these are the same people that had saved her great grandmother from the clutches of starvation, she reasoned. As Tehfariah strolled through the courtyard, Terri admired her confident stride. To this point no one had noticed them and Terri was thankful for that.

Once they were inside, Terri was surprised. The apartment they entered was neat and clean. It showed signs of dilapidation, and the stench seeped inside the apartment somewhat. But it shocked her to see that someone had taken the time to decorate it and quite well at that.

The people were friendly and in good spirits. Still Terri couldn't relax completely. A unanimous greeting went up as soon as Tehfariah stepped through the door. She was welcomed there. Tehfariah introduced Terri to everyone. There were about six girls already there. Terri watched them eye her with curiosity, but still they received her warmly, on Tehfariah's account she was sure. Tehfariah fit right into the on-going conversation. Next to them Terri felt over cultured, but at the same time inmature. Their conversation went from who was getting it on with whom, and who got kicked out of the projects, to the latest records and dances.

Terri felt as if no one noticed she was even there. As she was beginning to resign herself, one girl turned to her and spoke. You so quiet, she addressed her with a soft, rasphy drawl. Terri just sat there unsure of how to respond. Where do you live the girl inquired kindly. In Wellsley Township, Terri answered shyly, with her eyes looking down on her fidgety hands. Wellesly Township screamed one of the girls, who Terri thought wasn't even listening and surely wasn't in their conversation. She seemed to be the strongest of the group. She was by far the loudest. Her voice scared Terri and she cringed inside. Everyone stopped talking and stared at Terri with their mouths flung open. The silence was piercing. My boyfriend lives in Blue Rock, the kind girl said trying to divert the awkwardness. She was an attractive, mild mannered girl. My name is Toni, she continued.

Do you know a David Spears she asked. He goes to Central University. Terri shook her head no, but replied the name sounds familiar. He's a football player there Toni continued. Are you a student there too, Terri asked, realizing that was the first intelligent thing she had said all day. Yes, I'll be a sophomore this fall, Toni answered. Terri didn't dare say that her father was the president of the university. She had finally found someone she could relate to in the room. Terri chatted with Toni one on one during the rest of the visit. The others resumed their conversations, but Terri caught more than a few of them cutting their eyes at her. She was hoping the visit would end soon.

Just as Terri thought the visit was winding up, someone suggested plans for hanging out that evening. We ought to go to the Palace Club tonight. A unanimous yeah went up in the air like confetti, including Tehfariah. Terri was scared to death and tried to graciously back out. Oh that's alright, I don't have nothing to wear she explained. You can wear something of mine Toni offered. Terri was flabbergasted at the offer. You live here, Terri asked with her voice full of surprise. Toni nodded her head yes and searched Terri's eyes. Well I don't have any money, Terri was sure that was a showstopper. I'll get you in, Tehfariah announced. There you're in snarled the loud girl. Now let's go she snapped. They finalized the arrangements and scattered to get dressed for the evening.

Terri had never stepped foot in a real night club in her life, and was overwhelmed. She felt ill all over again. What if we get busted she asked Tehfariah as they sat in Toni's bedroom waiting for her to find an outfit. I got fake I.D's all over the place, Tehfariah said, digging through her purse and flashing them one by one. Eighteen, nineteen, twenty one, twenty five she announced each age as she laid them across the bed. Yaw'll think I can pass for twenty five, Tehfariah asked shaking with laughter.

When Toni opened her closet, Terri could see she had a nice wardrobe of clothes. Some of the labels were the same as her grandmother's wardrobe labels. Toni loaned Terri a very well made pair of black slacks, with a glittery white shell. As luck would have it, they wore the same size shoes. Here try these she shoved a pair of black and white platform shoes in her face. They were a perfect fit and match. Toni put a touch of eye make-up, and lipstick on Terri. She styled Terri's wavy sand colored hair into and upsweep of cascading curls. You look beautiful Toni complimented her. Terri reluctantly went to the mirror. In just a few minutes, Toni had changed her appearance from a fragile, shivering schoolgirl into a sophisticated young woman. Terri stared at her beautiful transformed face in the mirror. She had never seen herself in make-up, except on Halloween. Needless to say, there was no comparison. She began to feel slightly more mature and secure. Toni changed into a classy yet conservative outfit. It suited her personality well. She styled her own hair in a fluffy ball of curls on top of her head. She was quite elegant.

As they approached the door of the Palace Club, Terri felt her knees weaken. She wanted Toni to hold her hand like her mother did when she was a little girl. Her eyes stretched, and her heart beat faster than she could breathe. She felt faint as they handed the doorman their I.D.'s. She tripped on the step entering the club. Linda who was already inside the door snapped her head around and pulled her brows down, scolding Terri with her eyes. Terri kept her eyes moving all around the club. She watched the other girls dance and flirt with guys. They were very uninhibited, and Terri wanted to imitate them. She stretched her face to get the tightness out. She slouched in her chair a little to appear more comfortable. A young man approached her and asked her to dance. She froze. Toni stepped in and politely refused for her. She thanked God for Toni again. She seemed to understand her private turmoil, and saved her once again. As the night drew to a close she had grown to trust Toni.

All in all, the whole day had been a series of new adventures for which she was now grateful. More than that, her eyes had been opened to a new found freedom for which she had always longed.

Chapter Three

New Friends

Terri returned to the Whittenhall Projects several times with Tehfariah. This time was unique, for it was the first time they had entered through the front entrance. As they approached the tall wall and steps, Terri recognized a few of the many girls and guys sitting on the wall. She was still secretly afraid of this environment and people, except for Toni and Tehfariah. Tehfariah introduced her to the new faces. She saw the suspicious frowns and scolding eyes as they met her eyes. She wondered if she would ever fit in this environment. In any case they all welcomed Tehfariah, and immediately pulled her into the conversation. Within minutes the crowd was laughing and joking as usual.

They had been listening to music and talking about an hour when a loud raggedy Buick 225 pulled up to the wall. Apparently everyone knew who it was before the driver exited the car. They seemed quite happy to hear the familiar sound and were making jokes about his car. Everyone shouted his name in unison. Charles, they all hollered. Terri laughed inside loving the feeling of camaraderie this man had bought.

He shook hands and gave the power sign to all the guys, completely undisturbed by the jokes and name calling. He worked his way across the wall, speaking to the girls. He seemed to be the sweetheart of all the girls there. He didn't notice Terri, who had slyly pushed herself behind the faces in the crowd. She wanted to watch him secretly without him knowing she was watching. Tehfariah, of course, wouldn't allow it. She pulled Terri out front and introduced them. Charles stared at her hard, as if he recognized her. Terri discretely inspected him as well. He was handsome guy she thought immediately.

He was tall and slender with a defined muscular chest, which she could see through his unbuttoned shirt. He had a caramel brown complexion, and a soft fluffy afro. Terri could see the signs of street life in his face. Dull, tired eyes and a poorly postured body with long bold scars were the tell tale signs. A quick chill went through her. Their worlds were totally different, she thought as she watched him. Still, Terri felt something common hit her deep within the soul of her heart. The way he walked with a swaggering limp, and the way he talked with the streetwise zip, made her eager to get to know him like the other girls did. You live here, he asked pulling himself easily up on the wall next to her. He began a long series of questions, each one delving more deeply into her personal life and psyche. They talked to one another for at least two hours. His easy mild tempered spirit stole through all the questions he asked, revealing a surprisingly kind person. He was very understanding. He didn't make her feel like a fish out of water when she told him where she lived. She felt she could tell him anything. He was easy to talk to, and his unpolished street appearance was growing on her. The group had slowly departed one by one and in small groups as she and Charles conversed on. When they looked away from each other's eyes, there was only Toni, Tehfariah, and Linda remaining on the wall with them.

Charlie, Linda, who happened to have a beautiful falsetto, crooned. Take us out for lunch. All the other girls crooned in to help Linda convince him. Are **you** hungry he asked extending his hand to Terri. Not really Terri replied honestly. What squealed Tehfariah. What, she shook Terri by the shoulders. She hasn't eaten since last Tuesday boy Tehfariah joked. This girl is delirious she joked grabbing Terri by the neck and playfully choking her. Linda and Toni jumped on Charles and grabbed him by the neck as well, dragging him to his car. They were laughing deliriously by the time they all got into the car. That small display of camaraderie created a bond between the girls that would carry them through a mountain of trails.

That weekend Tehfariah left for college. Until then Terri had paid no mind to the fleeting time. Now she had only two weeks before her venture to Atlanta. The summer had been filled with a host of new adventures, especially Charles.

Over the next couple of days, Terri busied herself shopping for school and digging through her grandmother's treasures and pictures from Africa. She stayed close to her Grandma Rena's house. She didn't feel confident enough to venture to the Whittenhall Projects alone. She found her grandma's wedding pictures and asked if she could keep them. Her grandmother promised them to her as a graduation gift.

She was just laying across the bed, thinking about Charles, who she knew she wouldn't forget even after she left for Atlanta. The phone rang and her grandmother called her to the phone. Hello Terri the voice inquired from the other end of the phone. Terri didn't recognize the voice. Yes this is Terri she replied curiously. Why haven't you come over to see us the female voice went on inquiring. We thought you liked us. There was an awkward silence, then a burst of laughter shot through the phone. This is Toni. They both laughed. Why don't you come over today Toni invited. Charles has been asking about you she crooned. Terri agreed quickly.

She was so excited that first of all the girls had invited her without Tehfariah. That was a major step forward. Second, and most importantly, Charles wanted to see her. Things were working out well. It took an hour for her to decide what to wear. She had to look hip but not anxious, and clean but not pristine.

When she reached the front of the Whittenhall wall, Linda and Toni were waiting for her. What took you so long Linda snapped. Don't pay her any attention Toni said shielding her from Linda's face. We're gonna go to a party tonight. Wanna go Toni asked anxiously. Before she could back out she added, Charles wants to take you. Terri's eyes lit up. This was a complete change in social venue for her. She had never been on a date. Her father came to mind. He had never allowed them to date or even attend community parties. Their social life consisted of frequent week end travel from coast to coast, and summer vacations abroad. In fact they had just returned from the Netherlands over their spring break.

Terri loved traveling, and seeing the world and appreciating cultural experiences. It was funny she thought how little she had seen of her own city and culture. She figured this date with Charles was just the introduction she needed. She had grown restless and quite bored with her secluded proper life. She was now craving action and excitement.

Linda put on some music while they dressed. You know how to dance Linda asked suspiciously. Terri's mouth dropped open and she looked down at the floor. No not really she answered sheepishly. Linda roared with laughter. Terri's innocence touched Toni. I'll show you some steps before we go, Toni comforted her. Toni shushed at Linda who was still bent over in laughter.

Toni pleasantly put an outfit together for Terri to wear. It was a colorful checkered mini skirt with a solid cream colored halter top. Terri was mortified. She tried to argue with Toni. I can't wear this halter top. I have to wear a bra she fussed knowing her father would not approve. Toni's reply was kind but firm. You have to look like a woman for Charles. Terri found she couldn't argue with that. Besides Linda piped in, your little pokies will be fine in a halter. They all laughed and Terri relaxed a little. Toni styled Terri's hair in a French roll with soft curls hanging around the edges of her face. She did indeed look and feel like a woman. Toni also wore a halter top and a French roll to ease Terri's fears.

A loud knock at the door startled them all. It was one of the Star divas of the projects there to announce that David was parked outside at the wall and waiting for Toni. I'm not ready Toni squealed. I want to be all together when he sees me, 'cause I haven't seen him all week. Stall him for me yaw'll. Linda and Terri left with the Star to stall David.

When Toni joined them outside at the wall, David was mesmerized. Terri watched them both as Toni walked down the stairs. She was indeed gorgeous. Her cinnamon brown skin was silky smooth, and her jet black wavy hair was shinny. Definitely model material, Terri thought as she watched. David's eyes sparkled and he couldn't take them off of her. Terri envied Toni. Toni was so poised and elegant, Terri thought. She had a way of always displaying that grace and maturity no matter what she was doing. Whether she was casually descending a flight of stairs or just sitting on the wall outside she was a confident woman in every sense in Terri's mind.

David was quite a gentleman. He treated Toni with lots of tenderness. He kissed her hand and complemented her outfit. Terri could see their love, and respect for each other. It made her realize her own immaturity. She only hoped Charles looked at her the way David looked at Toni. David and Toni wanted to be alone and left Terri and Linda to wait for Charles. Terri looked to Linda for support, as they watched Charles's car pull up to the wall. Linda always had that desperate, angry look, no matter how nice she dressed or how much make-up she wore. It was easy to see that she was broke and without a man.

Charles complimented Terri in his own loud, manly kind of way. With lots of oooouu babies and doggy grunts he applauded Terri. It actually embarrassed her. She hid her embarrassment as best she could, and took his hand, trying to secure her maturity.

It was a house party. It was given at the home of David's cousin. They descended the stairs into a black light basement. Terri feared she would stick out like a soar thumb. In fact, Toni had forgotten to teach her some dance steps, and she knew she would look stupid trying to learn. To her surprise the basement was so packed full of people that no one noticed her particularly.

Terri immediately began searching for Toni throughout the dimly lit room. She spotted Toni sitting on David's lap, and an empty seat nearby. She made her way quickly to both. Charles disappeared in the crowd. Toni made her feel comfortable again, but her and David left her alone frequently to dance. Terri panicked when Toni pulled her on the floor to dance. Toni insisted that she dance at least once. It was David that made her realize no one could tell what dance she was doing because of the strob light. Then she slowly relaxed. To her surprise, she learned a few steps and was not so out of rhythm as she thought she'd be. The party proved to be wild and fun after all.

Charles drove her home early. Her grandmother was lenient, but she still insisted upon an eleven o'clock curfew. He walked her to the door, and wrapped his arms around her neck. Terri didn't know what to say so she kept quiet. You are so beautiful he said staring into her eyes deeply. There was something that Charles wanted to say to her. She could tell by that curious look in his eyes. She was worried for a moment then watched his eyes soften. I love high yellow girls, he went on to explain. She was relieved. It was nice to know he appreciated her as she was, and wasn't suspicious of her blackness. He pecked her on the lips, and held her close, swaying from side to side. Terri could feel the fullness swelling between his legs. Then he kissed her full open mouth. Her body grew rigid, while he grinded against her. His grip was strong and his body stiff. He was intense. Terri was struck with paralysis and silence, until they heard the door unlocking. Charles ran back to the car, and drove off. The suddenness of his release left her cold and shaky.

Terri lay awake all that night. She couldn't get the kiss off her mind. She was still amazed by the fullness of his manhood. She wanted to feel it all over again and her coochie was throbbing. She hadn't expected her first kiss to feel so powerful, or so comforting. She kept pondering how to get to see Charles again. She needed to feel this feeling again without provoking his manhood to much certainly without begging, which seemed like a likely option.

She felt comforted when Charles called her the next day. They agreed to meet at the Whittenhall wall. She didn't feel totally comfortable going to theWhittenhall Projects alone, but she felt the familiarity would make it alright. She left a half hour early in order to stop by Toni's apartment. She reached the Whittenhall wall around eleven thirty. There were only a couple of girls and a couple of guys hanging out there. Terri didn't recognize them and didn't stop to speak. When she reached the top of the steps, she heard an angry voice call, you too good to speak redbone? Yeah high yellow don't mean you can't speak to nobody, another voice called. She looked back in astonishment. She was at a loss for words or gestures. She headed toward the courtyard at an accelerated pace. Apparently that was the wrong response. The two girls jumped up and started following her calling out insults. Before she could reach the door to Toni's building, they were right on her heels. She felt something grab her hair and yank her head backwards. Something then came thundering down on her face. It felt like a ton of bricks. She fell to the ground, and began to scream at the top of her voice. Just as suddenly as it started it stopped. Charles was there picking her up off the ground. She fell into his arms wailing. Get me out of here she screamed. Charles headed toward the wall where his car was parked. Terri was too afraid to pass her attackers again. Charles didn't have time to think. He had no choice but to take her to his secret place there in the Whittenhall.

He carried her past the last building to the back entrance of the projects. Her face was buried in his chest and she was sobbing. There was an abandoned building. Charles reached into his pocket and pulled out a key. He opened the door and stood Terri on her feet. He hurried to the bathroom to get some first aid for her.

Terri lost track of her whereabouts as she looked around. It was one small room with a bathroom in the corner. There was a large island with a countertop, near the back of the room. It looked like it was used for handling construction materials. On the left side of it were built in shelves from the floor to the ceiling stacked with paper supplies like large reams of brown paper towels and plastic liners, even medicinal supplies like gauze and band aids. There was also large strange looking equipment and tools in open boxes throughout the room. It was a weird mix of items. Terri couldn't tell if it was an abandoned office or a garbage dump.

Out of the ordinary, there was a raggedy urine stained mattress in the middle of the floor, and a broken legged sofa next to the door. The place was filthy like it housed heavy foot traffic during the day. The smell turned Terri's stomach into knots. She thought she'd puke again like she did the first time she walked through the Whittenhall courtyard. She turned for the door, but was more sickened by the thought of facing her attackers again.

Charles bought wet paper towels and band-aids. Where are we Terri sighed like she had been escorted to another planet. When he studied the look on her face, he apologized. I'm sorry baby. His face was full of shame. His eyes were still very concerned. You live here, Terri stammered. Some sometimes he mumbled then dropped his head. Just for a night or two here and there he stumbled on awkwardly. Only when I can't find anywhere else to sleep he mumbled. Terri just stared at him in disbelief. He shrugged his shoulders then turned his attention back to Terri. He gently patted her face with the wet paper towels, and aided her cuts. He embraced her gently, while she began to cry again. They stood there embraced and silent.

Calmness and strength slowly returned to Terri. She didn't feel like talking, but she had to ask why. Why did they do this to me Charles? I didn't do anything to them. Charles cupped her face with his strong slender hands. They're jealous baby, he whispered as if not to shock her. Jealous of what, Terri snapped. Look at you, he explained, you're beautiful. Your skin is light and beautiful. Your hair, he lifted it softly, it's so long and pretty. You're so much more beautiful than they could ever hope to be, and they know it, he growled. And they're jealous of that fact he nodded for emphasis. Terri looked totally puzzled. She didn't know whether to believe him or not. It didn't sound logical. You mean they attacked me because of the color of my skin. I thought I was part of the "*rainbow*", Terri curled her fingers in the air, indicating quotation marks. I'm black too, she went on. But they are jealous baby because you are so pretty and they can't have *your* kind of beauty, Charles snarled. But don't worry. I'll be around to make sure it don't happen again. Charles pulled her closer to him and held her tenderly. They began to talk more, and Terri felt better.

Charles did most of the talking this time, and Terri lay in his arms and listened. She fell in and out of awareness as he talked and she pondered on his explanation about beauty. Charles carried on with his story unaware of Terri's attention span. He felt compelled to explain what led him to this place in his life. Terri did find out more about his life, and her heart ached for him. She stood quietly. She didn't know what to say. She hugged him with all her strength. Charles said nothing either, but the look in his eyes said it all. He lifted her face and kissed her passionately. He continued to kiss her non stop, until her body felt limp. Still holding her tightly, her unbuttoned her blouse, and lifted her bra. Within a matter of seconds he had loosened her pants and discarded her blouse and bra. He did likewise to himself with the same ease and skill. Terri loved the feel of his bare chest against hers. Before she knew it they both were completely bare. Terri felt him push his manhood between her legs and rub against her flesh. She sighed and forgot about her pains and her curfew. It was the most satisfying feeling she had ever felt. Charles started rubbing against her faster and harder, along with long wet kisses. Terri felt herself throbbing. It felt so warm and comforting she was lulled into momentary paradise.

Charles's grip was so strong, she forgot about the urine stained mattress. She forgot the stench that made her nauseated. His manhood commanded her full focus, and she was in ecstasy. He lifted her slightly and slid his manhood deep inside her. She screamed abruptly. Terri wanted him to stop, but the experience was far too intense. Charles was well experienced and worldly. He pushed with all his strength, while he covered her with wet wild kisses. Charles slowly stepped backward in order to lay her down on the mattress. Terri put her hand on the mattress to brace herself. Something fuzzy brushed the palm of her hand. She tried to raise up, but couldn't stop the momentum of his weight, bearing down on her. His weight forced her body flatly against the mattress. Something wet and fuzzy was squashed underneath her shoulders. Terri was mortified and could feel a warm wetness oozing down her back. When she felt it move again she raised slightly against Charles's weight. She could barley move against him. Charles was groaning with ecstasy and suddenly exploded into a convulsing animal. His weight lightened when he went limp and a warm fluid oozed down her leg. She pushed Charles with all her strength and hurried to her feet. She looked back at the mattress and only saw a quick flash of movement. She didn't know what it was, but she thought for sure it was a rat. She opened her mouth wide and screamed until her tonsils quivered. She rushed into the bathroom and swished the sink water all over her, leaving Charles on bended knee with his hands cupped around his manhood, and a groaning expression on his face. She puked for the rest of the evening. Her first sexual experience had been a disaster.

Her grandmother was enraged that she had broken her curfew. She grounded her for the remainder of her stay. She even threatened to send her home. They both knew it wasn't a real threat, but the thought was scary for them both. Each had their own agenda for the rest of the visit.

Grandma Rena wanted Terri to connect more to her black roots. She wanted her to integrate freely with her people. As freely as she'd integrated on the other side of town, she wanted her to feel as free and comfortable there. Grandma Rena didn't want her to be afraid of her own people like her father. Rather she planned to show him that being black was not an automatic sentence of failure.

Her father could never accept the success of black doctors, lawyers, accomplished business professionals. They're just tokens he'd say. Besides he felt they provided substandard service. Grandma Rena figured as long as she kept Terri from boys on this side of town, she'd show him how successful a black person, woman at that, could be.

Terri begged her grandmother not to send her home early. Her agenda was to be with Charles as long as possible. She knew if she went home she'd never see Charles again, but by an act of God. In spite of her first sexual experience, she felt something very strong for this man.

It took her grandmother all day the next day to calm down and soften, then only enough to use the telephone. She called Linda's house and asked her and Toni to accompany her to the Whittenhall and to contact Charles. When Toni and Linda showed up at her grandmother's house, Grandma Rena was impressed. She was reassured that Terri had made friends with her black colleagues.

This arrangement worked for Terri for the remainder of her stay. Charles would be waiting at the wall when they reached the Whittenhall. He was always happy to see her. He grinned wide, showing his straight teeth, and dimples. He slid off the brick wall easily and hugged her. He whispered I missed you baby in her ear, and opened the car door for her.

Terri glanced over at Charles as he sped through the streets of the ghetto. He was so handsome, Terri thought. She felt like Lena Horne riding alongside Harry Belefonte, and she wished she had the poise and grace to match. All she needed was a scarf to keep her hair from blowing in the wind, and a pair of white gloves to make her feel sophisticated. She'd borrow one of her grandmother's many scarves tomorrow, she thought.

She still felt immature, and square pegged considering Charles's worldly experience. He paid more than the usual attention to her knowing their time together was short. He wined and dined her as they whizzed around the city in his raggedy Buick 225. He seemed to sense her insecurity. He was careful to keep the conversations playful and light. All the while, the look in his eyes let her know he wanted more than a new pal or playmate.

She was learning a lot about him and the ghetto neighborhoods in the city. Charles seemed to know them all and know everybody in them. Terri was content to ride around with him all day in his car, while he conducted his business. She actually enjoyed seeing ghetto streets that she was sure the post office didn't even know about. Some of the dilapidated houses reminded her of her trips to Mexico.

She was careful not to let Charles see the shock on her face. She slowly began to feel safe and at ease with Charles.

What Terri thought was casual visits, were actually business ventures. This was Charles's means of survival. He sold clothes, shoes, small appliances, cigarettes, and other contraband from his car trunk. Frequent stops and visits were sometimes just promotional. Sometimes a quick visit was to stir up lagging business. On occasion, when no contraband was sold, Charles invited Terri in with him.

Terri felt good being at his side watching him wheel and deal. They laughed and played a lot. He told her hilarious stories about his growing up in these areas. He told her how he would be running and hiding from the police, dogs and older guys all wanting to kick his butt for some mischief he'd done. Charles had a honesty, and genuine misfitting about him that made him humorous. He was also as kind as he was street wise.

She felt herself yearn to be alone with him as the hours closed in on her curfew. Sensing her ease, Charles took her to a neighborhood motel for dinner, then got a room for the evening. Terri became unnerved as she walked into the room and saw the bed. At least the room was neat and clean. She felt her immaturity surfacing as her mind wrestled with all the little trivia that she could find to distract it. She tried to play it cool as her eyes continued to search every corner of the room for dirt, spider webs, paint splatters or whatever would take her mind off of what she knew was expected of her.

Charles, ever so smooth and worldly put her fears to rest immediately. He turned on the radio and dimmed the lights. He took her hand and asked her to dance. She eased into his open arms. I don't really know how to dance she stammered, knowing she could trust him. He wrapped his arms around her tightly. Don't worry about it, he whispered in her ear, and kissed her cheek. Just sway from side to side like this he instructed softly. He was gentle and patient. Terri relaxed and picked up the rhythm. Charles, Terri broke the silence again. I'm not really very experienced in in, she paused. I don't really know how to . . . she took a deep breath. I don't know how to kiss or anything like that. She exhaled hard trying to blow away her embarrassment with it. Charles leaned back and looked at her quizzically. Terri hid her eyes from him. She was sure she was red as a beet by then. Charles didn't say a word. He just leaned down and kissed her lips. He leaned back again and looked at her. He smiled softly and said there, see, it's not that hard is it? No she smiled back. He kissed her again, and again. It's getting easier, he joshed with her. He then proceeded kissing her from her neck to her mouth. This time he pushed his tongue in her mouth, and pressed his manhood hard against her. Terri felt a twich in her panties. I'll gladly teach you these lessons he said in almost a groan. He continued kissing, sucking and licking her mouth until she was breathless. He stepped back and unbuttoned his shirt and pants. He undressed her as well, all the while staring deeply into her eyes. Terri's heart was racing, and her coochie throbbed erotically. He laid her on the bed and climbed on top of her. He spread her legs apart with his thighs, then slowly eased his manhood inside her. Don't be afraid he whispered in the quiet. Don't be afraid he groaned. His chest hung in the air. His arms were straight pushing down on his palms. His head was tilted upward. I'll take good care of you, his voice moaned in the darkness. Terri opened her eyes. His silhouette scared her. He looked like a wolf on the edge of a cliff, howling at the moon. She closed her eyes quickly and shuttered. He stroked her hair then sucked her breast. Just relax he panted again. His voice was baritone and smooth. It gave her the courage she needed to relax. He pushed up and down quicker. He became wetter with each stroke. His wild wet kisses were fast and sloppy. Terri slowly joined his rhythm building a relentless, fiery pressure panting toward explosion. Terri herd herself spurting out short squeals and moans.

Charles exploded with a fiery rush that drenched her with his perspiration. He continued to hold her close soaking not only her but the bed as well. They lay awake in silence with their ecstasy still ringing in their ears and in their groins. Finally Charles broke the silence. You a fast learner, he joked. I give you an A+ on your lesson. I'll expect you back here tomorrow for your next. They laughed and held each other until they fell asleep.

Terri now looked forward to the next lesson. She liked the dark to hide her facial expressions. Charles however loved a dim light which let him see her shameful gratitude. Charles showed her body senses and physical positions she never knew possible. She trusted him and let him pose her and bend her like a double jointed doll. At last he posed her with her face in the pillow, she was most grateful.

It wasn't long before she realized it. The lesson had become gratifying and necessary. She longed for Charles's body when they weren't together. His love-making style was compelling. Charles was a bed-wetter. Even though his wet body was sometimes uncomfortable, Terri loved his full, commanding wet manhood. She found sharing their deep, inner most feelings as they talked afterwards most genuine. It was hard for her to decide which she loved more. Their intimacy grew quickly into deep love and closeness.

Charles had purged all of the mysteries of his past during their lessons. He also shared his deep feelings he had for her. He explained how ashamed he had felt to be homeless, motherless, and loveless. He talked about his recurring dream of falling into a wet darkness that lunged him straight up in his bed every night before she was there to hold him. He relayed that she had allowed him to free himself of his shame and guilt and pain. He had come to rely on her for this freedom. Now with her he could dream and believe in the things that seemed impossible. He shared that he needed her in his life to help him achieve what he longed for, which was a loving family and a successful career.

Charles took her hand and asked her to stay with him and give him the strength to pursue the baseball career he thought he could have. After a life of hardship, being pushed aside and slighted, and of laying his head wherever he could, he longed to be someone respectable. He promised he would make her life easy and wonderful. Before Terri realized it, Charles had slipped into her heart and found a permanent residence there.

Terri tried to figure out how to explain to him that there was no way possible for her to stay with him. She had to leave in two days. It would be hard for both of them. Maybe she thought, he could move to Atlanta too. Nope she thought, he'd have nowhere to stay. She pondered how to tell him this was the end of their student-teacher adventure. She decided to wait until tomorrow.

That night Terri lay awake thinking about all the wonderful adventures ahead of her. Atlanta would certainly offer its' thrills and experiences. That's what everyone expected her to do. But a new option had been introduced. The new option of staying home to support and nurture her relationship with Charles, was a viable option, but no one wanted her to do that, except Charles.

She loved her family, but she loved Charles in a different way. Plus his love was so exciting. She tossed from side to side. Stay. Go. Stay. Go. Finally she checked the clock again. It was three o'clock in the morning. I'm staying here she insisted. They'll have to accept Charles or loose me, she lamented. She tossed on her side again and went to sleep.

That morning Terri fixed breakfast for her grandma and herself. Her grandma looked totally delighted. I just want to talk to you since I'll probably be leaving today Terri explained to her grandma. Probably, her grandma's brows raised. Well yeah Terri sheepishly continued. I really don't want to go now. I wish I could stay here and attend Central University. Central her grandma shouted. The softness in her face turned hard. Terri had never seen that side of her grandma. Central she shouted again. Her hair even looked hard by now. For the first time she saw the survivor-warrior sista come out in her grandma. Terri tried to appease and soften her countenance. I was just thinking about it grandma. Well you might as well not she replied. Forget about it she went on. You're going to Atlanta tomorrow. Terri became highly offended by her tone, and demanding voice. I'm not she blurted out before she realized it. Her grandma's mouth dropped. I just want to stay here with you, Terri tried to soften her words. But the battle lines were drawn now. I'm calling your daddy right now. Terri stormed out of the room.

Terri hurried and dressed, then called Linda and Toni. She had them meet her at the wall, and contact Charles. When she reached Whittenhall, she found Toni and Linda at the wall. Charles wasn't there yet, but they knew he'd probably show up sometime soon. True to character, Charles showed up around noon. He entered from the back entrance, as if he had been there all along. He convinced Terri to join him in the storage room. Terri finally gave in since they needed to talk privately.

They stepped through the door. She stopped to look around for a moment. Charles wrapped his arms around her and kissed her hard and long. They danced, kissed some more, laughed and sang together. Terri couldn't remember having so much fun alone with Charles before. They were having a ball when Charles blurted out; I wish you would stay here with me. Before she could speak he held his hand nervously in front of him. He began to explain. I he swallowed and took a deep breath. I have deep feelings for you baby. You are just the kind or woman I want by my side when I make it. He went on to explain his attempts to try out for the city's professional baseball team. You have given me the courage and motivation to make it this time. He explained that he had been practicing all summer, and had finally gotten his speed up to draft level. He explained that several teams were interested in seeing him now. Terri was so flattered and touched. They began to talk intimately about their dreams and plans for the future. His voice humbled and tears welled in the corner of his eye when he took Terri's hand and told her with you I'm strong and most of all happy again. The emptiness of losing everything I ever had, the loneliness of not knowing who I belong to, the weakness of not knowing if anyone will ever love me is all gone now. I'm free now because of you he went on. I love you Terri interrupted him. She pushed him backward on the sofa and jumped on top of him. They made passionate love right then and there.

Terri came home that evening resolved to stay and bursting with the wonderful news. Her grandmother drew the war lines immediately. Terri wasn't swayed. She was fighting for the love of her life. Once she and all the family met Charles they would see what she saw in him. Besides a professional baseball career, no one, even her father could sneeze at that.

Chapter Four

Charles's Story

In the dark utility room of the storage building of the Whittenhall Projects, Charles Matthew Johnson was born to a dope addicted welfare mother. High and crazed from years of drug and alcohol abuse, she cut the umbilical cord herself. She immediately wrapped the baby in a dirty towel, and gave him a long kiss that saturated his tiny soul. She tied him in a garbage bag and pitched him in the dumpster right outside the door of the storage building.

Later that morning a utility worker entering the storage building heard a baby crying. He followed the cry to the dumpster. He jumped in and lifted up bag after bag of garbage until he heard the cry of a baby. He tore open the bag to find a newborn baby wet and frightened. He called the police.

The mother's identity remained anonymous, even after the official investigation. Speculation was ramped throughout the projects. The Stars of the projects made sure everyone knew all the details. They had pinpointed the suspect woman and solved the mystery. The Stars condemned her and waited for her to return to the Whittenhall again. They had determined she was not a Whittenhall resident by their account. No one except the Stars knew the truth.

Charles was taken as a ward of the state. He was adopted into a home at approximately three months of age. The mother was a Caucasian woman and the father was black. Charles fit in quite naturally, with his golden skin and sandy colored hair. He could have been born to the couple naturally from all appearances. After a ten year marriage, both were first time parents. The mother's desperation for children overtook her patience. She was unable to persevere all of the artificial attempts available. She finally convinced her husband. She would leave him and find another man to give her children. They adopted due to the father's low sperm count and unlikelihood to produce children.

Their home was financially sound at that time. The father was an electrical engineer. The mother was essentially uneducated. She had managed to finish the tenth grade, and had no desire or money to go any further in school. Anxious to leave a poor and torn home, she took to the streets immediately. She ended up dancing in a strip club on the other side of town. That was where she met her husband. After being a regular customer for a year, he proposed marriage to her and she accepted.

He provided a stable home, and gave Charles his first and last name. For seven years, they composed a happy family. Charles became accustomed to all the conveniences and many luxuries. His mother was a very kind and soft spoken woman. He loved her and felt very secure there with them. His father was louder and much more stern than his mother. In any case, he showed lots of attention and love to Charles. He was an avid baseball fan. He drug Charles to every home game of the city's professional baseball team. He also drug Charles out to the baseball field on every warm day to pitch and practice hitting and batting. Charles had natural talent and became quite good. Charles too became a lifetime baseball fan.

All was happy and well until one normal day a sudden change took place. His father came home from work as usual and pitched some balls to him in the backyard. After dinner, his mother put him in the tub to bathe and sent him to bed early. He could hear their voices rising. So he listened at their bedroom door. His mother told his father she was with child. He was not convinced that it could remotely be his child, considering his physical restraints. He didn't even believe in the immaculate birth of Jesus Christ. He would never believe she conceived by a barren man that couldn't even jack off as he put it. The argument escalated into a fist fight. His father beat his mother unconscious. Charles flung open the door and saw his father standing over an unconscious body. His father turned and looked at him but didn't see him. His eyes were tear-filled and hollow. He walked past him and out the front door. Charles never saw him again. The mother suffered terminal brain damage. The state removed Charles and placed him in a foster home.

Charles knew immediately that he was misplaced. He felt the cold and chill from Ms. Turentol immediately. There was no Mr. or anyone else to soften her harshness toward him. Ms. Turentol ran the foster care home alone. She currently had five other foster children in her home. She didn't expect or want Charles. That was clear. Ms. Turtentol had determined that Charles was lazy right from the beginning. She could just tell by the look in his eyes, so she said. She presumed to remedy this by teaching him to work. She loaded him with chores, and senseless errands. The workload was distributed quite unevenly. In fact, it appeared to Charles that he was the only one with chores. He was treated like Cinderella, while the other children were the ugly step siblings. Charles ran away repeatedly to avoid the constant workload. He was only found and returned to that same foster household.

Ms Turentol was a heavy set, middle aged black woman. She was so opposite of the mother figure he was used to. Ms. Turentol was loud and harsh, and hateful. She seemed to make a good living off of the foster care income. She provided daily meals and clothing, but her love was sparse.

Everyone called her Ms. Ma'am. She got that name because she only accepted yes Ms. Turentol ma'am or no Ms. Turentol ma'am as a response to her instructions, commands, or questions. Over the years, since many of the younger ones had difficulty pronouncing her last name, the response got shortened to Ms. Mam. It was fitting since she was very strict.

Among the several children, she had a few favorites and a kind of love for them. It was nothing close to the full blown love his mother and father had taught him. The other five were all older than Charles. They adhered closely to the hierarchical order. Steve who was sixteen was the oldest resident, and had been with Ms. Ma'am since he was two years old. His word was as good as gold in that house and Ms. Ma'am protected him fiercely. He had a savage hatred for Charles. Jerome, fourteen and Perry, thirteen weren't fleshly brothers, but the most tightly bonded of all the residents. They were always together and kept their circle closely guarded. They didn't seem to have any feelings toward Charles either way, but he was not invited to play in their circle. Anytime he opened his mouth to speak he was scolded harshly. Everyone took issue to anything he had to say. They didn't consider whether it was right or wrong. They just didn't allow him any words besides yes and no.

Silencing Charles hurt him the most since he was used to not only being heard, but being an important voice. The boys teased him about being soft, since he would cry often, in place of the words he was not allowed to speak.

The two girls, Gina, twelve and Kelly, nine years old both pulled rank over him like strings on a puppet. But like all girls with the littlest authority, they were the bossiest people on the planet. And like most girls, they were sometimey. Sometimes they liked him and sometimes they didn't. The girls would strangely however, agree on any issue regarding Charles. That was strange since they couldn't come to agreement on any other issue at all. They argued constantly, but were inseparable. In any case, right or wrong, Charles was at their mercy. Any disagreements between Charles and the girls, was always favored on the side of the girls. Ms. Ma'am actually only favored one of the girls, which was Gina. The other girl squabbled for her approval. Gina understudied Ms. Ma'am in every way. She was loud just like Ms. Ma'am, and mean toward everyone just like Ms. Ma'am.

The overriding opinion in the household, mentored by Ms. Ma'am was that Charles was too high yellow for their taste. The other kids used that as a weapon against him, calling him any names of defamation they could think of using the word yellow.

Charles seemed to be particularly annoying to Ms. Ma'am. He wanted very desperately to please her. He didn't understand why, but he longed for her love. He decided to learn her routine, and try to assist her in any way he could. He cleared the dinner dishes without being told. He emptied the trash without it being his turn. He washed dishes forever it seemed to him and mopped the kitchen floor nightly. He made his bed and cleaned the bedrooms weekly. He was slowly gaining ground with a couple of the boys, but Ms. Ma'am seemed to smell his desperation.

After endless effort and exhaustion he found he couldn't please her no matter what he did. She knew he needed her love, but she purposely withheld any sentiment except disdain. She yelled at him constantly. She picked apart everything he did from the way he combed his hair to the way he chewed his food. Charles remembered her reaching across the dinner table and smacking him across the face so hard that his food flew out of his mouth. Ms. Ma'am said that he was making a funny noise when he chewed. The other kids laughed merrily. It was like entertainment for them, and Ms. Ma'am enjoyed putting on a show for them. It didn't take him long to realize he couldn't do anything right in her eyes. He was stuck in a world where he was resented and meaningless.

Charles tried to shrink his soul. He tried to be invisible, but he couldn't. He was too used to being important and loved, and he yearned for that attention. Occasionally he attempted to share his day with the family at the dinner table. Dinner was mandatory family sharing time for Ms. Ma'am's foster home. They literally took turns sharing something from their day with everyone. Charles had learned that it was generally better to pass when it came to his turn. He knew the least little thing he said could set not only Ms. Ma'am, but the other kids off as well. He really wanted to stand up and scream; I'm smart not stupid, but that had become his nickname at the house. Oddly enough all of the children, even the others that Ms. Ma'am didn't love much, had the dubious privilege of calling him that nickname, as well as treating him any way their little moods dictated. He was always punched and pushed around by the older boys. It was part of releasing their aggression and frustration. The girls were much more cruel. They set up schemes against him by telling lies against him and enjoying the punishment and pain he'd have to endure. They would get mad at him at the drop of a hat. They would spit on him, even in his face. It was all allowable by the law of Ms. Ma'am's rules.

Every time he thought of the unfairness it sent tears pouring from his eyes. He couldn't stop them or control them. Like everything else in his life it was so unfair. The pressure defeated his spirit and his innocence.

His world grew darker day by day. He lost interest in everything around him. He even put away the only thing he had left from his father, and his life before this hell, his baseball. He couldn't find anyone in the world to love him. He was a little curly haired boy unwanted and unloved. Charles felt his heart was so irreversibly torn and crushed, it could never be mended.

Charles regressed into the darkness of his broken heart and life. He performed poorly in school. The notes sent home from school teachers went completely unattended. Ms. Ma'am was never interested in his grades or report cards. He signed them himself, forging her signature. She never responded to the phone calls from school. She plain just didn't care. Knowing that no one cared, caused Charles to conclude that he was unloveable.

He suffered at nighttime especially. Sweat would bead on his forehead, as he lay in his bed. He wrestled with his cover trying to fight off the demonic dreams. But if sleep came the dreams came. He felt as if he were falling, wrestling, kicking, screaming from inside a dark, tight, wet, smelly plastic bag. He could feel himself bound with no way out. A gut wrenching scream, then sudden light would end the dream. That had been his nightly horror since he laid his head at Ms. Mam's foster home.

His hurt soon turned to anger. His anger turned to rage. When he turned sixteen he'd had enough. He stole three hundred dollars from Ms. Ma'am and brought enough dope to start a small business. He wandered the streets aimlessly day after day. He eventually found his way to the Whittenhall Projects. There he found a storage facility. It was a one room building with a working bathroom. Charles secretly made it his home. He only entered late at night and left very early in the mornings, being careful not to be seen. It wasn't comfortable, but had a strange familiarity. He quickly got to know a lot of the residents, and made quick customers and friends there. He slept there often in the summer. As dirty and nasty as the place was he rested well there without his usual nightly horrors.

Charles stumbled into a life of petty crime and brief incarcerations. He learned the coldness of the criminal system. In jail and in crime he knew he could never be close or love anyone. It was all in the name of survival according to his story.

Although he was fully engulfed in the drug business, and his bare existence, he never stopped yearning for a career in baseball. Nothing could erase the fragile wish buried deep inside his heart. It was so fragile he couldn't even speak it aloud. He just felt if he could ever find someone to believe in him it might just be attainable.

Charles's affairs with women were just a series of small battles, with the conquest of physical satisfaction. He was quite successful in his conquests. It wasn't that black girls were easy. Actually, they were much harder to get undressed than the few white girls he'd dated briefly. Black girls needed much more dining and wining. Be it all a hamburger and fries, and a bottle of Maddog 20/20, they needed the initial coaxing. In fact Charles thought they were quite forward and of course loud regarding their "*pussy*" rules. Dinner was a mandatory requirement. If she was pretty, then a movie, and a drink might well be expected too. For the most part though, in his mind, they all were basically the same. Black women were all loud and sassy. He had grown to hate their brash, head swinging, hand on hip, careless, foul mouthed ways. Of course he removed himself from his feelings as easily as he washed his hands. He had learned to let them hoop and holler, with his head hung down and a silly smirk on his face. He only continued to put up with the black women because their bodies were extremely sexy and irresistible to him. They knew it and used them skillfully. Yet he reserved deep in his gut that he'd never marry a black woman. He believed they were certainly not gentle enough to spend a lifetime with, along with their lack of class. But for now, he concluded he'd have to select from what he called the lower ranks. He as well as all other black men simply learned to ignore the dramatic gestures and mute the loud mouths of their women until bedtime.

In any case, Charles's good looks got him off fairly easy with the women, sometimes without even buying dinner, but only sometimes. Charles was very selective, choosing only from the lightest skin tones, then according to hair texture. Even though Charles ranked *high* in both categories, he felt that was another silly idiosyncrasy among them.

He was friendly and polite toward everyone though. He had a mild seeming way of joshing with everyone. He was careful not to let his prejudice show. The slightest whif of that kind of prejudice would ruin his business. He was nobody's fool. He needed to sale his goods to everyone, every complexion from light to dark and everyone in between.

Business had been good lately and was picking up especially in the Whittenhall Projects. He actually had more friends and business associates there, in one place, than anywhere else in the city. In fact, Whittenhall was his most profitable stop. He always chuckled under his breath at the irony. He could never figure out how the poorest people in the city spent the most money on clothing and items of pleasure. It really needed no justification in his eyes, he just made sure he took good care of them. He even spent the night their frequently, if not with girls then in a storage room he'd made into his make shift apartment. He was clever enough to keep it secret from everyone, even though that was difficult to do. All in all Charles had learned the ropes of ghetto life, and made many alliances. It was a demanding hard life, with its moments of fun.

In actuality, Charles loved only one black lady. Her name was Linda. She was a lifetime resident of the Whittenhall Projects. Even though she was the typical loud mouthed sister, Charles loved her. She had taken him in when he was a wandering teen. He left Ms. Ma'am's foster home without thinking or realizing what awaited him in the streets. He wandered into the Whittenhall. He had tried many times to remember how he landed there. The last thing her remembered before landing there was attending a party the night before. His last vision was of seeing himself bend over to do a line of Cocaine, then darkness flooded his mind. His next memory was of a fair skinned, heavy set black woman rubbing his sweaty forehead, while he laid on a couch in a strange apartment. Linda took him in, nursed him and loved him without question. Till this day Linda and he never discussed their introduction, but shared a love that was unusual and unbreakable. Theirs was a brotherly love.

They never made love to one another even though they had slept in the same bed, and both naked on a couple of occasions. Those two occasions were stored away in the archives of their pasts. In any case, Linda was desperate for the love of a man. Charles felt Linda's broken soul and took careful note of her pains. She was always needy and begging. He didn't mind though. She was never to weighty for him. She was the female version of his own soul. Being a black female, she could vocalize all the pangs his own soul felt, that a man would never vocalize, but longingly admired her courage to admit. It was the double standard in reverse, what a woman could say without penalty, but a man would be ostracized for. It was the true pains and heaviest weights of the system to bear.

Chapter Five

Battle Cries

Terri had been so engulfed in war with her grandmother, she hadn't seen Charles. She was due to leave for Atlanta the following day, and wanted to spend possibly her last day with him. When she came downstairs to leave she was surprised to find her mother and father there waiting for her. Her grandmother had called them and explained her concern about Terri not wanting to leave.

When her father laid eyes on her he hit the ceiling. Why are you dressed like a whore he screamed. Terri had wore a halter top and some hot pants to impress Charles. Terri didn't yell back, she felt more mature than that. She took a seat and spoke firmly and directly without stuttering or pausing. I have made my decision. I am not leaving tomorrow. I plan to stay here and support Charles. I love him and he loves me. I am going to marry him and support him in pursuing a professional baseball career she raised her voice a little to emphasize the career. And just how in the hell do you plan to support anybody with no education and no money her father shouted back. His eyes were wide and the vein at his temple was bulging out. Terri sat motionless with a non-chalant expression on her face. Her father rose from his seat and pointed his finger directly in her face. He stood towering over her. You are going to pack your bags and go to Atlanta right now young lady he continued shouting. Terri gently pushed his finger away. He was furious. He snatched her from her seat and flung her across the floor. He ran over to her, and grabbed her by her arm, and pulled her to her feet. Get up those stairs and pack, he spoke through clenched teeth. I'm not going Terri screamed directly in her father's face. He swung his powerful arm and smacked her across her face. Both her mother and her grandmother screamed in unison. Her grandmother ran to her rescue. It's all your fault mother he yelled and pushed her away. His mother hit the floor with a thud and Terri ran upstairs. She could hear all the commotion downstairs, but was afraid to come down and face more of her father's wrath. After a few minutes she heard the door slam and was glad it was finally over.

The house was unusually still. Terri took several long deep breaths and then eased down the stairs calling for her grandmother. She sat on the stairs for a few minutes waiting for her to respond. She fiddled with her fingers while she tried to organize her thoughts and plans. She probably walked to the corner store to cool off she thought as she continued down the stairs and into the dining room. She eased throughout the house peeking and calling her grandmother. She sat at the dining room table waiting for her grandmother to return.

As dusk began to set in she was quite worried, but figured her grandmother was visiting relatives telling them about the fight and blowing off steam. She suddenly remembered she was supposed to meet Charles. She took off running and didn't stop until she saw the Whittenhall wall. Strangely no one was on the wall. Good she mumbled to herself and headed for the storage room.

Charles held her tightly, stroking her hair and face. She was surprised to find he had cleaned up the place. He had bought rugs to cover most of the cold cement floor, and more candles to give off light. It was still retched, but it had a crude romantic appeal to Terri. I wanted to surprise you he whispered. Why'd you do this Terri asked. I'm getting the place ready for us he answered quietly. I know this is not suitable, but for now babe, just for now, this will be our meeting place. Terri was naively flattered. She began to tell him about the fight with her father. They may not accept us or believe us until they see we're serious he replied. And we'll just have to stay together until then he added. Charles's words gave her more strength and conviction. Remember this is for me and you Charles coaxed her on as he opened the car door for her at her grandmother's house. They walked to the door hand in hand together. She felt safe and reassured and she had a gloating smile on her face, as Charles rehearsed calmly how he was going to explain to her father.

They rang the bell and knocked for more than ten minutes before they realized no one was home. Terri checked under the flowerpot for the spare key. It was not there. Her emotions swelled into a panic. Had her grandmother turned her back on her she thought. What a hypocrite Terri mumbled in anger. She of all people should understand forbidden love Terri thought becoming more angered by the minute. She checked under the flowerpot again and then on the window sill. Bitch, the word slipped out of her mouth as they headed back down the steps. She flinched for a moment realizing that she had never used profanity before. The regret was fleeting in lieu of anger. She apologized to Charles as she explained that she would have to go back to her father's house to settle matters once and for all. She felt it best that Charles didn't come along. She promised to meet him in the morning at the Whittenhall wall. Charles gave her cab fare and took off on two wheels.

Terri shuttered at the thought of her grandmother's betrayal. She cursed her all the way to her father's house. She heard some of the words slipping out of her mouth audibly as she pounded on the door back home. Her sister came to the door and grabbed her by the arm and pulled her into the house. She dragged Terri into the living room and pushed her on the sofa. She explained that Grandma Rena was taken to the hospital suffering from a broken hip. She went on to explain that their grandmother was due to be released the following morning. She demanded that Terri tell her all the details of the event.

Terri eased up the stairs to her grandma's bedroom. Grandma Rena was lying on her back staring at the ceiling. She tip-toed into the bedroom and put her arms around her grandmother. I'm sorry Grandma, Terri whispered. I'm so sorry. Her grandma just stared at her blankly for a while. Tears were streaming down Terri's face. Her grandmother hugged her and said softly, that's alright baby.

Terri continued to refuse to leave for Atlanta. She vowed to stay with Grandma Rena and help her recuperate. She knew it would interfere with her time with Charles, but she felt she owed her grandmother the service. Her grandmother would need around the clock care for a while and Terri was loyally committed. She promised her father that she would sit out of school for the first quarter and leave if she and Charles weren't married by then. If worst came to worst she promised she would attend Central University the following quarter.

Her decision finally won out. Terri realized she was victorious over her father again. This was the independence that she wanted. She knew from this point on she no longer had to take orders from him. Her father threatened to disclaim her if she continued to see Charles. He also forbade her to enter his home.

Terri didn't take him seriously. She remained in residence with her grandmother, caring for her every need. Grandma Rena was a good patient. She didn't complain or ask for much. She slept a lot. Her body was like a busted glass plate, and very hard to mend. Her mind and heart was strong as ever. She thanked Terri for nursing her to health, and confided in her that she planned to change her will to make Terri the beneficiary of her estate.

Terri continued to see Charles. For the next couple of months, they'd meet every evening at their meeting place. Terri's sensitive nose and stomach had turned to cast iron. The sight and smell of that place no longer nauseated her. In fact they often bought dinner in and served it on a wooden crate in their little slice of hell. She figured if their love and relationship could be happy during such hard times they'd be in paradise when Charles made the pros. She felt grateful to Charles for making her a mature woman, and making her akin to her black culture. Most of all, she was grateful to him for giving her the experience of loving a man besides her father. The fact that she was Charles's lady was well established throughout the Whittenhall Projects, and that made her swell with joy and pride.

While the seasons pushed onward, things were slowly changing for Charles on a professional level. He had finally been selected as a walk-on for the city's major league baseball team. He had to leave town in two weeks. He was full of joy and ideals for the future. He reflected on his retched beginnings and opened his soul to Terri. He told her again about the thrown away little baby boy found in the garbage of some projects, he didn't know where. That little baby was then thrown into a system of negligence and abuse. He had struggled to stay alive for as long as he could remember. All his heart and soul poured out night after night, as he thanked God for this golden opportunity. He believed that this opportunity had come as a result of Terri's love for him. They found themselves embracing one another for the support. He was grateful for Terri's love and this chance for a life of happiness and ease. Terri assured him it would happen and he deserved it.

Terri's heart was broken when he left for training, but she couldn't leave her Grandma Rena. Charles promised her that after this short three month trial camp he'd return home to make her his wife. He promised she'd be the queen in his life of ease and luxury. He promised her that they would never have to see that stinkin' room again. Terri couldn't wait to rub it in her father's face.

Their relationship had survived a scorching tempermental summer, but now the autumn days were beginning to grow chilly. In Charles's absence Terri visited Linda in the afternoons. Her grandmother was on the mend, and beginning to move about freely. Terri was spending long days and some nights at Linda's apartment. Terri stepped lively, headed for the courtyard, keeping her eyes moving. She still feared some resentment from the residents at the Whittenhall. She had tried hard to befriend as many as she could. It had been quite difficult. Without Linda as a buffer, few of the girls liked her. It hurt her deeply, and she couldn't understand why. She didn't want to believe what Charles had once told her. He was absolutely certain it was because of her skin color. Terri was certain that was wrong. Black people had too many oppressors to be quibbling over skin tones.

As she approached a crowd of men standing in the courtyard, unexpectedly a brightness and sharpness came into focus. The veil had lowered over her eyes. She could vaguely hear a conversation on foreign diplomacy affecting the economic balance of America, while her eyes changed focus. She stared at the men closely. She couldn't believe this was the same conversation she'd heard her father have many times with his friends. She wished he could be there right now and even challenge some of the points they made. She had always been taught that these people were so ignorant, they had no clue why they were in the rotting conditions they were in. Terri was curiously impressed. While their voices faded into the background, their clothes suddenly changed from the dingy tee shirts and jeans they normally wore. They were now wearing royal African styled garb. They each had a crown of weighted gold, encrusted with brilliant diamonds and exquisite gems, on their heads. Their faces were no longer racked with the signs of frustration and suffering. Their conversation became jovial and relaxed. The peace and serenity among them was apparent. Just as abruptly an unseen force snatched their crowns violently from their heads. They became confused and bewildered. Their clothes quickly returned to rags. They began to accuse one another for their losses, and vicious battles ensued. The peace zone they once inhabited was now a war zone, and no one was innocent. The fatalities were tragic and epidemic. There were pools of blood that rose up to their knees as they waded about in it searching for spoils. The peace and serenity they once had never returned as Terri watched their faces grow old and wrinkled ignoring the rising blood level. The saltiness of the tears hanging on the corner of her mouth intruded on her sharp vision. As the veil lifted from over her eyes, she let out a loud sigh. Terri shuffled past them wishing for what could have been.

Terri was now enlighted to a new reality. There would not be as much violence and poverty among black people if they could see their own kingship and wealth. If only they could see the crown upon each black man's head and respect his kingship, the ramped violence would cease. If only they could see the self destruction they've caused as a result of the systematic frustration, then their wealth would return. If only they could appreciate the genuine wealth they're born with, taking the life of any black man would be an unacceptable atrocity. They would largely be inventive, creative and productive citizens of this society. They would invent and own many new communication systems. They would create and patent new medical tools and operations. They would launch rockets into space. They would seize new medicines for the world. Then their worldwide reputation would be glorious, and they would not allow its' racism to suppress them. They could ignore the few ignorant racists, because everyone else would be in awe of their contributions to the world. Terri heard the words self destruction, tisk tisk tisk roll off her lips. First they have to appreciate what they have naturally; their kinky hair, their beautiful rainbow shades of brown skin and their genuine creativity. Before they buy red and blonde wigs, before they burn their hair out with chemicals to gradually fall out of their heads, before they suppress their own creativity and production to chase after someone else's; they have to stop the self destruction. Terri wiped a tear from her eye and knocked on the door.

Chapter Six

A New Ballgame

Terri fortunately found her brief association with Linda had left it easy for her to talk to Linda. She came to rely on her. Winter set in early that year. Terri found that Linda's apartment was the only warm place she could go in the Whittenhall. Being at the Whittenhall somehow made her feel close to Charles. Linda fed her and schooled her. She grew to love and respect Linda, something she never thought would happen. She never thought she'd see Linda as more than a baby dropping welfare star. Now she could see Linda as the true humanitarian she was. She never turned away anyone that needed help, at least no one cool. She was like the mother hen of the star class. Linda's apartment was always full. The stars shared their joys and pains with Linda. Linda was also privy to the first rumors and gossip of the projects.

In fact it still amazed Terri how hospitable Linda was toward her and all her friends for that matter. Actually, Terri realized it was the most common part of love there in the Whittenhall. In fact, when Linda ran out of food, she took Terri to her mother's house to eat. Terri was terrified to meet Linda's mother. She tried to refuse and leave, but Linda wouldn't hear of it. When Sue opened the door she immediately laid eyes on Terri. They just stared at one another, both with eyes of desperation and longing. Terri could see her neediness and she was sure Sue could see hers as well. For some reason they seemed to need each other's acceptance. Sue spoke first. Make yo' sef at home she said kindly. Terri felt something inside her relax. Sue could see the fear in Terri's eyes and pulled out a chair for her. Terri smiled and said thank you. She saw the light come on in Sue's eyes. They both smiled at each other. Sue fixed Terri a plate of collard greens, fried chicken, and candied yams. They started off with light conversation and were soon talking like best friends. When she left Sue's house, she knew Sue had a big golden heart, and she felt her love.

Linda made sure Terri felt right at home in her apartment. She fixed her a bunk in her oldest child's room. That room directly faced the storage building. That way she could see right out the window to the suite, in case Charles came home.

On the same day as their fourth month anniversary, little did Terri know, Charles was signed to a contract with a professional baseball team down south, a life changing event for him. Little did Terri know she was committed to a life changing event herself. One evening while talking to Linda and hoping for Charles to show up, she asked Linda for advice. It had been months since she could talk to her mother about womanly things, and her grandmother was too occupied with recuperation to bother with petty concerns. So she decided to get the opinion of the next most experienced person she knew-Linda. Linda how can I get some birth control pills, she asked shyly. Linda's mouth dropped open. Do you mean you're not already on the pill Linda asked in disbelief. Well no we've only had sex like two, three, her voice faded while she thought back and counted on her fingers. Her mouth dropped open as she began to realize it had been more than she thought. When was your last period Linda asked nearly holding her breath. Terri thought back again. Her concentration was overtaken by a small voice in her head repeating uh oh. Oh no, wait a minute she blurted out trying to stop the voice, as well as Linda's pressing stare. You're pregnant girl, Linda stated in a flat, pitiable tone. The words whirled around in her head like a cyclone. She was so blindsided that she couldn't see Linda standing right front of her face. The voice in her head kept screaming no no. I can't be pregnant. She exhaled after having held her breath for the last three minutes. Her mind cleared as soon as she took a deep breath. No no she yelled sharply to Linda. See I had a period in June, and then I think July too she explained showing Linda her hasty error. Linda went into the kitchen and got the calendar. Terri nervously flipped the calendar back to July, and pointed to the ending date. Linda looked at her with sympathy. It's the end of September darling, you're pregnant, Linda said softly as if the softness would take away the pain. It didn't. Tears began streaming down her face. Terri headed for her grandmother's house to let the thought sink in.

Her grandmother was recovering nicely at this point. Grandma Rena was getting about on her own and didn't need round the clock care any longer. Besides she was a very independent woman. She didn't want Terri to fuss over her. So Terri obliged. She checked in on her regularly, but was careful not to make her grandma feel helpless.

Terri stayed in her room the next few days. She didn't bathe or eat. She just found herself repeating the words over and over again. I'm pregnant. She couldn't imagine facing her father in such a state. She knew she was still the apple of his eye, and his disappointment would pass as long as she accomplished the goals he had expected of her all her life. But this all had to be a mistake. If not there had to be a way out Terri pondered. She knew she wanted children, but not until she finished med school and established her career. She couldn't disappoint her whole family. And most of all she couldn't disappoint herself. She decided she'd run away with Charles and get married before her parents found out anything. At least that would make her child legitimate. All she had to do is find Charles and quickly.

Terri hurried to Linda's apartment early the next morning. Surprisingly she found Toni there and another friend of theirs, Tina. Some other familiar faces of the Star class were there as well. But it was Toni who was a sight for soar eyes. She hugged Terri and looked at her hard. You alright she asked in her soothing soft voice. Terri nodded quickly. They were having a large breakfast and talking. Here sit down and eat Linda insisted. They caught up on old times while they ate and Terri found herself laughing soon afterward.

The other girls cleaned the kitchen while Terri, Toni and Linda reclined in the living room. Linda leaned over and stared at her hard. You look like hell girl. What's happening Toni asked. Terri tried to talk but the tears started again. Toni sat on the sofa next to her and put her arms around her. What's the matter Terri, Toni rubbed her shoulders. I know something's wrong she went on. Has Charles been treating you right she asked. She fell into Toni's lap and sobbed. She told Toni she was pregnant and her family would reject her without question. I'll have no one she sobbed. Toni held her and rocked her, and comforted her. We yo' sistas girl. You can always come to us, Toni assured her. If you want to have Charles's baby we'll be here for you. They gave her so much comfort and hope she almost felt invincible. That' gon be a pretty little baby Linda piped in. Terri managed a grimaced smile. They wrapped Terri in her coat and scarf and dragged her to the neighborhood clinic immediately.

For the first time, Terri thought of the baby. She hoped that Charles would be home soon so she could, share the news with him. She decided she would wait until they were married, and Charles is on the team before she told her family. But the days flew by, and she watched her belly getting harder and rounder.

Spending time with Linda turned out to be good for her. It was hard for Terri to imagine Linda having a soft side but Linda was very supportive of her. Linda turned out to be a big sister, and at that point Terri was glad Linda had the experience to help her. She helped her accept motherhood and womanhood. She helped her toss away that moral shame and guilt that kept her fastened to depression. Being around Linda made her days easy and fun. Linda's apartment was lively and exciting. She began to gather understanding of the codes of the projects. Yet she still wasn't sure where her place was in that environment.

It was one of Linda's habits to check the window regularly, just to see what was going on. Terri found herself imitating that habit, and before long she was there more than Linda. She found herself there mostly at night. She still wasn't used to sleeping in such a noisy environment. There was loud music, and laughter and fighting and arguing until all hours of the night. These noises often woke her. She'd go to the window and stare into the black sky, and wish on every resting star. More often than that, she'd awaken with beads of sweat popping on her forehead, and her coochie aching. She wasn't used to this pain. She tried ignoring it and going back to sleep. That was not the correct response. It literally seemed to be screaming at her, keeping her awake. She sometimes tried walking it off. That also was a poor response. It seemed to be crawling up and down her leg clawing fiercely to get out of her panties. She tried eating some food but unless it was the first of the month, Linda had none, or very little to spare. Finally at wit's end, again having been awakened by the growling feline, she stuck her hands in her panties and cupped her coochie with both hands. She tossed from side to side, squeezing her legs shut as tightly as she could. Sleep was impossible. Her head was pounding, and she was clammy and dewy. The moisture spread in her palms. She sprang straight up in the bed and let out a moan. Afraid Linda or one of the kids had heard her, she peeped out of the bedroom door. The apartment was quiet and still, with the exception of the roaches stirring about. She knew she could never get used to them. She raced to the bathroom, sat on the toilet and grabbed a handful of toilet paper. She grabbed the aching feline monster by the throat and squeezed it, until it went numb. Slowly she brushed the toilet paper over it. She stroked it again. She stroked her coochie again and again. Terri was pleasantly surprised. The savage monster inside seemed to calm down the more and the faster she brushed against it. She brushed quicker and quicker until a fiery hiss slipped from her lips. Her coochie monster was tingling and singing happy songs of climax. Tra la la la la she heard herself belt out. She covered her mouth with both hands and listened for footsteps. All was quiet. Terri sighed, then cried lonesome tears for Charles.

She never expected that her body would harass her so frequently. Her nights were never peaceful until she made that little trip to the bathroom. Terri could never get used to the crudeness bought on by this necessity. One in which she had just so recently become familiar. Nothing could replace the grandeur and ecstasy of having Charles intertwined with her body, but the cheap, ruff toilet paper that Linda supplied was her only choice. From that point on whenever she was awakened by the feline monster she rushed to the bathroom and grabbed the toilet paper. Linda constantly roared about the toilet paper disappearing. She threatened her kids, but to no avail.

One Saturday evening, as Terri sat watching television with Linda and the kids, a loud knock at the door startled them. Linda rushed to open it. A crowd of Stars flooded into the apartment all commenting loudly on what the latest word was on the streets. Guess who's here they enticed Linda. Linda couldn't answer fast enough. Charles is back they crooned. Charles is in the city and he's got a new car. Terri sat straight up. Where is he she shouted to match the level of noise in the apartment. He'll be here tomorrow before he leaves again for his new home in Georgia.

Terri was thrilled and danced around the apartment like a kid at Christmas. She told Linda she'd have to leave to prepare for Charles's arrival. She made Linda promise to send Charles to the storage room for dinner and some private time with her. Terri rushed off to her grandmother's house to prepare for her king.

Terri turned soft music on the battery operated radio. She chuckled to herself as she threw her grandmother's beautiful table linen across the wooden crate. It was quite cold in the storage room. The candles and the hot food were the only heat in there. Terri placed her hands on the hot pots to keep them warm, but soon they cooled off too. She draped her head with her grandmothers wedding veil she had bought along to make the evening ceremonial. In the back of her mind she had hoped that Charles would whisk her off to Georgia with nothing but the clothes on her back and her grandmother's wedding veil. It was an expensive African lace with gold flowers on it. Terri had longed to be married in it ever since she saw her grandmother's wedding pictures.

Charles arrived extremely late, and blatantly agitated. He gulped down the cold dinner without speaking. He reached for Terri with his long arms and embraced her tightly. Linda said you had something to tell me, he snorted. She was baffled and slightly afraid of his demeanor. She led him over to the couch on which she had thrown a plush blanket from her grandmother's linen closet. She sat on his lap. I missed you she began and smothered him with kisses. She questioned him on his stay at the training camp and his signing with the professional team. I want to be with you she pleaded like a naïve child. Charles didn't speak. He slowly unbuttoned her blouse and unfastened his pants. He finished undressing them both, and laid Terri underneath him. He plunged himself inside her as he pushed with all his strength. His body muscles were tight and strong. Terri could feel the benefits of his workouts as he lay stretched across her. Terri cupped his buttocks in her cold hands. This is what she had been longing for all those evenings in Linda's bathroom. They humped and grinded their bodies together violently, until they were exhausted. Charles jumped up suddenly as if he'd heard an alarm clock. He was drenched with perspiration. As usual Terri, the blanket and everything underneath him was soaked. He grabbed the veil which had slipped on the floor, and wiped his manhood with it. He carelessly tossed it back on the floor. Terri was mortified. That's my wedding veil she screamed. Oh I thought it was a rag, Charles growled shrugging his shoulders.

Terri was quite angry but didn't want to show it. Now what did you have to tell me, Charles snapped, while he slid back into his pants. When are we going to get married, Terri asked naively. Charles shrugged his shoulders again. What did you want to tell me he raised his voice to show he was annoyed. Terri hesitated for a moment. She decided to blurt it out and get it over with, since Charles seemed to be pressing her for time. I'm pregnant she said slowly and softly. Charles just stared at her for a moment. Then without notice he became angry. You women he ranted. His voice was full of uncontrolled disdain. You think all you have to do is get pregnant, and a man is trapped, he continued with his voice getting louder. I ain't getting trapped for nobody, he yelled. He looked around the room in disgust. He reached into his pocket and pulled out a fist full of dollar bills. He spread them out like a fan. It was ten one hundred dollar bills. He wiped his brow with the bills then pitched them on the dirty dinner plates. Here take this he growled and headed for the door. He turned and faced Terri squarely as he opened the door. You need to do something with this place, he snarled. It stinks he yelled, then slammed the door behind him. Terri stood there frozen in disbelief. She could hardly breathe. This had to be a nightmare she told herself. She wept bitterly.

Charles refused all her attempts to contact him. Terri's belly was growing large quickly and she had to face her family. She now realized she had been a fool just like her father had called her. Now she sat in front of both her parents and her grandmother trying to explain that Charles still loved her, and would provide for their baby. Her father was furious. He again blamed his mother and slapped her across the face. He flung Terri across the room and was about to punch her in the belly when Terri's mother grabbed him. She dragged him by the arm into the other room. All the while he was screaming names at Terri and promising her that she was disinherited. Terri knew he really meant it this time. He forbade her to ever enter his house again and never to bring the illegitimate child there.

Terri's father had all of her things shipped to her grandmother's house the following week. Her grandmother assured Terri she could have a home with her. She had had to disclaim her only son and she felt Terri and the baby were the only family she had left. Grandma Rena promised to change her will to make Terri the beneficiary of her estate. They grew closer and relied on one another.

Early in the spring Grandma Rena died unexpectedly. To her surprise Grandma Rena hadn't changed her will, leaving Terri's father the beneficiary of her estate. He came to the house the day after the funeral, and posted a for sale sign in the yard. Terri tried to converse with him but he flatly refused. He didn't look at her or speak to her. Terri screamed at her father, look at me. Instead he would stare off into space. Terri tried to cling to his arm. He simply shook her off like a pest. When he finally spoke he told her, you chose to live like a dog so you're gonna have to deal with the fleas. He walked out of her grandmother's house and slammed the door, rattling the whole house.

Terri's father continued with her eviction and sold the house. Terri had no legal recourse, and she was homeless. Her father flatly refused to allow her back in his Wellesly home. He worried that the neighbors would find out. What a disgrace she would be on him and the rest of the family. For the sake of appearances, she was left out in the cold.

Chapter Seven

A New World

Terri had no alternatives. She had to move. She cried in disbelief. She had nowhere to go. She couldn't believe her mother would leave her out in the cold. But the message was loud and clear. Terri was on her own. She could not depend on any help from her mother or sister.

Linda helped Terri get welfare aid and an apartment in the Whittenhall Projects. Whittenhall *always* had vacancies. It was like the edge of the city threatening to collapse into the river and disappear. No one wanted to stay there long. Terri was grateful for the apartment. It was a mixed blessing. She appreciated having a place to live, but she was sorely transplanted. She could have survived nicely in her grandmother's house. The location wasn't far from Whittenhall but it was a much cleaner and quieter area. She would have loved to visit Whittenhall at her leisure. Somehow being pressed into the soil there was not a good match. For one thing the cultural differences made her stand out. Another thing was she was not used to being poor. Plus everyone in the projects knew and spread your business and all other gossip like wildfire.

All of her thoughts were painful at this point. If she thought about her family, she longed to go home. If she thought about Charles, she cried. If she thought about the baby, she felt regret. There was no safe haven for her in her mind or residence. Terri took a deep breath to hold back the tears she felt welling up in her eyes. She walked through her small apartment and cringed. She told herself that she could fix it up, but the pit of her stomach ached when she smelled the foul air that permeated the premises.

Terri squeezed her eyes tight and tried to imagine her tiny abode filled with African décor, and the pleasant order of potpourri. A smile slowly spread across her face. She started remembering her grandmother's beautiful home. Now that's a home she heard herself say out loud. Let me get some fresh air she said out loud again. She hesitated for a moment. Humph. I'm talking out loud to myself she said curiously. She glanced at the clock on her way to the door. She realized she had been in her apartment all day and hadn't spoken to anyone. I guess the loneliness is getting to me she spoke again out loud.

She stepped outside her door and immediately coughed, gagging on the thick stagnant air. She waved he hand in front of her nose. Yuk, pee yew, she mumbled stepping lively. She didn't know where she was headed but just needed to run away from her scenery for a while. She passed through the courtyard without seeing anyone and straight to the wall, and down the raged steps. She turned on Warhigh Street and into the corner store before she realized how far she had walked. Her heart raced as she grabbed her pockets and scrounged for some change to buy a candy bar. She didn't want the people to think she was lost or worse yet a drifter. She found two dollars and thirty seven cents in her pockets. She sighed a long sigh. She looked around the store for a candy bar to grab and eat on her way back home. It wasn't until then that she noticed all the vitamins and the juice bar. She also noticed the fresh clean herbal smell. She scanned the store amazed at her ignorance. This was a health food store. There were no candy bars there. She drifted through the store trying to soak up the herbal scented air, and let it sink into her clothes, while she read some labels. Can I help you a baritone voice startled her. She turned quickly to fall into the eyes of a handsome, tall, dark older gentleman. He watched her eyes slightly intrigued, and slightly bored. What can I get far you he said aiming his ear toward her mouth. Terri was still off guard. Oh, I'm just browsing she stuttered. Well is there anything in particular you were interested in, his voice sounded authoritative now. She just froze and stared ahead. He seemed to feel her discomfort. We have our natural juice drinks on sale today. Would you like to try a spinach, carrot, guava he said leading her toward the juice bar. Terri twisted her face. Oookay, no he laughed. Terri laughed with him. How about a cranberry he paused while he was searching for a complimentary juice. Terri scanned the menu board. Orange she blurted out. He looked at her surprised. A cranberry orange she said solidly nodding her head affirmatively. She tried to convenience him she was familiar. He smiled but wasn't fooled. Where are you from he asked. Wells, she caught herself about to say Wellsley Township. Um Whittenhall I mean. He stretched his eyes. Whittenhall he asked surprised. Yes, Terri answered firmly, then took a sip of her drink. He watched her face. Terri made sure she showed no emotion. That'll be two dollars and fifty nine cents he replied still watching for a response. Her mouth fell open. Um um I think I must have dropped some money outside she tried to act as if she was surprised she didn't have enough. She acted as if she was searching the floor. Oh that's alright he said smiling slyly. Terri felt stupid. She realized he must have heard that excuse about a million times.

What is your name dear heart, he asked politely. Terri she said looking down into her drink. Alright I'm Al he said extending his hand. You can come by anytime for a juice he said mildly. Okay thanks, Terri looked up to find him waiting for her eyes to meet his. He smiled wide. Terri left in a hurry still embarrassed.

Her sense of direction was not as poor as she thought. She had subconsciously remembered certain landmarks. She gradually realized she was near the barber shop where Charles had headquartered his business empire. She grinned as she passed the street still stepping lively. She landed back at Whittenhall just before dusk.

A few fierce Dons were on the wall as well as a few fierce, desperate looking girls. Hello everybody, Terri spoke loud and clear. A couple of the guys hooted and howled at her. A couple of the girls scowled their faces at her. High yella bitch one blurted out loud enough for her to hear once she had passed by. I'll kick yo' ass for good measure she continued on with her threats. Terri looked behind her to see the girls headed toward her. Luckily Linda had been watching out of her window and had made her way down to the courtyard. Linda stepped in front of Terri. Naw yaw'll can't be jumping on my cousin like that, Linda warned them. If you wanna fight I'm here. Let's go, Linda spread out her arms. The girls stepped back from Linda's mean retched face. They tried to quickly explain to Linda that they were just joshing around with Terri. Linda warned them again. If anybody put a hand on my cousin they'll have to answer to me, she growled. The girls snarled and walked away.

The word of the incident spread faster than wildfire. The high yella girl is Linda McRay's cousin. Enough said. No one wanted to test Linda. Linda had been tried several times before. She was truly a fierce, evil, wild competitor. Her last opponent was literally broken in three places, while Linda walked away virtually scratch free. That sealed it. Terri had one of the most powerful forces in the Whittenhall Projects behind her. She no longer had to worry about those attacks. The worst thing was that she still heard hateful remarks and scowls directed toward her. Terri hated the mistrust and hatred her light skin provoked in them. She had tried to relate that she didn't think she was superior or better than her ghetto sisters. She wondered what she'd have to do to prove herself.

She rushed back to her apartment. She could feel herself still shaking. She went into the bathroom to wash her face. She stared at herself in the mirror. Why, she questioned out loud. Why can't they see my blackness she sighed aloud. I am one of them she went on. Why do they hate me just because of the color of my skin. It's so unfair. She wondered if she would ever look black enough or act soulful enough for them to accept her. Of course she had only intended her visits to Whittenhall to be a temporary playground. Now she was so entangled she'd never get out of the projects she thought. How would she survive under the politics in this environment she asked herself. They're racists she concluded. They would fight and kill if they were called that, but the principle is the same. They hate me because of my skin color. She stared at herself long and hard. She had to concede that her features were more European like her mother's. Her hair was too straight and sandy colored, and long. She opened the drawer and pulled out the scissors. She cut her hair a half inch. It made very little difference in her opinion. She cut another half inch. That did very little to change her appearance. Finally she cut it all off to about three inches long, brushed it straight back. It laid in soft rolling waves across her head and curled up slightly at the bottom. Her long locks fell to the floor. She had some make-up Toni had given her. It gave her skin a slightly darker hue. That's it she smiled at the mirror. At least now they'll know I'm on their side, she mumbled to the mirror. Now we can get over the color issue Terri said aloud nodding her head in approval.

She tried to busy herself in her apartment, but she was still homesick. She picked up the telephone, then hung it up before she could dial the number. It was only a few minutes later and she did it again. The third time and only a minute later, she tried to stop herself but couldn't. She dialed the number and called her daddy. She begged him to come home and wept in his ear. Although her father was completely disappointed in her, hearing her cry like that melted his heart. He got in his car and drove over to the Whittenhall Projects to reclaim her.

He pulled up to the Whittenhall wall where several of the Dons and Stars were sitting. He made the crucial mistake of showing his disdain for the people sitting on the wall. He walked right past and turned up his nose. You got a problem pops, one of the young Dons yelled out. He kept walking without responding. Before he reached mid court, five young Dons threw him to the ground and beat him mercilessly. They left him in the middle of the courtyard bleeding profusely.

The next morning Linda rushed around the complex knocking on doors, spreading the latest news. When she got to Terri's apartment, she was glad to find that Terri still hadn't heard. Linda anxiously told her the news. For some reason Terri was curious about the person's appearance. She asked Linda to describe the victim. When Linda described a fair skinned man with a silver blue Mercedes Benz, her heart sank. She took off for Wellsley Township immediately.

A neighbor met her at her father's house and took her to meet the family at the hospital. When she arrived, her mother and her sister both gave her a cold stare and didn't speak. Pains shot through her heart from the daggers in their eyes. Her sister turned her back to her. Terri quietly eased into the hospital room. She screamed when she saw her father's condition. His head was swollen to the size of a watermelon. His eyes were the size of golf balls and his mouth was still oozing blood. Terri was hysterical. She threw her arms around her mother who pushed her away. Neither her mother or sister comforted her. She could feel their blazing hatred.

A nurse detained her in a private room until she could get herself under control. She was heart broken and needed her Grandma Rena. She stayed the night by her father's side along with her mother. Neither of them left his side for the first week. Her mother didn't utter a word to her. They were two strong women, both determined in their mission. They sat fixed on her father. Terri was just barely preserving. Regret and shame grew along with the heaviness of her belly. Her mother refused to look at her, or hold a conversation with her beyond cold greetings and questions about her father's condition. They sat side by side at his bed day in and day out. The silence played its own games. Sometimes Terri swore her mother had spoke. Huh, she'd ask, only to have her mother totally ignore her or give her a sympathetic look. Her mother purposely sat with her back to her to rub in the rejection. It took every ounce of Terri's strength to keep from clutching her mother desperately and sobbing. She was in pure agony.

In spite of her euphoric hopes and dreams, her father's health deteriorated. He slipped into a deep coma. The doctors came in and spoke with her mother. They informed them that this could last for weeks or maybe even years and they'd no longer be able to keep this bedside vigil. Terri was quite put off by their cockiness. How dare they think she would ever leave his side she thought. She stared at her mother's face to see how she was receiving the news. She seemed to be thinking the same thing.

Her mother spoke to her for the first time in weeks, when she suggested a visitation schedule. I'll come in the evening about seven and stay the night her mother said. Why don't you come and relieve me at nine in the mornings she stated piously. Terri readily agreed without a second thought. They may think we can't keep up the routine Terri thought, but they don't know the McDaniels. We'll show them what the McDaniels's are made of Terri blurted out in her rising optimism. Her mother cut her down quickly with her icy glare. It was all be it clear, that she no longer claimed her or considered her a McDaniels. Let alone her mother's small grunt to let her know she was not worthy of family affiliation.

The days were long and lonely. As they dragged by, Terri talked, sang and read to her father daily. She was sure he could hear her, but he never moved a muscle. She left the hospital crying most days, worn out from the battle.

The only part of her day that she looked forward to was her stop at the health food store. She got off the bus everyday at that stop. She'd arrive just before closing. Al would let her in and lock up for the evening. They'd talk for hours, while Al prepared for the following day. He had become a dear friend and a wealth of encouragement to her. Come along dear heart he'd say as he escorted her to the bar. What will it be far yah today he'd ask in his smooth Jamaican accent. How is yer papa today? By now Terri had confessed her whole story to

Al. She'd report on her father's condition daily and her struggles. Al listened as she cried out her pangs of distress.

It was quite clear, in her mind at least that her mother despised her more and more each day. She wore her emotions on her face like a cheap brand of make-up. It was also clear that this routine was wearing her mother down as well. Terri shouldered the blame for it all.

Al's wisdom was one of the most comforting things in her life. Ah lit til baby gurl, you musn't allow such a big comfortable room far that doubt. Squeeze it out of yer mind, and make no room far it at tall. Yer papa is just needing a good long rest. He will soon be himself again. But you lit til baby gurl, you must take kare of yer selv. You must have a healthy lit til baby. Come drink Al commanded. Al's words would restore her hope and the juice, her health. Al wouldn't allow her to walk home in the dark alone. He'd drive her to the wall, and then escort her to her door.

One morning, Terri came into the hospital room to relieve her mother. Her father had been in a coma for about three months now. Her mother's face looked especially fatigued. Did he have a bad night, Terri asked kindly. He had some sort of a seizure her mother explained. Terri was surprised that she spoke to her. I thought he would wake up from it her mother went on, careful not to mention the word coma. She put a tissue to her eye and brushed away a tear. Terri wanted to hold her, but was afraid of the rejection. When her mom left, she opened the curtains. The sun poured in directly onto her father's face. He smiled widely. Terri was ecstatic. For the first time since he was admitted he showed some sign of life. Terri rushed to his side and tried to wake him. Finally, she took a deep breath, this will be the day he wakes up, she mumbled under her breath. She heard a loud rush of air. Suddenly a crew of doctors rushed in the room and started pounding on his chest. To Terri's dismay he passed away with the sun and a smile still on his face.

Chapter Eight

Out of The Ashes

Terri gave birth to her son, April 7, 1974. Toni and Linda were there to support her. He was an almond toned sandy haired little boy. She named him Rahjeem. She instantly realized how much strength she would need to raise him alone. Though she saw no way through her circumstances she insisted that she'd make a good life for her child.

She hadn't spoken to her mother or sister since the funeral. They both vowed through clenched teeth to make her pay for the losses she had cost them. They also were unsure of their financial status without her father to support them. They shuttered at anything other than their cushy Wellsley life.

It was tremendously hard living on her own, especially in the Whittenhall, but she had nowhere else to go. She was a resident but she was still treated like an intruder. Someone was always there to object to her presence. She didn't want to run to Linda or Toni every time someone called her a name. She'd take her worries to Al and he'd comfort her again and again.

She envied Toni and Linda. They didn't have to endure such cruel punishment. They didn't even realize what a heated battle she was in most of the times. It was like an invisible war, and the brown complexions didn't even know it existed. It seemed to be waged against the lighter skin tones and the very dark skin tones. It felt like such an attack on her blackness. Terri had always honored her blackness. To have the constant suspicion and frontal attacks really disturbed her. There has got to be an end to this non sense she thought.

Terri could now see why the Master's had laid blame on the racists society they lived in. She'd never forget that conversation. She saw the true genius and royalty of the African American people as they spoke about the oppression of their people. Terri was no longer observing black people from her lofty Wellsley mountain. She was down in the trenches amongst them.

She could now understand why they reveled in instant gratification, since these were small victories they could claim. She understood their pressure from being in a poor and separate society, trapped like a caged animal. While people gulked at your desperation and rage, they claimed there was no reason for it. She could feel the frustration that resulted from the systematic struggle. That was the royal run around that ran you in circles and lead to nowhere.

The system or ruling class would promise you can get a good job if you get an education. They say you can get an education if you pay the price. They say you can pay the price if you get promoted. They say you can get promoted if you have a blue suit. They say if you have a blue suit you have to sound like us. They say if you sound like us you have to look like us. And they're back at square one, imitating something they were never meant to be. No wonder Terri, blurted out loud, realizing how shielded she had been. No wonder black people can't see their genuine God-given wealth, Terri thought. They keep looking at themselves through the eyes of the ruling class. They have been running in circles and fighting the systematic struggle. If only they could see what I see she mumbled. If they could only love and accept their original characteristics and strength, they'd be Kings and Judges over the world. If they reject these, their prosperity will be sparse. Terri for the first time in her life prayed to God to help her impart some understanding among the people.

Al was her protector and mentor. He was kind enough to visit with her daily after he walked her to her door. They had fun together. One night Al asked if he could stay. Terri was shocked by his forwardness. Al pulled her close to him and kissed her mouth. His warmth felt surprisingly good to her. He kissed her again. Terri wanted to stop him but it felt right. She kissed him open mouth. She felt his manhood swelling between his legs. If felt good to feel a man's bulge between her legs. He unbuttoned his shirt and pants. Terri unbuttoned her blouse and pants. They went to her bedroom and fell on the bed kissing and grinding. Terri spread her legs as wide as she could and Al eased his manhood inside her. He grinded and pushed his hard manhood inside her wildly. Terri heard herself panting and moaning. She felt herself explode on his manhood pumping until she was breathless. Al rolled over and kissed her once again. She was afraid to look at him. She was afraid he'd see her satisfaction. He finally whispered thank you in her ear. She hugged him and pulled him on top of her again. They made love over and over again until they were both exhausted. At last Terri said thank you this time.

They spent all their nights together for the next couple of months. Al was trustworthy and genuine. She knew she was no cheap thrill for him. But it was still a shock when he secured a safe babysitter, Linda's mom, and took her to a fancy restaurant for dinner. Terri hadn't been anywhere so nice since her father took her to that nice French restaurant on the Riviera.

After dinner Al took her hand pulled her close to him. He pulled out a little black box from his pocket. He flipped it open and showed her a sparkling diamond solitaire. Terri gasped and covered her mouth. I want you for my wife he said softly. Will you marry me he asked politely. Terri was speechless. She just nodded her head quickly. Al moved her hands from over her mouth and kissed her passionately.

She was thrilled to have Al in her life romantically. He loved her insanely and had adopted Rahjeem as his own son. But she still felt something was missing. She still walked to the store everyday and waited at the juice bar while Al closed the store. They talked freely while he cleaned up and prepared for the following day. She told Al she didn't feel complete. Al inquired about her goals and Terri realized she wanted to go to school. Al was supportive. He encouraged her to go to the University and take some classes. As soon as she made up her mind to attend Central University she contacted Toni. Toni was more than happy to help her apply and secure financial aid.

The years crept along while she studied psychology and accounting at the University. She wished her father could see her now. She knew he'd be proud. She had organized and took control of her life. She had an agreement with Linda to babysit Rahjeem. She had Linda's mother as a stand by babysitter. And she had Al as a finance'. Things were well.

She was well prepared for college. The Wellsley school system had equipped her nicely for the work load and academic level of the classes. She had very little trouble passing them handily. Even though it was difficult to study and take care of the baby, her ghetto sisters eased the load a lot. She still missed her mother and sister. She wanted to share her news with them, but still felt the time was not right. She persevered and completed all her classes. After graduation her momentum was still racing. She felt Medical School calling her. Al, Linda and Sue all consulted to take care of Rahjeem while she completed this mission.

Medical School was much more challenging. She found she had to study non-stop, but she knew Psychiatry was her calling. Psychiatry would help her figure out how black people could deal with the emotional unbalance that has crippled them as a whole, and this society has left them with. Terri found joy in her pursuit even though it kept her away from her family most of the time. She kept remembering the greater good of it all.

Again the years crawled by and were merciless. She again persevered and completed her mission. Graduation finally rolled around. This time she sent an invitation to her mother and sister. They didn't respond. She was broken hearted but she knew time would heal their wounds. She persisted with her goals. She passed her CPA exam on the first attempt. It would took a little while longer before she passed her medical board exam.

She didn't want to delay her wedding any longer. Al had been more than supportive and patient. She sent a wedding invitation to her mother. She didn't respond. She married Al anyway. Linda, Toni, Rahjeem and Sue were there. They were her family now.

Al moved her out of the Whittenhall Projects and into a nice home not far from her grandmother's house. While she was packing the last of her things in the Whittenhall, the door bell rang. She answered surprised to find a delivery man standing at the door. Sign here ma'am the delivery driver said impatiently. He then wrestled three large boxes through her door. Terri thanked him and wished him a nice day. That's the way it's done in the ghetto she thought. There is no money for tips.

She anxiously checked the label on the boxes. They were from her father's address. She tore open the first box. To her delight she found many of her grandmother's African artifacts and clothes. The second and third boxes contain more of the same. All in all her mother had sent her all of her grandmother's belongings. She hoped it was a peace offering.

As Terri hung her grandma's mirror on the wall in her new house, she caught a glimpse of something colorful. She stepped back and stared into the mirror. She saw a tribunal of African Warrior Queens. They were all shades of brown and black from the lightest to the darkest. There were all races and colors of women. She watched as one queen crowned her head with an exquisite jeweled crown. Terri felt the joy and love of their sisterhood. She knew instantly that she now belonged to the sisterhood and that she didn't have to prove her blackness to anyone ever again. Terri blew a kiss to the mirror and felt the warmth return to her. She tried on one of her grandmother's African outfits and felt whole and complete. She sat down on the bed to rest for a moment, and the phone rang. It was her mother.

Terri was now so fulfilled she wanted to return some of the strength and knowledge she had gained in her life. Her lesson from the veil had never left her mind. She believed she could help reduce the self destruction in her community by patiently teaching literacy first, and secondly wealth building techniques. She realized from her lesson that appreciation and respect grow through building dreams and accomplishing goals.

As an accountant and a psychiatrist, she paired simple savings and wealth building tips with lessons in self esteem. She watched her students grow in both wealth and self esteem. In time Terri was able to help some students purchase homes and investment properties in their own community.

She cherished her classes above all else because she had become the sister and healer of the people she had always wanted to know.

TINA'S STORY

Chapter One

Strong Fences

Tina Douglas stood staring out of the back window of her fifth floor apartment. She took a long deep breath, and quietly watched the movement below. Rayshaun and Trey will be better off here with me she mumbled to herself in a pensive trance.

Living in the Whittenhall Projects was a step up for Tina. Even though it was the roughest, most dilapidated of projects in the city, it was better than "*bunking*." Bunking had claimed a major part of her life until now. Bunking was when you stayed in a different place almost every night. Bunking didn't suit her style, and Tina was determined to stabilize her life. Most of her young life with her mother was spent bunking from one relative, friend, or even stranger to another.

She had scattered, vague memories of living in a nice home with her grandmother, but that part of her life had ended quickly. During that time, she didn't know her mother very well. She only saw her mother on holidays, funerals, or some other rare occasions. She remembered her being very kind and generous to them when she did see her. She longed for that security once again, but it seemed as if it had all been a dream.

Her grandmother died when Tina was eight years old, but somehow they were the ones that ended up in hell. When Aunt Sally came to live in her grandmother's house, she didn't expect or want the responsibility of three small children. It seemed to Tina that no one did. Her Aunt Sally was her grandmother's sister, but she was much different than her grandmother. Tina could barely believe they were sisters. She had never met her before, and couldn't clearly remember mention of her or her whereabouts. So this Sally person could be and most likely was an impostor according to Tina's reasoning. If not, Sally and her sister were not very close apparently.

Sally was quite delighted with the house itself. She admitted that she didn't own one, nor much of anything important that Tina could see. In any case, this was a pleasant surprise willed to her by her younger sister. Tina never knew how her grandmother came about having the nice house. The only work she ever recalled her grandmother doing was domestic work and not for that long a time. Somehow she had acquired this large four bedroom, three bath colonial house. The rooms were large and drafty with cold hardwood floors. Once Sally settled down, she began to rearrange and decorate immediately.

Sally was quite bossy. She ordered the movers around like low ranking soldiers. When she finished decorating to her taste, the house was very fancy and frilly looking. There were fancy little whatnots all about the living room, and lacy pillows and curtains. It was nowhere near the well suited casual home for kids that her grandmother kept.

Rayshaun and Trey were drawn by their childish curiosity, to the funny looking little statues and dishes that now sat about the room. Sally however, didn't like them touching her precious porcelain or hand me downs as she called them. Tina thought they were all ugly and wondered why so many of them were naked since they were supposedly so precious. Yet to Sally, their dirty, grubby little hands all over her things was the start of contentions. It was clear that Sally didn't have any patience for kids and pushed them around like stray pets.

Sally also resented the attention that these three children required. She did everything dutifully with such displeasure. She mumbled and huffed and puffed while she cooked their meals, or cleaned up after them. They had three square meals, clean clothes, and a warm bed, but not without hearing the complaints about the inconvenience. She'd constantly inform them that if she had wanted to change diapers, clean up after kids, or wipe runny noses, she would have some kids of her own.

After three of four months, Tina could see the change in Sally. She could barely perform these duties any longer. The wear and tear of child care had exhausted her. She would fix their meals and slam the plate on the table in front of them. All the while she'd be glaring at them with evil eyes and pulsating temples. She looked as if she was set to strike at any minute. Tina had to comfort the younger ones. Little Rayshaun was so scared that he'd eat the tears that streamed down his face and plopped into his food, never tasting anything at all. Trey was too little to understand what was going on, but his face was fear struck. Tina kept him on her lap and fed him from her plate. It was terrifying for them all.

Aunt Sally was also very strict with time schedules, and order of operations. But once she started watching her favorite soap operas, there was a period of freedom for them. The soap operas lasted several hours a day. During those hours, they had to be still and quiet, but most importantly, out of sight. Sally demanded no one disturb her television viewing. Tina tried very hard to keep

Aunt Sally happy, but Rayshaun's unexpected wetting accidents, and needed clothes changes took her over the top. Her spankings were hard and cruel. Tina shivered and sobbed as she'd watch Aunt Sally spank Rayshaun. She seemed to particularly dislike Rayshaun.

Tina began to change Rayshaun herself. She'd hide the soiled underpants behind the dresser, to keep him from getting his little hinnie spanked everyday. They all soon learned to avoid Sally, and ask for nothing. Tina kept her little brothers out of harms way as much as possible. Just the threat of encountering Sally or hearing her heavy footsteps across the hardwood floor, would send Rayshaun into shakes. He'd wet his pants, out of fear. Rayshaun's little hands were shakey and dewy all the time. The rambunctious, confident little boy, had become a nervous, timid kid. He wanted Tina to hold his hand all the time. Tina held his hand all the time.

After what seemed like a lifetime to the kids, Aunt Sally finally gave up the attempt, to care for them. She made the official call to their mother, for a meeting. Tina vividly remembered that fateful meeting. It was July, a little over six months after her grandmother's funeral. Her mother showed up at their house, wearing a corset starched, blinding white, cotton dress. Her wavy auburn dyed hair was snatched back into a tight, orderly bun. She wore the faintest touch of makeup over her cinnamon brown skin. The soft glittery gold lipstick across her pouty mouth made her look like a movie star to Tina. She looked very clean and sophisticated.

Tina sat on the hallway steps with her face pressed between the spindles. Rayshaun sat pressed to her hip, while she held his small hand. Trey was on her lap. Aunt Sally promptly informed her mother that she was planning to turn the children over to the Welfare Services. Aunt Sally was a stoic, well educated, bottom line type of person. She left no room for discussion in her words. Her mother who had been on the most proper behavior, was sipping a cup of tea, with her pinkie finger sticking out. At the sound of those words, her mother dropped the cup and sprang from her seat. Tea stained her fresh white dress, and she looked tainted in the face. She screamed and sobbed at the foot of her Aunt Sally's chair. No don't put my children in the system, she pleaded. She was completely pitiful. Her pleas were heart wrenching and her moans were guttural. Even stark, stoic Aunt Sally was visibly moved.

Tina stretched her eyes. She gripped the spindle tightly, and held her breath. After several minutes of bickering and threats, Aunt Sally resolved that the only other alternative was for her to take them. Just as Tina was about to sigh relief, her mother burst into tears again. For some reason, that Tina didn't understand, this wasn't a suitable option to her mother either. Her mother appeared generally capable and sound in mind, yet she continued to argue that that was not an option. They bickered for the better part of the afternoon. Aunt

Sally was growing more and more frustrated because she was missing her soap operas. Tired and aggrevated with her mother, Sally made one last offer. She offered to let her mother stay there temporarily with the kids and take care of them. Sally over emphasized, with a hint of threat, that she and only she was in charge of the house. She also laid down the law on Gloria's financial obligations, and household expectations. Tina listened carefully, while Sally ranted on. I'm a Christian woman, Sally lamented. Ain't gon be no late night moves up in here she went on. Aunt Sally spokes as if she knew something secretive about her mother, Tina thought. Her mother agreed sullenly.

Tina found her mother's presence only a thin buffer between them and Aunt Sally. She warded off the mean resentful stares of Aunt Sally. Her mother didn't seem to mind fixing them supper or drawing their bath. She did it lovingly, unlike Aunt Sally. But her mother couldn't seem to meet Aunt Sally's rigid schedule. Gloria really didn't mind taking care of her own kids, she just resented Aunt Sally's strict regiment of, up by seven in the morning and lunch precisely at noon, come what may. A simple exotic dancer, Gloria was used to sleeping till noon. Tina could see Aunt Sally's frustration rising up again. She understood that it wasn't her fault. She didn't expect to inherit three children with the house. She had no children of her own, and no husband or man to speak of. While her mother's presence took some of the pressure off of them both, the arrangements came unglued quickly.

Gloria just couldn't seem to keep up her end of the bargain. She never contributed enough money for her Aunt's satisfaction. They constantly bickered about finances. This took Aunt Sally to her wits end. Finally she gave one last ultimatum. She demanded that Gloria find a job and a new place to live, giving her two weeks to exit.

Gloria began spending most of the day away from the house pretending to look for a job. Tina and her brothers were thrown right back into Aunt Sally's fury. The objective was doomed to failure. Her mother had quit school in the ninth grade, and never held a "*respectable*" job. Tina pretended to be asleep each night when her mother rose very late. She was sure all the kids and Aunt Sally were asleep by then. She'd dress up in her high heels and stockings and sneak out of the house and really go to work. She'd return late or stoned or both. Still she didn't seem to bring back enough money to please Aunt Sally.

The straw that broke the camel's back was the surprise search and seizure. One evening around supper time, there was a knock at the door. They had just sat down at the dinner table. Aunt Sally peeked out of the window and nervously announced that it was the police. Her mother immediately ran and hid. Tina thought it strange and listened carefully. We're looking for a Gloria Johnson ma'am, the police staunchly announced. She's wanted in the slaying and murder of a Philadelphia man and woman he continued on. Murder Aunt Sally screamed. We have a reason to believe she might be in the area he explained. May we come in and take a look around. The officers brushed past Aunt Sally before she could answer. They peeked through the house for a few minutes. If you see her or know of her whereabouts give us a call, he instructed shoving a card in Aunt Sally's hand. She nodded still awestruck.

Aunt Sally demanded her mother leave the house immediately, and she would call Welfare Services first thing in the morning. Tina's heart pounded at those words. Her mother looked petrified, but didn't argue or explain. Gimme till dark Sally, she pleaded with her Aunt. Tina could hear the fear and urgency in her mother's voice. Later that night Gloria woke Tina and her brothers up and dragged through the neighboring backyards to an adjacent street. So began their life of bunking.

In the beginning they bunked with other relatives a night or two, and sometimes even a week or so. It wasn't that bad in the beginning, so Tina thought. Everyone was sympathetic to her mother's sob story and the scrawny little faces tagging along behind her. It took about six months before they had gone through the familiar members, the ones Tina recognized, of the Douglas family. After that it reached the point of embarrassment. Explaining on a stranger's doorstep whose sister's, cousin's uncle's child you were was humiliating. But her mother had a silver tongue, and no shame. She'd run down the lineage while walking through the door, and have the stunned relatives laughing before she reached the couch to seat herself. Mae Ray Connell she'd call the surprised person at the door. I'm your Uncle Pete's, cousin's, sister's niece, Gloria she'd run it down smoothly. You remember me, don't you girl, she'd ask. She'd go on before they could answer. You used to come to the family reunions up Ma Dear's house didn't you, she'd offer again. A hesitant yeah would slip from the stranger's lips. Girl I remember that time you was running from Uncle George's son at the family reunion and you had an ice cream cone in your hand, Gloria continued. You fell and got ice cream all over your pink dress and Aunt Liddy tore your legs up, she'd round out the story. Naw that wasn't me that was my sister Nina the stranger would offer while they both laughed and headed for the couch. Tina was sure some of those people weren't kin folk at all. They were just too embarrassed to say they didn't remember.

But finally welcome was worn out. All the relatives, and friends were aware of the scam, and they were tired of them. They began to refuse Gloria's tall tales and promises, and leave them on the porches cold and hungry. Gloria never seemed too depressed over it for she knew she always had a trick or treat or scam that someone would buy. When all else failed Gloria still worked the bars. She'd have Tina and her brothers wait in a nearby alley or storefront and find someone who she could dance privately for at their place of choice as long as her three kids could come.

Gloria seemed at peace with their life of bunking. She prided herself on finding a place each evening. Be it a stranger's house, a new friend's apartment or an empty basement of a dilapidated drug house, they slept indoors. Gloria seemed to accrue just enough money to buy them each a hot meal and they weren't hungry when they went to sleep either. That was sufficient provisions according to Gloria Johnson. Once this was accomplished Gloria would drink herself into a stupor until the next day.

When Gloria was at an impass or too drunk to con anyone she always had one refuge. Gloria gathered her children and hailed a gypsy cab. Her pretty face always stopped traffic and somehow to her advantage elicited trust and innocence. On this night she smiled at the cab driver and instructed him to drive them to the WarHigh Apartments. Tina remembered the way the cab driver looked at her mother with desire in his eyes, then scanned the back seat to look at their faces. Tina was frieghtened. She squeezed Rayshaun's hand and he squeezed back. The driver was quickly distracted by her mother's conversation.

When they pulled up to the apartments her mother unlocked the back door and waved them out of the car. Wait on the steps she ordered them. Tina obeyed. She heard the driver repeat the fare to her mother. Tina looked back to see if her mother was alright. She was still afraid that her mother would abandon them. Tina could only see her mother's head leaning toward the driver's lap. She heard him squeal and howl for a few minutes while they waited on the steps. Afterward her mother rushed toward them and the cab sped off. Gloria ushered them toward a door with a crooked sign on it. She knocked on the door hard while she fiddled with a black pouch that appeared to have lots of money in it.

A rough voice from the other side of the door hollered, who is it dam it? Tina's heart sank. It's me dam it Gloria hollered back just as rough. The door snatched open. Tina watched the man's face. It was sleepy but excited. He held out his arms for her mother. Gloria stepped in gave him a quick hug then pushed him aside. She pulled Tina's arm and slammed the door behind them. She locked the door and double checked the knob as if she was worried about burgulars. She ran from window to window shutting the blinds and curtains. Finally she turned her attention back to the man waiting patiently for it. In her usual, cool witted tongue she joshed with him. How you doing Ray? I'm glad to see you got a dam lock on yo' door. When'd you get in town he asked. They headed for the kitchen conversing like old friends. Several minutes later, Ray noticed the kids still standing by the door. As he approached them Tina felt herself start to shiver. Ray sensed her fear and spoke in a soft calm voice. Come on in children and have a seat. His eyes were gentle and he smiled wide. Tina was still holding Trey in her arms and holding Rayshaun's hand. He continued to speak with them. I can't believe yaw'll dun grown so much he said kindly. Just as pretty as a picture he pinched Tina's cheek softly. He motioned for them to follow him. He gathered up some pillows and linens. Tina was delighted since she was so tired.

Occasionally Gloria would interrupt the conversation and peek out of the blinds that she had closed. Suddenly they heard a car horn blaring. Gloria ordered everyone to the back room. They could hear somebody walking up and down the hallway beating on doors. An angry voice yelled I'm gon kill you bitch. I want my money back bitch. The voice grew louder and stopped at their door. I'll be waiting for you bitch. I know you got my money. Don't let me catch you slut. The yelling went on for what seemed like an eternity. Then the voice finally faded as it headed toward the sidewalk. What you dun done now Ray asked curiously, and shook his head from side to side. Gloria shushed him and pulled him by the arm to the kitchen. Ray fixed the kids a chicken sandwich and a glass of milk. Gloria ordered them to bed as soon as they finished eating. The covers were fresh and clean. Tina pulled the boys close to her and curled up in a fetal position and went to sleep.

Tina was awakened what seemed like ten minutes later. Actually it was seven the next morning, Tina happened to notice the clock on the wall. Gloria ordered them to dress quickly and ushered them out the door. It was light but chilly. They walked and walked and walked what seemed like ten miles to Tina. She was carrying Trey and holding Rayshaun's hand. When they finally reached the corner of Del Mar and Taft streets, Gloria told them to wait in the alley behind the corner bar. Tina obeyed. But she checked frequently to see if her mother had abandoned them. To her surprise, there were several people on and moving about the corner too. There were all kinds of people, Tina noted. Well dressed, working people, neighborhood bums and hungry people like them, all waiting for something Tina wished she knew. Her mother was quite comfortable among them all. She congregated with the people, drank beer, sang and fought with them as the day poked along.

Tina managed to keep Trey and Rayshaun busy and distracted. She played hide and seek, patty cake, and four square with a dirty deflated ball she found in the alley. At certain times throughout the day, the alley was just as busy as the corner bar. The alley proved to be a pathway of exchange. There were exchanges of merchandise, money, drugs, and even bodily fluids. Tina was glad it was a long alley with little coves in it. She didn't want her brothers to see all the sins of their elders. She wanted to leave it all and go to school, but she was afraid of what would happen to her little brothers.

At the hottest point of the day, her mother came to the alley and bought them three sandwiches that looked like they had been made in someone's kitchen. She came back about and hour later and bought them two sodas. Tina thanked Gloria loudly. She wanted Gloria to feel they were appreciative. If not Gloria might abandon them. She was even more grateful for a few private moments of Gloria's attention. That gave Tina energy to play some more with her brothers.

A couple of hours later, Gloria returned. She beckoned for them to come to her. Tina picked up Trey and grabbed Rayshaun's hand and ran to her like playful pups being summoned by their master. She directed them to a shiny new Cadillac. Gloria opened the back door for them. The man was waiting there with the car door open for her mother. Tina scanned the man from head to toe, and was very impressed. The man looked at her as if to read her thoughts. Who's this lil black one with the nappy hair, he growled at her mother. Her mother hit the man hard. Tina dropped her head, and caught a glimpse of the man's shoes. She was afraid to get in the car or look the man in his face. He motioned impatiently for her to get in the car. She kept her head down and reveled at the man's shoes. They were so black and shiny that they looked like mirrors to Tina. She knew then, he must be a King.

She climbed into the back seat as quickly as she could. The interior of his car was red velvet, and perfume scented. Tina was worried that he would have servants at his castle and they would harass her as well. She hoped if she kept her head and eyes down they would overlook her. So that's what she decided she'd do.

His palace wasn't far from the bar. Tina walked in carrying Trey and holding Rayshaun's hand. She kept her head down. She still stole peeks around the palace. There were two colored televisions and a large stero. The man pulled out the sleeper sofa and made their bed. Her mother had several drinks with the man. They finally went into the bedroom. She heard them giggle and howl, while they lay in the dark wondering where they were. Slowly the boys drifted off to sleep.

Tina heard the man stumble out of the bedroom and into the kitchen. He poured another drink. She pretended she was asleep. The man stumbled toward her with the drink in his hand. He was cursing because he was spilling his drink everywhere. He stopped right above her and spilled some of the drink on her face. She opened her eyes. He was furious. He put his finger to his mouth and told her to hush. He stuck his hand down her pantys and pushed his finger up her coochie. She jumped and screamed. He muffled her scream with his hand and threatened to kill her and her mother if she told. You black and ugly ain't nobody gon want you he added as he stumbled off into the bedroom where Tina could hear her mother snoring. She lay there shivering and bleeding the rest of the night.

Her mother woke them again early in the morning. Tina washed them up in the bathroom. Her mother noticed her bloody pantys. What did you do she snapped at Tina. You don started yo period already, she questioned her suspiously. You awfully young for that, but I'll get you some sanitary napkins she agreed softly. Tina just nodded her head without looking at her mother's face. Tina was afraid if she told her mother she'd think they were too much trouble to care for and she'd abandon them. They returned to the same corner bar, and waited again in the back alley. Tina watched again for her mother. Again Gloria socialized and drank beer standing on the corner. As the day grew hotter, Gloria again brought them three homemade sandwiches, and two sodas. She instructed them to hurry up and eat. When they finished she beckoned for Tina. Tina grabbed the boys and rushed to her mother's call, naively hoping that they were going home wherever that was.

Instead her mother gave her brief directions to the shoe store about two blocks down. She instructed her to go to a man she pointed to named Black Mac and get the money. Tina approached Black Mac with her head down. When she reached him she realized he's black like me she thought. I don't have to hold my head down. She looked him squarely in the face and smiled slightly. To her surprise his eyes narrowed and his black face twisted. He stared at her for what felt like a century to Tina. Finally he spoke. Can you count blackie he snapped. Yes sir Tina answered gently. She held her head down again. I want my right change back he growled. Yes sir, Tina answered quickly. He pressed a ten dollar bill in her hand. Tina caught a glimpse of his shoes as she turned to walk away immediately. They were black and shiny like sun drenched tar. He must be rich she thought. He must be a King.

With Trey on her hip and Rayshaun on her hand, she walked quickly. Walking quickly helped press down the swelling in her coochie and the indignation in her heart. She purchased the items at the store and turned to leave. Trey pointed to some candy and began to cry. The man in the next line asked with a scowl if Trey was her baby. Tina replied gently in a soft voice. He's my brother. They both are. The man surveyed the three of them carefully. He pulled out a dollar and handed it to Trey complementing him on his "*good hair.*" He then complimented Rayshaun on his pretty light complexion and handed him a dollar as well. Tina encouraged them to say thank you. The man looked at her and laughed. How'd you get so black he asked with hatred in his eyes. Tina held her head down and didn't reply. He was a well dressed man. His shoes were clean but not shiny. He is not a King she thought. But he is so well dressed he must be a Judge she figured. She purchased some candy for Trey and Rayshaun both and left the store immediately. When she stepped outside the door, she realized he was standing by the door. She instantly dropped her head and hoped he didn't see her leaving. She caught a glimpse of his glare as he lit up a cigarette. She could feel the heat of his glare burning a hole in the back of her blouse as she hurried away. She promised herself she'd never go to that store again.

Through the next million Tuesdays of her life, Tina learned the codes and wisdom of the streets. While Gloria targeted her next victim, Tina ran errands throughout the ghetto neighborhoods. This made the days pass more quickly and she earned nickels and dimes for herself and her brothers. Tina found her niche being subservient to all the ghetto high rollers that she privately nicknamed Kings and Judges. But while the streets taught her survival, they also taught her shame, self hatred, fear and worthlessness. She chose to wear black and dark colors to be less noticeable by the Kings and Judges. Tina held her head down in their presence, and learned to con them out of a few cents at the same time. Oh Mama Kaye said for you to give me a quarter, she'd tell the deliveree, or Daddy Cane said give me fifty cents she'd proclaim. It was big enough for a small treat, but small enough to be forgivable, should there be any misunderstanding. Over the weeks Tina taught Rayshaun and Trey to beg and steal. When she heard Sister Sue say that the Lord answers prayer. Tina prayed that God would make her skin lighter or make her entirely invisible, so that the daily barrage of insults would end.

Tina and her brothers were waiting in the alley as usual between errands. Her mother had gone on a quick "*run*" as she called them, and did often. Trey was very irritated. Tina checked his diaper and realized it was heavily soiled and his bottom was red with diaper rash. Tina panicked when she realized she had no clean diapers for Trey. Trey's little bottom was so soar she couldn't carry him. She still didn't trust Rayshaun to the dangerous ghetto streets alone. She had no choice but to leave Rayshaun in the alley with Trey while she tried to bum up nickels and dimes to buy diapers. She ran to the corner store. She wanted to shout at the patrons and passers by, and insist that they all rush to her and dump their change on her immediately, but good sense prevailed. She politely approached them one at a time. She had come to expect the scowls and scorns and the curled lips she knew she'd receive, but she dared not be so bold as to offend the mighty Kings and Judges. She was very slowly getting nickels and dimes by the afternoon. She was tired and needed to get back to the alley with her brothers. She was worried her mother may want to pick them up soon. She didn't know what else she could do to speed up the collection. She approached as many of them as she thought she should. She knew by looking at some of them not to approach them. She knew they judge you first on your skin tone and second on your hair texture. Tina knew she passed on neither of these test in their eyes. She was happy when she could maneuver in and out of crowds without being noticed. She knew then that God had answered her prayers. He had made her invisible. But today she had to approach them-The Kings and Judges without delay.

Just then she spotted a gentleman leaving the store. He had a kind face and a bag of diapers. Her heart leaped for joy. Surely he would understand and help her. She approached him, still polite and apprehensive. Sir she addressed him. Could you please spare a dollar. I need some diapers for my little brother she explained. He stared at her for a long time without saying a word. Tina held her head down and swallowed the lump in her throat. She saw him reach into his back pocket and pull out his wallet. He pulled out a five dollar bill, and looked at her with a strange expression on his face. He then harked and spit right in her face. Tina jumped then lifted her eyes slightly. He had on shiny shoes. You black she heard him say. She took off running and ran all the way back to the alley with the tears and spit rolling down her face.

When she got back her mother was waiting there impatiently with her trick for the evening. She was sloppy drunk and angry. Tina told her about the mean man spitting in her face. Tina knew her mother was incapable of doing anything but she clung to her and sobbed. Gloria swore she'd get him then passed out on the man's kitchen floor. The man stepped over her and locked his bedroom door behind him cursing and swearing. Tina rummaged through the apartment and found some clean undershirts. She bathed Trey and oiled his bottom and made a diaper out of the clean undershirt. Trey hugged her with all his little strength, then kissed her tenderly. Tina ran Rayshaun's bath and cleaned him as well. She scavenged through the man's refridgerator and made them some sandwiches. She poured Trey a fresh bottle of milk and played pillow fight with Rayshaun. She could feel their relief, so she laid on the floor beside her mother and stroked her wavy hair. Tina cried as she outlined her mother's beautiful face. She wondered how someone so beautiful could be so miserable. She heard her mother grunt and felt relieved. She put her arm around her mother's shoulders and laid her face next to hers praying for a smidget of her mother's beauty. The boys laid down on the floor next to Tina and fell into a deep sleep.

Tina felt her arm being tugged. Her mother was standing over her calling her softly. Tina opened her eyes and looked around, trying to remember where she was. C'mon her mother whispered softly with an urgent expression on her face. She watched her mother rummage through the closet. She seemed to hit the jackpot as she slapped the papers on the palm of her hand. Bingo Tina heard her mother mumble. She instructed Tina to go through the drawers in the bedroom while she slipped the gold watch off the sleeping man's wrist. She was smooth as velvet and quiet as a cat. Gloria gathered a few more valuables then tugged Tina's arm. Let's go she whispered. Tina grabbed Trey and Rayshaun off the floor still sleeping and ran out the door without even shutting it. Tina felt victorious for her mother, as they waited again in the alley.

Tina ran errands as usual that day. As she was walking back from one of her deliveries, she thought the surroundings looked familiar. As she walked farther down the block, she realized it was the nice man's house, Ray. She immediately turned around and walked back. She went to the door, but she hesitated before she knocked. What if he wasn't the nice man she thought he was she asked herself. She stood there staring at the crooked sign for several minutes. Then it suddenly occurred to her that he didn't have shiny shoes. She took a deep breath, and knocked softly. The voice from inside yelled, who is it dam it. Tina smiled and sighed relief. The door yanked open. Ray was surprised, but still pleasant. He welcomed them in. He asked about Gloria. Tina answered politely with her eyes down carefully remembering to say sir to every answer. Ray watched her curiously for a few moments. Then he turned his attention to the boys as if he read her mind. He cuddled them for a few moments. He straightened Rayshaun's pants and called him man. He put Trey on his lap and tickled him making him smile fully. Let me get a tissue and wipe your nose lil man he told Trey sitting him gently on the floor. He tickled him some more with the tissue. Trey and Rayshaun both laughed. Tina watched and snickered. Ray then put the boys to the table and fixed them a bowl of cereal. Tina held back her tears. She found herself wishing that he was their father and they all lived with him, including her mother. She heard him call her to the table too. Trey and Rayshaun were happy and relaxed. Tina slowly began to unwind. Ray began to ask her kind but probing questions. How's school young lady? You getting good grades he questioned on and on. I know you are getting good grades cause I know you smart he flattered Tina. He said the word "smart" with punctuation and a warm smile. Tina giggled. After his questioning ended Tina could tell he had gathered all the information he was seeking. He got up and picked up the telephone. Mr. Ray Tina called softly. That man spit in my face she went on shyly. Ray froze and stared at her for a long time. What man he asked barely moving his mouth. That man at the store. Ray took her hand and said I'll take care of him baby and patted her hand. C'mon he said slowly. Get the boys and come wit me he instructed. They got in Ray's car and drove to the store. Where he at Ray asked solemnly. I don't see him Tina cried. That's alright we'll find him. They drove around for what seemed like hours. As they passed by the store for the tenth time the man was approaching the store. There he is Tina yelled. As Ray opened the door to get out of the car, Gloria appeared out of nowhere screaming. She was running down the street in a turquoise blue dress with shoes to match. There was a Jewish man running after her. She looked as if she'd been at some sort of business meeting. Get me outta here she screamed. They all heard a bang. It sounded like a firecracker to Tina but it scared them all. Gloria's face looked panicked. She jumped in the car and screamed at the top of her lungs. Go! Ray put the car in gear and floored the pedal. What's goin' on Gloria he asked her roughly. What you dun done now he asked in a voice pitched higher than his usual baritone. Tina looked back to see a man waving a gun. Gloria must have been up to her usual con games Tina thought as she shrunk in the seat and shivered. Gloria looked back in the back seat. Ray was driving wildly down the street. Gloria shoved a small paper bag into Tina's hands. Hide it she said sternly. Tina's hands were trembling. Save that for mommy she said pitifully. Tina was terrified to look inside the bag. Yes ma'am she answered quickly. Suddenly Gloria shouted let me out here Ray. Ray tried to reason with her but she was insistent. They all watched silently dismayed as she disappeared. They made a few stops and returned to Ray's house.

The boys were tired and irritable. Ray fixed them dinner. He appeared calm but still concerned. He fixed their beds and instructed Tina to stay there and let no one into the house except him or her mother. Tina watched Ray prepare to leave. He stuck something in the back of his pants and left. He checked the door for safety and disappeared into the darkness. Tina prayed for him and her mother. She suspected it was a gun in the back of Ray's pants. She wasn't sure if he was mad at her mother or not, but she prayed to God that he didn't kill her.

She was barely asleep when she heard the door creak. It opened slowly and she heard whispering. Shhh Ray hushed Gloria. Don't wake up the kids he scolded. Tina laid back down and pretended to be asleep. Ray and her mother tip toed pass them into the kitchen. Their argument was progressing. Their voices gradually grew louder and louder. Tina peeked from behind the door and listened. You can't take care of dem kids and be no streetwalker Gloria, Ray insisted. Streetwalker her mother yelled. Streetwalker she repeated in disbelief. I ain't no streetwalker she stressed with disgust. My kids eat everyday and they sleep under a roof every night Gloria lamented. Tina couldn't believe her mother was bragging about their living conditions. How could she be so proud of being so unstable and drunken Tina thought, shaking her head quietly and still watching. Gloria continued screaming with her hand on her hip. Those triflin' hoes screwing in that alley and shooting up drugs those is yo' streetwalkers, she explained. I I she patted her chest for emphasis, ain't no streetwalker. She pulled a gun from her purse and handed it to Ray. Here she shoved it in his chest. You get rid of it this time Gloria. She stared at him coldly with her mouth twisted then slid the gun back into her purse. Ray shook his head at her and headed for the door.

When Tina woke the next morning, Ray was in the kitchen fixing breakfast. C'mon eat doll baby he invited her. Tina smiled. She asked where her mother was. She stepped out for a minute he answered. She'll be back in a little while he reassured Tina. Tina nodded her head. Tina felt a quick chill as she watched Ray. Gon on and get you brothers up so they can eat Ray instructed mildly. Tina shrugged and obeyed. They played indoors and watched television all day. Ray stayed indoors with them and made several calls throughout the day.

Ray let them run and jump and make as much noise as they wanted. They were enjoying themselves but Tina noticed that Ray was mildly unnerved and distant. As night fell, Tina became more worried about her mother. After everyone else had gone to sleep, Tina stayed up late hoping that her mother would show up. Finally she heard a knock at the door. She heard Ray tiptoe to the door. She instantly knew it was her mother. Gloria and Ray went straight to the kitchen. Tina was straining to listen to their conversation and watching the television at the same time. When the television came into clear focus, Tina gasped loudly. It was the man that spit in her face on the television screen. Tina listened closely. This father of three was gunned down and killed in the alley at Del Mar and Warhigh Streets said the announcer. Tina was frantic. She pulled the covers over her head and shivered. She couldn't believe a King was dead. She thought Kings never died and never in a dreaded alley. Tina was puzzled and haunted all night long. She strained to hear her mother and Ray's voices again. Their voices grew louder and more enraged. The last thing she heard was her mother screaming, dem is my dam kids Ray. Then she heard a lot of shuffling and scuffling without words, then dead silence. The silence lasted for what Tina thought was hours. Without hearing any resolution, she fell asleep.

The following morning, they dressed quickly and left Ray's apartment again. Her mother forbade her to return to Ray's house under any circumstances. It seemed to Tina the last couple of days had all been a dream. But reality was staring them straight in the face again. They were back in the alley with the same old familiar faces. Nothing seemed to have changed there. It was as if no one had seen her mother run for her life down their street. It was as if no one had heard about the King that was gunned down on their street. It was as if she had dreamed it all. So back to the routine they went. She was running errands and doing chores for all the Kings and Judges. Occasionally Ray would pop up and check on them. Sometimes he would even locate them in the dead of the night. Always in a different location and always in need, Ray would find them. He'd hug and cuddle them. He'd straighten the boys twisted pants and wipe their noses. Sometimes he even bought dinner that he had cooked at home. Sometimes he just bought a treat. But he never left without giving them their "mad money." He'd drop a quarter or two in each of the boys' hands and a dollar or five for Tina. They were never quite sure who they were supposed to call when they got mad, but they slept with the coins curled in their little hands like it was the Holy Deity. They loved him. This was their only shred of security and they clung to it.

Chapter Two

A Change of Life

Wednesday morning was drafty and dark. They had been on the street corners for months now with no stability or promises of better conditions. Tina kept an eye on her mother's comings and goings. The other eye she kept on Trey. His nose was stuffy and his breathing was strained. Tina hoped her mother got lucky early today so that Trey could be medicated and get some rest. Her mother did her usual song and dance with no urgency or interest in Trey's worsening symptoms. Tina decided she would walk to the store and see if they could manage to beg up enough money for cough medicine for Trey. They tried their usual store fronts and corners. It seemed that no one was on the streets. So Tina decided to venture further and further away from their usual spots and was becoming more desperate and urgent in her search. She felt herself getting tired and winded before she reached the next store. She put Trey down to walk for a little while she rested her arms. She noticed out of the corner of her eye a police car stalling close behind them. Her suspicion was aroused, but she felt no dread. She pressed on about her business. Tina took Trey back in her arms and cautiously entered the corner store. She was surprised by the quiet tension as all eyes landed on her and her brothers. She surveyed the store and hadn't realized until then that they had entered an all white area. Can I help ya a curt voice called from behind a tall counter. I would like some cough medicine for my little brother Tina answered shyly. The heavy set proprietor snatched a box off the shelf and slammed it on the counter. That'll be two fifty he snuffed. He rang it up on the cash register and held out his hand. I only got she started while she clumsily fiddled with her change. The proprietor interrupted waving his hand. Take the kid to the doctor's office over on Stargill he stated shooing her with his hand. Tina left quickly knowing she was out of familiar territory. She walked as briskly as she could. Her arms were aching from the weight of Trey's body. He felt like cement. She stumbled into the doctor's office three blocks later on Stargill Street. The receptionist questioned Tina about her reason for her visit. It was clear to Tina that she was annoyed by her presence. After the receptionist had collected all of the information she needed, she informed Tina that she needed an adult's permission to treat Trey. The weight of Trey's body seemed to double and her arms and feet ached and throbbed as Tina began to sob. She was so loud and distracting, the receptionist put her in a patient room and closed the door. A nurse curiously peeked in and saw her in tremendous distress. The nurse put her arms around Tina and asked what was wrong. Tina tried to talk but couldn't. Instead she cried harder. To her surprise Rayshaun spoke up. He sick Rayshaun said simply pointing to Trey. The nurse softly asked Rayshaun who's that. My brother he answered childishly. Who's that she quizzed Rayshaun again pointing to Tina. My sista he said sticking his little chest out proudly. Wait here the nurse instructed them calmly. Tina felt herself calming down as she wiped her eyes. The nurse returned quickly with the doctor. Where's your mother the doctor asked directly after stepping into the room. Rayshaun quickly shrugged his shoulders. The doctor sat in front of Tina with a quizzical look on his face. He repeated the same questions the nurse had just asked. Tina composed herself quickly to answer the questions. She was careful to protect her mother's identity and whereabouts. The doctor shook his head softly. Stay right here we'll get you some help. Tina sat back in the chair to relax. She had slightly dozed off when the police officers flung open the door. The doctor instructed her to go with them and they would help her. Tina backed away screaming. She resisted uselessly. The nurse followed behind them with tears in her eyes. Tina could feel her tugging on her pocket, and placing something in it.

The officers placed Tina and her brothers in the back of the patrol car. They rolled along slowly while they continued questioning her. Where do you live little girl? Where's your mother? We just wanna take you home to your mother. Tina cringed. She longed to be in the alley waiting for her mother and a room again. She naively trusted the officers. Del Mar and Delancey she spoke up hopefully. The car sped up and they were on the familiar streets in a few minutes. Where's your mother the officer asked more forcefully this time. She gon pick us up right here Tina answered slightly agitated. The driver parked the car. Alright we'll wait they responded in unison. Tina rummaged through her pockets nervously. The nurse had stuffed her pockets with sample cold medicines and antibiotics. Tina sighed happily, then began to watch out the window for her mother. She felt her nerves become more frayed as the minutes ticked by slowly. She spotted her mother approaching from behind the patrol car when her mother locked eyes with her and put her finger to her mouth and ducted into the alley. The officers began to question Tina again after a while. They were becoming impatient. They sat for a short while longer then one of them stated it's dinner time let's go in. They drove around the block a couple of times while they questioned Tina some more. She protected her mother fiercely. Tina watched out the window wide-eyed as they pulled off. She squeezed Rayshaun's hand to make sure he was there. Trey was sleeping in her lap. She spotted her mother once again and once again they locked eyes on one another. The dread on her mother's face frightened her, and she wondered how they would meet up for the night.

The officers escorted them into the police station. He seated them on a long bench and then left to make several telephone calls. Tina wasn't sure if they were being arrested, but no one paid much attention to them so she figured they'd just have to wait until the officers ate their dinner, then they'd be dropped off on the corner again. Tina sat back to relax and wait. She heard Rayshaun's little stomach growl. She looked at him sympathetically. He tried to be brave and strong. He smiled softly but his little eyes were pleading and scared and tired. I'll tell them to give us sandwich Tina said kissing his hand. He smiled again. Okay he said trying to be the man Ray had always told him he was. He straightened himself on the seat. They both waited with grimaced smiles and growling stomachs

Before they knew it the officers were approaching them again. This is Ms. Goettings they said. She's gonna take care of you. Ms. Goettings squatted down before them and began to speak calmly. My name is Betty what's yours she asked as she pointed to each one of them. Would you like to go with me to get something to eat. Rayshaun immediately slid off the bench nodding affirmatively.

Tina was scared and nervous. As bad as their lives were with their mother her biggest fear was abandonment by her mother. The thought of never seeing her again filled her with greater fear than sleeping on the streets. She felt the care of strangers would be worst than her mother's care and she worried what would happen to them. Where are we going Tina asked politely. You'll be safe where I'm taking you. Can we see our mother she continued asking questions. You will, she answered. Tina couldn't think of any other objection to raise. They followed Ms. Goettings

When they arrived at her office they watched Ms. Goettings fill out a bunch of papers. She then escorted them to another place. As they pulled up to the curb, Tina saw a yard full of kids playing. She got excited and asked is this where we're going. Yes, Ms. Goettings answered. Tina was happy, especially for Rayshaun. She instructed them to go play until dinner time.

They were called in about a half hour later and fed a delicious meal of hot food. Trey even ate all of his food. Tina still held on to Rayshaun's hand and kept Trey pinned to her hip. Ms. Goettings returned and led them to a room. She explained that this was to be Tina's room. There was one bed, one desk, a rug and a closet. Simple but clean. Tina started to enter the room. Then Ms. Goetting asked Rayshaun and Trey to come with her. As she was leading Rayshaun out of the room Tina screamed from the bottom of her gut. It was so loud everyone ran to her door to see what had happened. Where are you taking my brother, Tina screamed. Calm down Ms. Goettings tried to relax her rubbing her back. Rayshaun and Trey will be in the boys section, right down the hall she explained. No Tina screamed louder than before. I want my brothers in the room with me. Tina was screaming so loud she got a headache and was shaking. They'll be alright Ms. Goettings tried to reassure her. No. No. They have to be with me, Tina continued screaming. Just lay down Tina and try to relax she said trying to pull Trey and Rayshaun out of the door slowly. Tina ran after her pulling the door open. She pulled with all of her might. She pulled and screamed so hard that her nose started to bleed profusely. Tina paid no mind to the blood. She commenced to hitting and scratching Ms. Goetting's arm. She was shaking her head wildly and screaming. Blood was slung all over the room. Okay Ms. Goettings relented. Here they are. Here are your brothers. They're not going anywhere. The nurse came in and gave Tina a cold compress to put on her nose. Tina grabbed Rayshaun's hand tightly and would not let go. Ms. Goettings and some other ladies that had been watching stepped outside the door. Tina could hear them mumbling. Tina was afraid they were going to try to take her brothers again. She started planning like she did back in the alley. She wished for her mother and feared that she was dead. She knew whatever the case, they would not take her brothers out of that room with her alive. They stepped back into the room and explained the situation kindly. Tina this is an orphanage. Boys and girls are not allowed to sleep in the same room. It is against the law. She conceded that Trey and Rayshaun could stay in her room for the night, but that would be the only time. Tina agreed suspiciously.

Tina didn't know how or what to plan against this well organized enemy. They were under watch all day and night. She was told they were in the system now and had to abide by the rules of the state. But Tina didn't care what they said Trey and Rayshaun were with her all day and night.

The next night she slept in their room. Ms. Goettings and the other ladies tried everything short of drugs to get her out of their room, but her wild screaming and fighting was more than they could handle. The following night her brothers slept in her room. It went like that back and forth for the next three weeks. By then Tina trusted them (the enemy) a little more. They fed them well. They housed them well and educated the boys well. She gradually let the boys go to the" big boy" room together, without her. She finally got settled into her own school and study program.

After about a month later her mother showed up at the orphanage with Ray. She posed as a respectable mother with her fiance'. Gloria Johnson could fool the best of them, Tina thought as she watched her mother from across the room. She looked like a Paris run way model with her heavy make-up and eyelashes.

She knew how to speak the "King's English" like a champion orator, and she had impeccable manners when she needed. No one would ever guess she was a street drunk from the ghetto.

In any case, Tina watched her mother and Ms. Goettings and several other officials exchange papers and sign them. Tina almost believed the pose herself. She figured her mother would take them back to Ray's house and they all would live happily ever after. To her dismay, Ms. Goettings handed her mother a bunch of papers with the official seal of the state on them, and said your children will remain here until they turn sixteen or graduate from high school. Tina's mouth dropped open. Gloria turned her face away from Tina and left the room without a word. Ray visited with them for a while after the proceedings were officially closed. He explained that he and her mother would be back to visit them and this was the best for them all for a little while.

Tina carried the betrayal and the abandonment in her heart. But gradually the orphanage became a way of life. After a while Tina realized it was better than street walking and far better than bunking. She missed her mother sometimes and her grandmother all the time. Whenever she thought about Gloria Johnson, she knew deep down that she was a survivor. She kept close tabs on Trey and Rayshaun daily, and watched them grow into strong healthy boys. It was no surprise to anyone that knew her that Tina's eagerness for learning helped her advance quickly and catch up with her peers academically. Now it was time for graduation.

Tina had stayed in the Whittenhall Projects for about two months now. She was first the house guest of a good friend named Linda. With Linda's help and her after school job she was able to get her own apartment, now that she was eighteen. It was the most stability she could ever remember for the past ten years. She liked the feeling of controlling her own life.

The sound of glass breaking and loud voices shook her out of her trance. Tina saw the Whittenhall Projects just as most other projects. There were people fighting a system that only crippled them. She heard the people repeating, like parrots, to one another, every indignity and violation of self worth they'd ever heard. All the while they're wearing over priced designer clothes, and standing amidst a pile of garbage. The residents masked themselves from real freedom. Tina shook her head and sighed. Whittenhall had the same ole methodical madness, a systematic game of mousetrap for its' residents. She watched and just shook her head.

Tina refused to mask herself in any way. Her eyes had been opened at an early age. She didn't wear make-up or designer clothes. Most of the people around her insisted that she was too black and ugly to wear the natural look. They insisted that she, at least, straighten her hair. She refused. Tina didn't fully know why she insisted on fighting against the odds. She didn't even know why she insisted that she had to be natural, and accepted that way. But her childhood had shown her enough of the hypocrisy. She was in search of what was real love and she wanted to start with herself. She longed for someone that could see who she was behind the black face and crippled emotions. So far, her life had offered her no one.

She was suddenly reminded of her nickname. In the streets and alleys, someone had named her mudpie. That name was thrust at her like a knife. They said it fit because her face was as black as mud and as flat as a pie. Thus, the name stuck. It was just another indignity she had to bear in the presence of Kings and Judges.

The resentment toward her was clearly because of her skin tone. In fact, it was those very Kings and Judges who made it their grand duty to appoint ranks upon the withering masses of colored people who didn't know the proverbial color hierarchy. Even when they were playing in the alley, the Judges would compliment Rayshaun on being a very fine, good looking boy, always noting his light skin tone. Trey was a step below making him only cute. His brown complexion was noted along with his "good hair". But Tina had no redeeming qualities they could see. An instant scowl, and turned up lips was her general greeting. Insults usually followed close behind the mean expressions scolding her. Ooou wee you so black. Whose little black thing is that? Don't touch that little black one. Those taunting remarks were no surprise. There were a constant barrage of attacks. Tina tried to harden her heart to their burning remarks, but sometimes the sting still penetrated her immature armor. Her little heart was actually crushed and broken under her rough exterior. She hated showing her weaknesses and vulnerability to those foul insidious Judges. They deemed it their responsibility to render judgment and punishment against her. The only crime they ever cited was being blllaaaack. Then they'd stroll off satisfied with their pronouncement and proud like Kings. Tina wanted to defy them to their faces but couldn't muster the courage to look them in the eye. She kept her head down, but secretly vowed to each face, each time, that one day I'll be someone you'll respect.

Through her anger and pain, Tina learned from those early lessons, that black people judged you by your skin tone first and your hair texture second. They reinforced those twisted hypocritical lies that left them enslaved to their white counter parts. Tina didn't understand how they could hate an innocent little girl just for her skin tone. Yet, it seemed they didn't hate being slum dwelling scavengers. They didn't hate being two dollar, side stepping pimps and whores. They didn't hate the systematic rape of their dignity and freedom. They just hated her dark, mud-black skin. The greatest sadness was that Tina learned to be ashamed of her own skin.

It was a heavy cross to bear. Sometimes Tina felt it was unbearable. She realized even at her tender age, that her eyes had been unveiled to a painful reality that couldn't be denied. Even they didn't know how to escape the chains that bounded their minds and hearts, so they lashed out at her again and again. They saw their true essence of course nappy hair, and deep skin tone as through the eyes of their oppressors, with loathing and disdain. They had a secret yearning to shed the deep hues of their own skin. That's why they tried to beat her down with a single word, shot at her like poisonous venom. That word was black.

In spite of all the pains Tina realized she needed and loved her people. She promised she wouldn't allow their hypocrisy to misguide her as well. She knew she had to be the strongest link in the chain. She also swore to herself she would not only be respectable but she would be a high roller in her community just like the Kings and Judges.

Tina had managed through lots of force and persuasion to stabilize her life. That was a feat her mother could never manage. She wiped a tear away from her cheek and mumbled Trey and Rayshaun can come be with me. Her high school graduation was just a shuffle away. She had secretly dreamed of becoming a doctor. Although she'd never said that aloud to anyone, except in poking fun at herself. Comedy was like that in the ghetto. You laughed at your misery, as well as your dreams. Yet there was a place in her heart that couldn't erase this fantasy.

She hadn't kept in contact with her mother although she wanted to. It was too painful for them both she figured. She always knew how to search her mother out however. It was the usual detective game. She'd stand on street corners and question old neighbors and friends. If that was not successful, Ray Giles, was always aware of her mother's whereabouts.

Ray was the only true and lasting friend her mother ever had. Her grandmother had told her stories about him and his relationship with her mother. Ray had fallen in love with her mother many years ago. Before she had had children and become a drunk, Gloria was a very attractive, self suffient woman. They were in love and had planned to marry.

Ray was a local bar and club owner. Gloria was a dancer in one of his bars. She performed every night in his club. She also performed after hours in several locations throughout the city, even in many white clubs on the other side of town.

It was just one ordinary day when Gloria met another fine gentleman. He was a singer, travelling from town to town, trying to get a grip on the golden life. He serenaded her mother right out of Ray's arms. Gloria dropped everything and everyone in her life and followed the gentleman on the road.

They were in and out of hideaway motels and speakeasy's, working the chitterling circuit until she found him in the bed with another woman in their home. The following morning newspaper headlines read, two slayed in bed, and Gloria was back in Pennsylvania. She never discussed her reasons for returning home suddenly and without the singer or the fame she sought. In any case she kept his last name, Johnson.

Gloria never got her life back on track. She went back to Ray Giles for awhile, but he couldn't compete with the love she still had for the singer. Her grief and loneliness led her to drink. Poor Ray still loved her to this day. But he like Tina got tired of the continual saga of alcohol and harlotry.

Ray and her mother didn't seem to travel in the same circles any longer, but somehow he always knew where she could be found. Nowadays Ray was a true friend to Tina too. It was Ray who visited them regularly at the orphanage and reported on their mother to them. It was Ray that took them out to eat on the weekends and it was Ray that gave them the security of being loved.

When her mother didn't appear in her usual corners and cervices, Tina went directly to Ray for more insight. After checking three times already and not finding Ray at home, Tina was dismayed. It frightened her to think Ray could have moved without letting her know where he lived. This would cause more instability in her life than never seeing her mother again. She knew she had the right apartment because the crooked half broken "Welcome" sign hung on the door. That was Ray's welcome home sign that had hung on his door for years. He always said that it was his special way of welcoming himself home and being grateful for what he had. Tina was beginning to worry as she approached the door again. Graduation was that week end and she wanted her mother to be there, for some odd reason. If she didn't find Ray at home today she figured she'd call the police.

Tina approached the door cautiously, praying that all would be fine. She banged as hard as she could on the bent steel door, right above the "Welcome" sign. Ray hollered in an angry voice. Who is it dam it? Tina exhaled and snickered under her breath. She could hear him breathing on the other side of the door. It's me Ray, she called back. She heard him sigh and then heard the clanging of all the locks being unlocked. He hugged her tightly and rubbed her back. Come on in darling he said motioning with his hand. It's a good thing you woke me up. I put on these greens and fell asleep. Tina could smell the aroma of his dinner. What else you cooking Ray, Tina inquired anxiously. You always cooking something she went on. They laughed in unison. I got some smothered chicken and some yams and some good ole greens, Ray tempted her with the menu. You better sit down and eat, he commanded pulling a shallow dish of sizzling chicken out of the oven. The aroma overwhelmed Tina. Okay let me wash my hands. You'd better cause you gon be lickin' dem fingers. They laughed. Ray set the table. Tina hadn't realized until then how little food there was. She made no mention, but felt badly. I think I'll just have a taste of the greens Ray, she said sounding apologetic. Ray wouldn't hear of it and served her plate heartily. That was just like Ray to pretend that there was plenty Tina thought. She knew she was probably eating his portion of dinner for tomorrow. She also knew he'd be more insulted if he couldn't share.

Tina bubbled over the good news while they ate. I'm graduating tomorrow Ray, she said bouncing in her seat. The news came as a shock to him. Ray like all other old people had lost track of time. He got up from the table and came around and hugged her. He embraced her extra tightly showing his approval. Well that's alright baby, he said through a wide grin sitting back in his chair. Tina went on to relay the details of time and place and handed Ray his invitation. He handled it like a precious gem and read it slowly. Well what's your plans now baby? I'm just going to attend the two year college around the corner. Ray was well pleased. Do you know where my mother is Ray? I wanted to invite her too, Tina sighed. Last I heard baby, she was staying in the homeless shelter over there on DelMar St, he answered with his voice fading into a slight tremor. They both hung their heads in silence for a moment. Tina felt the fear and anger well up inside her. You know Ray, I promised myself I'd never let myself and my children live like that. I'm gonna make sure I have the money I need to take care of myself and my children. I'm going to go to medical school and become a doctor, she said with resolve. She looked at Ray sheepishly as if asking permission to state her dream aloud. Ain't nothing wrong with that darling he assured her. I know you can do it. So just put yo' hand to the wheel and don't stop until you get there. Don't stop no matter what happens you hear me. I know you can do it. Ray sounded commanding and warning at the same time. Tina felt his words and confidence lock within her chest. I will, she murmured quietly. Thank you Ray. I'll see you tomorrow.

Her mother and two brothers along with Ray watched her walk down the ailse proudly. They all went out to eat afterwards. There was a sense of old times amongst them, but everything was different. Her brothers were growing quickly. Rayshaun was twelve and Trey was seven years old now. Her mother was beginning to experience physical ailments. She had sudden onsets of tremors. It was the result of her poor care and repeated attempts to quit drinking cold turkey. She kept her eyes lowered. She seemed most embarrassed by the shaking. Used to attracting attention for her sexiness and prowess, the tremors hurt her pride. Gloria explained that she was confined to a shelter by a doctor to help her quit drinking and avoid walking the streets" looking crazy", as she put it. She belonged to the system.

Chapter Three

The Systematic Struggle

Tina started college in the fall. She attended the community college in her neighborhood and studied Medical Assisting. She still worked part time as a shoe clerk in the shoe store. She slid the shoebox from under her bed. She unwrapped the plastic bag and counted her savings. Four hundred dollars she had saved with one goal in mind. Barely an adult herself, Tina wanted to pursue legal guardianship of her two brothers. She knew it would take all of her savings and much more for her to accomplish this feat.

Tina opened the phone book and simply pointed to a name in the attorney's section. She said the name aloud to measure how professional it sounded to her. She checked the address. It was in an expensive section of town. They must be good Tina thought. She called the office using her best professional voice, and made an appointment. She checked and wrote down a couple more names. She wanted the best her money could buy.

She immediately dressed and left for the law offices. Upon entering the first law office, she noticed the typical shock and disdain registered on the lily white faces of the clients waiting in the lobby. The clerk approached her with horror and disbelief written all over her face. Her mouth barely moved from its' hung open position, as she asked, May I help you? Yes, I have an appointment to speak with one of the attorneys, Tina answered almost in a whisper. The clerk stared blankly with her mouth in the same hung open position. Um . . . um I'm sorry ma'am, the clerk was grappling for words while she shook her head in absolute refusal. We don't take walk-ins, she took a long breath and clutched her chest. Tina now stood with her mouth hung open. Our attorneys only see clients by appointment she quipped through a cocky smirk. I called and asked to speak with an attorney regarding guardianship, Tina snapped with her voice slightly raised. The clerk's nostrils flared as she requested the name and date of the call. Tina was holding off her backhand slap and her tears. The clerk flipped through the appointment book loftily. I'm sorry I don't see your name Ms. Douglas she emphasized the name. Tina stood firm, staring into the clerk's face. The clerk picked up the phone turned her back while she whispered into the receiver. Tina turned around to catch a long breath and found everyone staring at her. The disgust and terror on their faces accounted for the daggers in their eyes. The clerk hung up the phone and pretended to go back to work.

A tall slender young looking man came rushing from the back corridor. He had black stringy hair that appeared to be wet. His face was stern, and his brows pulled down. His eyes met Tina's about halfway through the corridor and widened as he entered the lobby. What can I do for you ma'am? I came to speak to someone about Guardianship. Well I'm sorry we don't take walk-ins. I called this morning Tina said punctuating her words. Oh well we don't handle those kind of cases anyway, he said seething through clenched teeth. Tina stood there at a loss staring into the man's eyes. His eyes narrowed as he shooed her away with his hand gesture. He watched her turn and walk away.

Tina left the law offices fuming with anger and frustration. She reached into her pocket and counted her change. She cried as she counted out her bus fare. She was disgusted and hurt. This was a different kind of hurt. She was used to the rejection from the neighborhood Kings and Judges, but this felt different. It was wicked and lowdown.

Up until now her world had been a predominantly black one. In the black world she knew how to handle things and get what she wanted. She had grown up in black neighborhoods, went to black schools. There was an occasional white teacher here and there, or the white store owner on one of the corners in the neighborhood. Essentially though, Tina's world had never spilled over into the white world. Her coat was now soaked with tears, and she grew madder by the minute. She turned around and marched right back to that law office. She had to slap that slut at the desk and spit in the face of that obnoxious attorney that shooed her out of the office like an infectious pest.

She got to the office door and jerked on the door. It didn't budge. She grabbed it again and again, before she realized it was locked. She screamed some obscenities through the heavy solid wood door, then listened. There was dead silence not even a footstep. They had totally dismissed her and made sure no other unwanted pest stepped through their door. She was even more angry and frustrated.

Tina prepared her dinner in silence with no television or radio in the background for her usual companionship. She couldn't get the piercing incident off of her mind. She was perplexed yet curious about understanding their motives for immediate loathing. There seemed no reason for it. She posed no threat whatsoever to them. It was just senseless hatred. It was too instant to be thoughtful or reasonable. Without hearing or knowing her, they condemned her. It felt somewhat like the loathing of the Kings and Judges toward her, but there was a difference she could not put her finger on.

It was finally the weekend. Tina wanted to sleep in then visit with her brothers, but her mind was still weighted down with finding an attorney. She forced herself out of the bed early, and began to prepare to seek out the right attorney. She examined herself closely in the mirror, with the last incident still fresh in her mind. Weekdays didn't allow time for that kind of introspection. She conceded that she wasn't the most attractive or alluring woman she had ever seen. She didn't consider herself pretty. She was chocolate brown in complexion. Ray was the only man that she could ever remember telling her she was pretty. The overriding opinion in the ghetto was that her dark brown complexion and short hair was not pretty. In most cases, it was to be pitied. Tina had both. She stroked her face softly and outlined her features with her finger, carefully studying each one. She had a round face with a long round nose. Her eyes were prominent, round and bright. She wore her hair in a neat close cropped afro. She stood back from the mirror and examined her profile. She stood in quiet contemplation for a moment. There was no monster there. It wasn't the hideous objectionable monster everyone else seemed to see, but she still felt a distaste for her complexion. After a long sigh she realized there was no time for that. She had to find an attorney right away. She bathed then rushed out of the bathroom. She headed for a reputable office in the Blue Rock section of town. She had seen it on a television commercial.

She entered the office slowly and took a long breath. The receptionist looked up from her work as Tina approached her. It was raining and Tina was shaking the water from her umbrella. Hi may I help you she sounded curious. Yes, my name is Tina Douglas. I have an appointment for a consultation she spoke politely. Oh well our appointments are done on a first come first serve basis ma'am. And all of our attorneys are tied up for the entire day she quipped graciously. But I called yesterday ma'am and the lady told me to come in at ten thirty. I see said the receptionist moving her eyes quickly. She was a mature lady of about fiftyish. She had auburn red hair and keen facial features. She didn't show any emotions as she removed her glasses and stared Tina right in the eyes. We set appointments but they're just rough estimates, she explained. We go by how many people come in and who gets her first. We never know how long each case is going to take to discuss, she stated apologetically. Tina felt anger welling up inside her. She caught herself as she got ready to blurt out a row of obsenities. Instead she said leaning over the receptionist desk. I'll wait. The receptionist looked stunned. Tina took off her wet coat and hung it on the coat rack along with her umbrella. The receptionist watched her every move. As soon as Tina was seated she made four quick calls. Tina knew she was warning each of the four attorneys. She waited impatiently for two hours. She watched the lobby fill up and empty over and over again. She watched the attorneys walk in and out of the lobby. They ordered and ate lunch. At one forty five she quietly left the office with her head hung down. She felt as if she had been kicked in the stomach. She wanted to go home and cry, but she had to find a lawyer that day.

She walked a block and found another law office. The sign said walk-ins accepted. She opened the door and faced a long staircase and dark corridor. A sign by the banister read Law Office with an arrow pointing up. She ascended the staircase quickly and quietly. She opened the glass door and found three men working at randomly spaced booths. The man nearest the door looked up when he heard the door open. Can I help you he asked rising from his desk and walking toward the tall counter. Yes I'm trying to find a lawyer for a guardianship case. Guardianship he asked obviously surprised. The whole office quieted. You mean like foster parenting? No like guardianship Tina restated. Hey Jim she wants a lawyer for guardianship he called over to the man directly behind him. Jim got up and walked over, you mean you want an a adoption case hon'. No I don't, Tina was getting frustrated. Guardianship she persisted raising her voice a little. She knew they were playing games with her, but didn't know how to counter their strategy. I don't understand what you mean Jim said waving his hand. Hey Nick you know anything about litigating guardianship did you say as he turned to Tina with his face twisted. Never heard of it Jim. Jim gave an attaboy snicker of conciliatory approval. Why don't you come back when you know what you want Jim insisted. Tina was exhausted by the mind games and left without another word. She realized the game was systematic. They didn't have to discuss or plan. They had mastered the game and immediate loathing and disgust of a dark face. Tina realized their method of operation was to confuse the issue. She could see why it was so successful. What she couldn't see is why black people would copy that method and use it on one another.

She busted into the next office like a gangster. I want to see a lawyer now, Tina demanded. She was dripping wet. The receptionist ran from behind the desk. C'mon in and have a seat hon' she said grabbing her arm, and pulling her to the back. What's the problem hon' she asked sympathetically. Tina took a moment to notice her face. She had dark brown hair and deep black eyes. Tina felt relieved for some reason. She explained what she wanted. The lady was very kind and explained that she needed a retainer. Tina pulled out the four hundred dollars that she had saved. Four hundred dollars the receptionist said as she counted the money and here's your receipt she said handing it to Tina. Your attorney will give you a call that should be sometime next week. Tina left satisfied. All it took was a little bit of forcefulness she concluded.

Two weeks had past and Tina hadn't heard a word from the attorney's office. She called repeatedly to follow up, and was stalled everytime. The attorney's not in right now, the receptionist would answer. She'd put Tina on hold for twenty minutes at a time, just to return and say I'm sorry he's with a client right now. She recognized the receptionist's voice. Tina found herself frustrated and out witted with no place to turn. It was times like these that she really longed for a mother. She concluded that she had to accept the cruelty, simply because she lacked the experience to handle it.

She was visiting with the boys one day at the orphanage, when she spotted her old high school counselor. A feeling of nostalgia gripped her and she called to her. Ms. Miller motioned for her to come over to her office. She kissed Trey and headed for the office. C'mon in girl she said getting out of her chair. She gave her a huge bear hug. It made Tina feel good to be so welcomed. They exchanged pleasantries and chit chat. Tina decided to relay her dilemma with the legal system to Ms. Miller. Ms. Miller immediately picked up the telephone and called the attorney's office. Her voice was extremely professional. Her speech and diction were impeccable. Tina snickered as she listened. Within three minutes, she had a four o'clock appointment to see the attorney. Tina suddenly understood why those stupid English classes were so necessary. She thanked Ms. Miller with a big hug and kiss. Ms. Miller called her back and said sit down and wait for me. I'm going with you. Tina's heart leaped for joy. She felt as if she had been rescued from a drowning boat.

On the way to the attorney's office Tina filled Ms. Miller in on the mind games she had been through while in search of an attorney. Ms. Miller educated her swiftly. Tina that's called the struggle, and it's systematic sweetie. The hatred is inbred and they do it automatically without even thinking about it. It makes them think they're not racists since they don't plan it. We're no longer in physical chains, but the system runs you around, never letting you accomplish anything, to make you frustrated and throw up your hands and give up. She turned to Tina and looked her sternly in the face. Tina doll baby don't you dare let them win that game. You've got to be stronger than everyone else Tina her voice was strong and curt. It's unfortunate but we black women have to be even stronger than our men sometimes, her voice broke a little. We carry the black nation in our bellies and the world on our shoulders. She went on slightly nostalgic. We as black women especially, must bond and help each other. Why don't we agree right here and now Tina to help each other and any sister carrying a heavy load. Let's pass on a helpful hand and a positive word. Do you go through these struggles Tina asked thinking Ms. Miller is so together she doesn't have to bother. Yes Tina we all do. You have to expect some struggles sweetheart she replied in her soothing voice. It's the systematic way of keeping us in our place. The only way to beat it is higher education, collective buying and higher tax brackets. She smiled slyly with one brow slightly raised. She held Tina's face and explained you are far too smart Tina to be chained to a poor man's salary. You should continue in school and become some kind of professional. Tina felt a chill run down her back. She confessed to Ms. Miller she had always secretly dreamed of becoming a doctor. Ms. Miller hugged her and unexpectedly began to cry. We need black doctors her voice trembled a little. Tina couldn't reply. She was in shock from Ms. Miller's reaction. Ms. Miller dried her eyes and straightened her posture, before entering the attorney's office. She looked poised and dignified.

The receptionist recognized Tina. The look in her eye told Tina she remembered all the games she had played with her on the phone. Ms. Miller didn't give Tina a chance to speak. We're here to see Mr. Engel, her voice was direct and confident, with a slight courtesy. He's expecting us, she added quickly. Just one moment the receptionist said without hesitation. To Tina's surprise, they didn't have time to take a seat. Mr. Engel was there to personally escort them to his office. He was so polite. The proper papers were filled out on the spot. All that was missing was a signature from her mother. Ms. Johnson's signature and one court date will be necessary Mr. Engle explained, handing them the papers. That's just a formality though he went on. They left the office with papers in hand and work in progress. It took all of a half hour. Tina couldn't believe the type of service Ms. Miller's presence commanded. All she knew was that she wanted to have the same type of respect from both white and black people.

Instead of taking her straight home Ms. Miller took Tina back to her office. Tina was a bit surprised but figured Ms. Miller had some loose ends to tie up or some things to pick up. Ms. Miller shut the door behind them, and pulled out some papers. Laying them on the desk in front of Tina she said, here you go Dr. Douglas. Tina stretched her eyes and examined the papers closely. Ms. Miller proceeded to show Tina the curriculum and financial aide she could take advantage of beginning immediately. Tina was breathless. She couldn't believe Ms. Miller had taken it so seriously. It was just a silly dream she thought about from time to time. Tina stumbled out a few excuses, but Ms. Miller was firm. I want an invitation to your graduation she blurted out, concluding all objections.

Tina was pensive the rest of the evening. What a difference a day makes, she thought laying across her bed. She kept looking over the curriculum Ms. Miller had given her and wondering if she could really do it. She couldn't subdue the excitement in her gut, yet she couldn't dismiss the judgments that had been handed down from the alley. She came to a conclusion. There was no way she could truly make it through medical school. I'm just a no named ghetto street brat she went on condemning herself. She sat straight up in her bed. I see no need to lie to myself she said aloud. I couldn't even get in most likely she went on with her reality check, let alone graduate. I have to be real. It would take all the king's horses and all the king's men to convince any school administration that I'm not a project brat. They don't let project brats study medicine. She got out of bed and threw the papers and notes right in the trash pail.

For the next several weeks the thoughts of medical school haunted her. She fought to keep the fantasy out of her head, but no matter how hard she tried she could think of nothing else. She kept picturing herself in a white jacket and thinking how nice it would be to hear someone call her Dr. Douglas. The thoughts began to interfere with her everyday functioning. She called Ms. Miller and explained that she was thinking about taking just a couple of pre-med classes. Her tone was humble and childish as if she were asking mother may I. Ms. Miller assured her that it was a wise decision to start off slow. Forcing the issue, Ms. Miller told Tina to meet her at the registrar's office at eight o'clock sharp the following morning. Sometimes amid her admiration and respect she resented Ms. Miller. Ms. Miller was so strong there was no way to say no to her.

Tina was so afraid and excited all at once. She didn't get any sleep that night. She altered between feelings of euphoria and depression. She thought about changing the plan, but she didn't want to disappoint Ms. Miller.

Ms. Miller was there at eight o'clock sharp. She hugged Tina firmly, and assured her again that she was doing the right thing. She tried to convince Tina that she would be successful. She helped her choose the classes she would take and to Tina's surprise paid the money she needed to get started until her financial aid came through. She could not believe the faith Ms. Miller had in her. No one had ever demonstrated such confidence in her before. She wanted to say thanks but no thanks. Yet she didn't have the fortitude to argue with Ms. Miller.

Tina decided she had to pass these two classes since Ms. Miller had put her own money on the line. There was no guarantee where she would go from there, or if she would continue beyond that point. In spite of all the self doubt, she had to continually wrestle down her excitement. It felt as if she were in a dream. She still felt it was more than wise to keep cautious boundaries on her dreams, but for some reason that fragile spark of hope wouldn't subside. It bounced up and down inside her courageously like a morning star. A morning star with the audacity to try to outshine the sun, but the hope was insistent with joy. From that point on the underlying joy kept pushing her forward.

It was eight months after their visit to the attorney's office that the guardianship papers came in the mail. Tina had been granted guardianship of Trey, but not Rayshaun. Rayshaun would soon be sixteen and not worth the cost of pursing legally, so the attorney advised.

Tina let the boys finish their school year at the orphanage, then moved all of their belongings into her apartment. Rayshaun was free to leave the orphanage since he was sixteen and he chose to test the waters of freedom. He promptly found his way to the streets and pursued a life of danger and crime. Within a matter of weeks he began living on a separate schedule from Tina and Trey. They only saw him once or twice a week when he stopped by for clothes or food. It was still hard for Tina to let go. Rayshaun had been her best friend for so many years. Now time had forced them down separate paths. As she watched time change all of their lives drastically, the emptiness weighed her heart down. She'd never be as close to Rayshaun again. Her blood ran cold at the thought of losing him, but she knew she couldn't hold his hand any longer. Her life had to move on down its' own course.

Gratefully she loved school. She had always wanted this wealth of knowledge, and to be respected for her mind. She was gaining the knowledge rapidly. The human body was fascinating to her. She finished her classes with a 4.0 grade point average (GPA). She called Ms. Miller to determine if she should continue. Strangely enough, she still hadn't begun to believe in herself. She needed to know that someone did. As long as Ms. Miller did she decided she would keep trying. She needed that gentle coaxing by all means, and Ms. Miller was a God send.

She chose to take a full time schedule of classes this semester. She talked to Ms. Miller daily. Trey grew close to Ms. Miller as well. She became like a surrogate mother. She'd wash their clothes, cook meals and taxi them around when they were in a bind. She also helped keep Trey on the straight and narrow path. She took Trey to church every Sunday, and Tina though her time was restricted would join them on occasion. Tina always found time for Sunday dinner at the Miller's however.

The Miller's lived in the suburb of Blue Rock, right next to the wealthiest part of town. It was a predominantly white neighborhood. Mr. Miller was the principal of a nearby high school. It had surprised Tina to find their house was strictly African cultured on the inside. She would have never thought Ms. Miller had as much soul as she had class. Her house reflected her awareness and love for her culture. Tina loved being there. She made a conscious effort not to extend her visit beyond its' welcome.

She continued her classes, adding a class each semester. She was still working at the shoe store and carrying a full class load. She often felt unbalanced. When she decided to devote more time to school and studying, Ms. Miller agreed that she could quit her job at the shoe store and just live on the government check she received for Trey. Ms. Miller usually filled in any gaps in finances so they were able to continue without harm. They had grown into Ms. Miller's family circle.

School was still fun and exciting for Tina. She studied ravenously. As a result, she was at the head of her class with an excellent standing. She felt she'd better hurry up and learn as much as possible before they realized she wasn't supposed to be there. She was sure that she would be kicked out of school as soon as they discovered that she was a street brat. She had stealthily slipped through the doors and gotten accepted. Now with every passing day she had to remain undiscovered. Keeping her grades high was part of her cover. She also broke the tell all ghetto cadence of her speech and spoke the King's English with perfect diction.

The semesters flew by. Tina took heavy course loads with electives favoring pharmacy and chemistry. It was addictive since she felt like she was cheating the system. She just hoped they never found out. Self doubt never abandoned her. When her advisor contacted her she was immediately worried that she had been discovered. She knew she had a favorable class standing so it could be nothing other than a request to leave school that he wanted to give her. She felt sick up till the time of her appointment.

She arrived at her appointment late. She had to delay the bad news as long as she possibly could. By the time her advisor called her into his office, Tina was annoyed and had worked up an attitude. He started the meeting off formally. Nice to finally meet you Ms. Douglas, he spoke warmly and extended his hand. Thank you Tina said flatly ignoring his hand. He looked puzzled but went on. I've been looking over your transcript and I see here that you've been taking quite a few biology courses. I just wanted to inform you that if you took a few more math courses and a couple more biology courses you'd be able to receive a double degree. Her mouth dropped open. She stared at him quizzically. Questions were speeding through her mind so fast she thought she had already asked them. But she hadn't uttered a sound. I mean that is if you wanted to do that he stumbled on, not sure of how to read her blank expression. You've already met your requirements for graduation. I was kinda wondering why you hadn't applied for your graduation package. I'm done Tina finally squeezed through her buckled throat. She instantly covered her mouth with her hand. Hearing her own words made her feel silly. She cleared her throat and took a deep breath. How much longer would I have to go she asked trying to sound sober. Oh just another semester he sneered. Tina tried to process the information quickly. She found herself overwhelmed. I'll tell you what he spoke up quickly. Why don't you just take this information home with you and look it over, and get back to me he advised. Tina left with the information and her mouth still hanging open. She returned the next day with all of her papers filled out. I guess one more semester won't be so bad she joked.

Trey was slowly becoming a problem child. He wanted to be a carbon copy of his big brother. He began skipping school and experimenting with drugs. He tried Tina's willpower as much as possible. To his surprise Rayshaun would team up with Tina against him. The two of them together forced him into submission. Trey wisely settled down and became a good student again. It was Rayshaun's promise that he'd always have an eye on him that convinced him to remain in school.

It was funny Tina thought, how Rayshaun was insistent that Trey remain in formal school. Rayshaun insisted that the street school of hard knocks was not right for Trey, and made it clear to him that he would not have him try it for a minute. Tina wondered what made it right for Rayshaun when it wasn't right for Trey. In any case, she shrugged everyone was getting an education of some sort for now.

Chapter Four

New Friends

Tina sat in the lobby of Sullivan Hall one afternoon cramming for a class assignment. She was completely absorbed in her studies, when she heard a loud thud. She looked up to see a strikingly handsome young man staring directly at her. He gathered up his books while he continued to watch her eyes. Hi, he smiled softly. How are you doing he asked. I didn't mean to scare you. I almost made it to the table. They both laughed. Tina grabbed a few of the scattered papers, and handed them to him.

My name is Greg Walton he spoke solemnly. Tina's heart fluttered. A fine brother Tina thought as she extended her hand to shake. Hi I'm Tina Douglas she stated suspciously. Greg took a seat beside her and started conversing and questioning her. Tina wondered what this approach was going to cost her in addition to her time. He surely wasn't seeking her friendship she thought. He was just too fine to be interested in her. He comfortably explained that he was a sophomore majoring in international business management. He continued on talking about his classes, his grades and his plans for the future. Tina hated to interrupt him but she had to leave for class. It had been a nice get aquainted meeting, and Tina told him just that as she stood to leave. May I call you a little later lovely lady he asked as he caught her by the arm. Tina's heart was beating fast. Yes you can she nodded affirmatively. She rolled off her telephone number and broke away from his grip. Tina felt a sensual craving welling up inside her.

Tina returned home that evening with the meeting fresh on her mind. She hoped but was doubtful that he would call. Most good looking guys like him wanted the model type girls and looks. Besides he was a few years younger, a rule Tina hated to bend. As she was preparing for a test the phone rang. It was him. He started up almost exactly where he had left off in Sullivan Hall. He talked comfortably and continually. Tina was amused and excited. He assured her he wanted to spend some time with her and asked if she would meet him at the same place again tomorrow. Tina agreed.

She was excited to find Greg already there waiting when she arrived. Again Greg picked up where he had left off the night before. Tina enjoyed hearing him talk. He had sparkling white teeth and soft curly hair. He had smooth golden brown skin and manicured hands. Tina still wondered what he wanted with her, but she decided to be patient and let time slowly reveal its' secret.

After a few weeks of meetings, things were very personal between them. Tina found it hard to pull herself away from their carefree conversations. Tina was afraid of the turn the relationship was taking. When Greg invited her to his house in Wellesly Township she knew she had to refuse. Tina warned herself repeatedly. She knew the time was not right for a relationship. She had too many obligations. She wanted to break away with nothing but a new friend. But her heart was desperate and led her right back to the same spot day after day.

Although Tina's study schedule didn't allow time for them to go out regularly, they managed through several hit and miss dates to seal their connection. But the closer they got the more Tina felt this wasn't the right relationship for her. Greg had revealed in their conversations that he came from money. That was scary enough for Tina. But not only did he come from money he had a close well functioning family. He had grown up in a home with both parents, a dog and goldfish. He was educated at private schools and with in home tutors. He was groomed to be a professional something and receive an inheritance. He had everything she had dreamed about in her childhood. Tina reasoned all the strikes against the relationship but all the excuses in the world couldn't save her heart from the eminent dive into love. She had asked him to move on to another relationship, but she knew deep down in heart that she wanted this man. She craved the touch of his manicured hands on hers. She loved his baritone voice. Besides that Greg was persistent, patient and understanding.

Their first intimate date changed everything. They met at her apartment for a quick lunch. Greg turned up the heat instantly. He backed her against the wall and slid his tongue in her mouth. He was slow and gentle. He pulled her panties down to her ankles. He pressed his manhood slowly into her coochie while she squatted and hissed. He grinded his well endowed manhood rhythmically pressing her buttocks in his soft hands. Their slow screw against the wall climbed until they both cried out harmoniously, and the heat dripped from inside them.

Tina graduated Summa cum laude from her pre-med program with a double degree in Pre-Med and Chemistry. Her life was transitioning in several ways. She was accepted into the local Medical School program. With help from her advisor and Ms. Miller she had enough financial aid to cover her first year tuition and books. She didn't have to worry about Trey. He practically lived with the

Millers now. There was no objection by either of them to that. Ms. Miller even transferred Trey to the high school in Blue Rock. Trey had gotten comfortable with the plush surroundings. Tina missed his presence at home but it was all for the best. Trey had truly been like her own child. She had carried him in her bosom, then on her hip for the first two years of his life. Now she had to let go of him, and watch him walk on his own. Tina felt she had found a place of security for him. She turned his check over to Ms. Miller, who usually turned more than half of it back over to her for her own expenses. Tina felt guilty taking it but Ms. Miller coaxed her.

Rayshaun was still in and out of the apartment occasionally. He swore it was still his primary residence and where he called home. He still proclaimed to be the man of the house. Greg was still in his undergrad program. Staying local proved to be best for all of her relationships.

Medical School took off like a rocket. It was a daunting challenge right from the start. It proved to be an endless succession of classes, study, study groups and patient cases to review. It was growing continually harder to see Greg regularly but he persisted. They had to be satisfied with ten and twenty minutes love sessions. They made the most out of them.

Tina fought to keep up the pace during her first year of Medical School. She pulled through by the skin of her teeth. She moved into her second year fretful and anxious. Greg graduated during her second year of medical school. To her surprise he proposed marriage to her. Despite their brief dates and briefer sexual escapades he saw hope of a future life together. Sometimes Tina wondered if those short stolen moments was what made their relationship so intense and strong. They talked on the telephone more than they made love, but not due to lack of desire. There had been so little time for them. Tina still was able to keep count all their blissful encounters. They were few, but even quickies were powerful. In any case Tina accepted. Just the thought of a happy more importantly stable family life made her giddy with joy.

Visions of herself preparing dinner while Greg read a book to their three little children by the fireplace filled her heart with warmth and a large dose of security. Tina thought this would kill the song of the Kings and Judges that played in her head over and over. How happy she felt to have an answer to their dreadful pronouncements.

There was no time to plan a large wedding. A small cozy wedding was the perfect solution given their time and financial restraints. Tina had never pictured a large wedding for herself anyway. She had generally accepted that she would probably never get married at all. She always felt no one would ever want her. But now she was tickled all over that someone wanted her. And not just someone, but someone with a quite respectable background. She had cheated the system again.

Although she wasn't having a large wedding, Tina still wanted a beautiful gown. She made time to shop for a gown. The bridal shops were crowded and busy. It was the bloom of the wedding season. It seemed everyone else in the world had decided to plan their wedding at the same time. The gowns were lovely and stunning. She had her eye on a few exceptionally gorgeous ones, but she hated pushing her way through the crowds, the long waits just to try on or ask a question. Most of all, the prices were far out of her range. Seven, eight hundred dollars for a dress, for one little day Tina snorted. I don't think so besides it was taking more time than she had allotted. She booked a Justice of the Peace, and sent out stock invitations, and ordered a cake.

The rushed pace and heavy school schedule were taking their toll. She hadn't found a gown in the crowded bridal boutiques or department stores. Tina decided to shop the thrift stores. They usually carried evening gowns and occasionally wedding gowns. She knew all the thrift stores in the city. She figured she could hit them all without the crowds and lord knows without the big ticket price tag. She did just that. To her surprise she couldn't find even one white gown. It was official everyone in the world was planning their wedding at the same time as she. She was terribly pressed for time by now. She felt this would force her back into the bridal boutiques. That she dreaded.

She had no more time to devote to dress shopping. Her exams and study schedule were demanding the remainder of her scarce free time. She felt the pressure bottling up inside of her. She felt she would blow at any minute. She pictured herself standing at the alter in her same soiled scrubs. She could feel the screams belting against her throat. She pushed the line to signal the bus driver that she wanted the next stop.

The fresh air was what she needed. She suddenly realized how precious little of it she ever got anymore. She usually spent a minimum of eight hours in clinical and roughly four to six hours at school or the library. Even the lower west end ghetto air smelled fresh for once. She sucked in a deep breath and stepped quickly on her way to the apartment.

At the corner of Drake and Warhigh Streets there was a rutty looking consignment shop. Through the window the sparkle of tinted glass beads caught her eye. She went inside with her eyes fixed on the sparkle of the beads. There they sat in a dusty white porcelain bowl, like chunks of gold nuggets, glimmering at her eyes. As she reached for the bowl, her hand brushed against a wedding veil that lay on its' side. It was almost as beautiful as the glass beads. She didn't know which to pick up first. The veil called to her. It was layers of white netting sheared onto a beautiful tiara. She lifted it off the stand and placed it on her head. She walked to the mirror and took a deep breath. It was stunning. It was perfect. It sat on her head like a crown of royalty. The layers of netting fell over her face like a grand water fall. As she stood there staring at herself in the mirror a flood of grandeur washed over her. She felt as if she'd awaken an ancient African queen who had rushed to the mirror in front of her to bestow her approval. A voice to the right of her kindly said that's beautiful. Would you be taking that home today? It was Al, the propeitor. He ran the health food store next door as well. Tina was afraid to take her eyes off the mirror. She turned her head slowly toward the voice. Al's eyes were shinning with brightness and joy. That is for you my queen he added as if he had heard her thoughts. Might this joyous occasion be yer wedding he asked. Yes, Tina answered still breathing shallow. Well this veil is the perfect compliment to any wedding gown he went on. Tina's eyes snapped back to Al's face. I haven't found a gown yet she admitted sheepishly. My wedding is Saturday and I don't have time to shop anymore. Please say you have a wedding gown to match this she pleaded. That I don't Al said almost humorously. Tina frowned and sighed. I do have the most beautiful piece of Egyptian cotton that would serve quite well, he added with slight tone of salesmanship. Come this way my darling he said as he dragged her to the fabric. She unfolded it. It was beautiful. It was a gleaming bright white like the dress her mother wore for the meeting with Aunt Sally. It definitely wasn't throw away or push aside fabric at all she thought to herself examining it slowly. How though could it work when she didn't have time or money to hire a seamstress, she thought. As if on que, Al said, I can show you how to tie this one piece of cloth seventeen different ways and more if you'd like to return for lessons. He gently took it from her hand and began wrapping it around her. He showed her one look after another. Tina finally stopped him. I like this wrap she said swaying happily. It's simple yet elegant. It's perfect for me. The snags and rips aren't visible either she said as she glanced back at Al who was smirking lightly. Al patiently taught her how to do the wrap. She then placed the veil on her head. Ah, Al sighed. Absolutely gorgeous he added. You must have this for yer ceremony. Tina agreed. She was sure the Kings and Judges would not approve, but she always wanted to defy them anyway. It's right for me she concluded, natural and regal. The whiteness of the cotton made her skin glisten, and the veil made the simplicity of the dress regal. Together it had an understated appearance of royalty. Then she remembered the beads. She ran to the window and added the bowl and beads to her purchase. Those are lovely Al complimented. What might one do with them he asked. I'm not sure but I think I'd like to make a necklace out of them, or she punctuated with her finger, put them around the edge of the veil. That would be superb Al agreed.

Tina rushed home to try on her wedding outfit again. She began matching her shoes and accessories to the gown and veil. She undressed and tried the ensemble again. Still stunning she murmered out loud in the mirror. She called Ms. Miller for her opinion and companionship. She fiddled with the beads while she waited for Ms. Miller to arrive at her apartment.

She twirled and sashayed in front of the mirror. She practiced her walk down the ailse. Everytime she turned away and looked back in the mirror her veil looked more beautiful and royal to her. It seemed to show her a new person everytime she looked and gave her a new message of confidence. Tina greeted Ms. Miller at the door in her full outfit. They didn't speak they just grabbed each other and clung on for minutes standing in the middle of the floor. After about five minutes of continuous screaming, they collapsed on the sofa. Ms. Miller took charge from there. Okay Tina what's left to be done she asked. She started sounding off the checklist. Invitations? Check Tina replied. Food? Check. Flowers? Check. No no no wait I forgot the bride's bouquet. Tina was instantly frantic. Okay don't worry, I'll take care of it Ms. Miller said calm as always. Is there anything else at all that needs to be done Tina? Tina shyly gathered the glass beads and asked if it would be an inconvenience. Not at all Ms. Miller replied sounding thrilled at the venture.

Tina hadn't heard from Ms. Miller since Thursday when she took the veil. They had agreed to meet at the ceremony an hour early, and that's what she did. Ms. Miller met her in the parking lot with all the finishing touches. She had hired a pianist, a singer and a photographer from her church with her own money. She had champagne and glasses for a toast and of course flowers for everyone including Ray who would walk Tina down the ailse. She had also made a fabulous necklace and earrings with the remaining beads.

Tina couldn't wait to see the veil. As she dressed, Ms. Miller unwrapped her veil last, heightening the suspense. She had had it cleaned and stiffened, as well as added some of the glass beads. It looked twice as full and twice as glamorous. It was unspeakably beautiful. They both watched silently as Ms. Miller placed it on her head then burst into tears. Tina cherished her wedding veil and vowed it would be a lifelong keepsake.

The wedding was held at a small chapel near the justice of the peace who officiated the ceremony. It started on time a three o'clock on July twenty first. The wedding was short and sweet, just like Tina wished. There was a brief cake cutting and reception immediately following. Tina wanted to keep everything brief since she had to be at school early the following morning. They had promised to renew their vows with a more elaborate ceremony once they were both established and successful. Tina was most proud that Ray and her brothers and Ms. Miller had attended. Her mother was nowhere to be found.

Practically all of Greg's family was there, which was the first time she had met them. Even though the meeting was brief, Tina was quite impressed and somewhat intimidated. His family didn't seem too smittened with her. They inspected her as if they barely approved of Greg's choice.

There was virtually no time to honeymoon, but they managed another blissful encounter. Greg had taken care of that. Greg had rented a suite in the most expensive hotel in the city. The Rothwell Inn. Rothwell was the richest community in the city and their clubhouse, golf course and hotel were all gated and private. Tina wondered how Greg had managed but didn't take time to inquire. There was something else demanding her attention. Greg was an easy lover. He was slow and gentle and aimed to please his partner. Tina was thrilled about his slow winding twisting maneuvers, and he sweet talked his way through the entire process. Greg was a slow grinder, and that's what Tina wanted and needed. They drank expensive champagne and slowly grinded the night away.

Greg's parents were still married after thirty five years, a marvel to Tina. She hoped this was an indication of how her marriage to Greg would be. Greg had two sisters and one brothers who all attended their wedding. Greg was the baby of the family and the only one of the siblings who wasn't a lawyer, stock broker, or engineer, or any professional of sorts. This seriously concerned his family especially his father. His father insisted that every last one of his children be professionals and nothing less. Greg guaranteed his family that he was well on his way.

Greg had always been the rebel in his father's eyes. His father felt Greg would surely be the one to fail or miss the mark. But Greg swore to them all including Tina, on bended knee that he'd go straight to graduate school and graduate Magna Cum Laude. Tina felt his success was eminent.

Marriage was wonderful for Tina. Marriage exposed her to among other things the close family circle she had always craved. She and Greg spent a suitable amount of time around Greg's family. They congregated occasionally throughout the week and most Sunday afternoons. Tina wanted to slip into their family circle with ease. His family was somewhat gracious but not completely accepting of her. For the moment their half hearted acceptance was enough. Any family cohesiveness was just the kind of security Tina had always wanted.

Greg reluctantly agreed to move into the Whittenhall with Tina for sake of convenience and finances. He was not comfortable there never having lived in the projects before. He conceded that it was the best place for the moment.

Greg found it somewhat difficult to ease into Tina's inner family circle as well. Greg and Trey gradually bonded over a few months of casual encounters. When Trey was home with Greg the household was peaceful. Not the case with Rayshaun. Rayshaun was in and out of their lives and home, but it was never a peaceful stay. He hated Greg with a passion. In his mind he was still the man of the house and refused to have Greg or any other man running his house. He let Greg know that in his own hostile words. There was always the threat of a fight between the two of them.

Rayshaun was headstrong and so was Greg. Rayshaun was set and determined to get Greg out of the house. He didn't like Greg's kind as he put it. Greg was too soft, straight-edged and intellectual for Rayshaun's taste. If it wasn't for Tina, Rayshaun would stop short of nothing to get Greg out of the house.

Tina insisted that Rayshaun respect her husband, and keep his cool in her house. He tried to respect her wishes but the tension was always thick. Tina tried to vary her schedule and keep Rayshaun from being alone with Greg, but her schedule was far too busy for that.

As circumstances would fall, Tina walked into the house one day from a long day of study, test and clinicals. She dropped her book bag and headed up the stairs. She suddenly heard a scrambling sound in the kitchen. She rushed in to find Rayshaun holding Greg down on the floor with a knife in his hand. Tina screamed at Rayshaun to let him go. She rushed over to them and pulled them apart. Filled with anger, she insisted Rayshaun leave immediately. His face registered the confusion, hurt and betrayal he felt inside. He couldn't believe Tina had asked him to leave his own house. You against me Tina, he screamed shaking his hand in the air. Naw Tina. Naw Tina. He da one you spose ta kick out, he continued straightening things out with her. This soft shoe loafer wearing punk spose ta be the one to leave. Tina repeated firmly looking Rayshaun square in the face. Get out. Rayshaun cocked his head to the side in total disbelief. Tina could see the pain and tears in his eyes. Rayshaun dropped the knife, and headed for the door walking like a zombie. They parted that day for the longest, and widest division of their lives.

Chapter Five

Finding the Way

Greg didn't go straight to graduate school. He decided he'd work for a while and save up some money. He didn't like the first job he got, so he quit after only one month. He had clearly defined his goals and his path to success, and he refused to alter it in any way. After about two months past he found another job which he said was closer to his path and goals. Greg was a method man. The problem was he had only one method for doing everything. Anything that was not acceptable to him he immediately dismissed.

He was highly intelligent, but he seemed to have a slightly arrogant trait about him, which is why Tina was so surprised he had ever looked her way. He seemed to expect the world to be waiting at his feet. Since it didn't work that way he dismissed his second job as well. The manager, whose position Greg clearly felt he deserved for himself, told Greg to take responsibility for filing away all their claims. Greg promptly refused, but of course in a dignified manner. He wasn't the grumbling cursing type of man. He was a proper diction and large vocabulary type of man. But he wasn't about to become as he put it a pussy-assed file clerk. So he quit. In any case due to his intelligence or good fortune, he moved right into his third job with little delay. Tina still had honeymoon eyes for him and was very deeply in love with him. In fact, she still didn't see what he saw in her. He was a thin man of five feet ten inches tall. His cooper toned skin had sudden brassy flickers. He had the shiniest curly hair and the longest eyelashes she had ever seen on a man. His teeth were perfectly straight and frosty white. She could just sit and stare at him for hours. Often she did just that when he was asleep beside her.

He was a gentle, methodical lover. He was well equipped with both romantic and physical skills. He was generous with both fore and after play. He understood a woman's needs and how they differed from a man's. He was a thorough, sensitive, and complete lover. Tina was totally fulfilled with him physically.

Greg's family was close knit. They had migrated from the sticks of Alabama to Pennsylvania. However, there was no southern drawl in their diction. His father, the all powerful tyrant of his household, insisted that they all suppress it. His father (Walton Senior) was a towering large boned man. He was caramel toned with soft curly hair. He was very demanding and critical. His wife, Greg's mother, was a soft spoken very pale skinned lady. Greg often spoke of the lessons of color, status and prestige that were drilled into his head by his father from the time he was three years old. He felt color was of the utmost importance. Tina's dark skin tone made her a loser in Walton Senior's eyes. He didn't care to hear Greg's description of who and what she was. He didn't allow Greg to discuss her credentials or accomplishments with him. Tina knew instantly he was a King.

They met again at the Thanksgiving Dinner of their first anniversary of marriage. Walton Senior's eyes narrowed ever so slightly when he looked at her. It was like he was really seeing her for the first time. He didn't smile. His lips were pulled to the side and curled upward. He barely touched her hand when they shook. Unfortunately Tina was used to this reaction. Most people were a little less obvious, but there were many black people who had no tolerance for dark faces. Even if slight, disgust and hatred were always detectable, and immediately at that.

While Walton Senior told dirty jokes, Tina received a shocking revelation. While the soft snickers and pinched grins faded, Tina was connected to the veil as it lowered. Suddenly she was viewing the family's nakedness. She was able to see beyond the well groomed bodies and proper diction. With just a brief flash of keen focus she saw the entire Walton family sitting in a magnificent castle. They were dressed in highly expensive garb and jewels. There were splendid statues and precious whatnots scattered throughout the castle. All their fleshly desires were satisfied. Their castle sat perched high atop a pyramid of sand which was the fast indication of wealth in that place and time. But suddenly the pyramid collapsed. Their castle came crashing to the ground. They were chained and taken captive to a hooded clan. Their pleas and promises of payment served them no good in that time and place. They were beaten and killed without remorse. Tina gasped as she watched the gun smoke rings dissipate around their heads. She quickly wiped a tear away and pretended to eat her meal again. As the veil lifted she now could see the hatred, prejudiced and bondage they were all in. She saw a well educated, well off, good looking family in mental and emotional chains. It swiftly occurred to Tina that the systematic struggle that Ms. Miller had spoken of would never end. It was the mental and emotional bondage left behind. This was a bondage that doomed a race of people to enslavement to expensive clothes and jewels and cars, while their economic status declined. They were constantly trying to prove their self worth with the things they possessed. They found a way to elude themselves into thinking they fit into the higher echelons of society by anesthetizing themselves with expensive material things. They are blind to the fact that they are emotionally crippled and their expensive things in no way gives them acceptance beyond the ghetto streets they inhabit. Tina's heart pounded and ached while she struggled to abbreviate her sudden focus.

Even though Tina had seen with sharp focus the horrid revelation of mental and emotional bondage through Walton Senior's narrow eyes and frown, it stayed on her mind. When she returned home with Greg, who had noticed nothing of course, she locked herself in the bathroom and cried. She realized she had somewhere in the recesses of her mind, believed this would someday go away. Now she was sure it would never. She thought she had painstakingly built herself into a realistic, strong woman. She grounded herself with the knowledge from her understudy of life and intelligence from her education. She thought the needy ashamed little girl had been put to rest. She thought she had carried herself with confidence and pride until now. No one had penetrated her wall of awareness and self respect for years, until Walton Senior. She couldn't figure out how to match his slick fast wits or cruelty. Her wall tumbled down like a wall of cards. She continued staring at herself in the mirror. Anger welled up in her and she flung open the medicine cabinet. Reaching to the very back of the cabinet on her tip toes she figited for the skin bleaching cream and started to apply it heavily. The tears running down her face left tracks in the bleaching cream.

With barely a year past their first anniversary, Greg was on his fourth job. They were getting further behind in their bills every month. This didn't bother Greg. He spent money like it grew on trees. He brought a new suit for every interview. He added to his fine collection of jewelry and gold. He gave generous gifts of perfume and jewels to Tina too. The best of everything was his mantra. He felt no measure of overdue pain or responsibility. Se la vie, k ciera ciera, have faith in me baby was his response to all of Tina's concerns. I know what I'm doing. It would all magically work out somehow, at least in his mind. When Tina expressed her concerns about money he'd shush her and have her standby for his rabbit out of a hat trick. Tina's unenthusiastic reactions or responses simply hurt his ego, and prevented him from achieving or functioning at his optimum level so he claimed. Hence he began to fail at job after job. Greg still displayed high potential and value, but was easily frustrated when opposed or distracted. Yet again he was having problems on his job.

With the pressure of overdue bills, and poor credit status, Tina was forced to become a part time student in order to work and help pay the bills. With this adjusted schedule, her dreams of becoming a physician were fading hopelessly away. Without dreams of being a physician she worked hard on her marriage.

She felt she might lose her medical career, but she wouldn't allow herself to lose her husband.

Finally Greg couldn't adjust to life in the Whittenhall Projects. He began to complain bitterly. The loud noises, the nasty, dirty environment, the thugs and Dons were all an aversion to his success he complained. He also hated having so little in comforts and such meager things at that. Knowing this was the only place they could almost afford with all the bills they had, he agreed that they needed to stay there. He made it clear however, that he had to fix up the place to his comfort level. He deserved to be comfortable at least.

He shopped at the most expensive stores. He simply went to the furniture store, Clondikes Exclusive Furniture, no less, and filled each room one after the other. If he liked the display he'd purchase everything in it, including the pictures and the flowers.

With a succession of job failures behind him Greg became confused and angry. Tina felt his wrath was unjustly aimed at her. In any case, he was quite tormented and had to vent his pain. His path was no longer clear or defined. He had become a sketchy, irresponsible worker. His pay checks continually decreased. He would take off of work just to watch a television program, or meet with the guys on the corner. Tina could feel their relationship deteriorating as well. The main culprit was financial pressure. She felt she spent all of her time pleading with Greg to stop spending such large amounts of money. She thought a job would distract him as well as pay for some of his purchases. Deep inside however she also knew Greg's torment was restless and he wouldn't be able to settle down.

Tina wanted to help Greg refocus his energy. She still believed in his potential. She helped him search through newspapers and trade magazines for any positions she thought might be of interest to him. She submitted resumes' and letters for him. After a couple of months things were opening up for him. He had the option of three different job offers at the same time. He had aced the interview as he put it and gotten offered top dollar at the investment company. He started his fifth job with a new suit and a new attitude.

Only a month later Greg was threatening to quit his fifth job. He couldn't function under the management he was working with he claimed and he needed his space and freedom. It was an insult to his manhood he complained. Greg told Tina he was too smart to walk into a trap that he could see. So he quit his fifth job.

Tina felt guilty for blaming Greg for her falling behind in her program. He was not actually the blame. He had tried very hard to support them on his own. The weight and pressure was just too much for him, and unfair too. After all medical school was her choice. She chose to commit to the time and sacrifices. Why should Greg be deprived and uncomfortable? He at least deserved the bare necessities, a comfortable home.

Tina wanted their second anniversary to be happy. She tried to console Greg by promising they would move in the near future. Greg couldn't wait. He became absorbed in finding a new place. His employment search was secondary to buying a house. He spent most of the day searching the swankiest neighborhoods and pricey condos.

It was another four months before Greg found what he was looking for in a house. It was another three years before they qualified for a loan. It had been torturous for them both. Tina had crawled through medical school. It had been six hauntingly long years and graduation was on the horizon. By then they were both at their wit's ends. Greg was disenchanted over their housing situation and Tina was bidding away her time for graduation.

Finally the time arose. Tina went to pick up Ray, and her mother. Trey and Greg rode with Ms. Miller. They all proudly watched Tina cross the bridge into her brightly cast future. With residency and the state board exams ahead Tina sighed. Her relief was cautious.

Entering residency at a local hospital was a major benefit. The pace was twice as grueling as medical school, but at least there was some compensation. Tina often chuckled about the fact that she had graduated medical school and was making on the average about the same as when she worked at the shoe store. It's a living Tina would shrug her shoulders and chuckle. She only got a chance to see her family when she was off duty. Then she was usually so exhausted she slept most of the time off. She managed to visit Ms. Miller, and Trey and Ray.

Ray's visit were requiring a little more time these days. Tina found that she had to cook him something to eat or straighten the place up a little. Ray wouldn't admit it but he was losing much of his strength and energy. Tina did get him to admit he hadn't been eating or feeling well. He assured her he would come in for a full physical.

Residency was exciting and exhausting at the same time. Tina enjoyed treating the patients, but her loyalties were divided, making it harder to concentrate. She worried more and more about Greg.

Lately Greg had made some new friends. They seemed intelligent and nice enough Tina thought. They were forming a partnership to employ themselves and their people. Tina was marginally relieved to see Greg focused on employment. Greg had managed to network his way into a banking position he felt "pretty good about". He was a computer operator, and was enamored with the technology. He seemed to feel this position fit into his long term plans, and added an exceptional skill. He saw himself using the computer technology in a very creative way to make a lot of money and become independent he explained to Tina. Tina was happy to see her old Greg resurfacing.

This new venture kept Greg on the move. He was harder to see than anyone on her list. He travelled in and out of town with his new posse on the weekends, and worked Monday through Friday quite long hours. Tina had to schedule an appointment in advance to see him. She insisted that they make time for each other and love making.

Trey was finishing school. With a little persuasion from her and a lot from his brother, Trey decided to attend college. With Ms. Miller's help he got adequate financial aid to attend the college of his choice. He chose a southern black college, and a computer programming degree. Until time for Trey to leave Tina was piping with joy. When it was time for him to go, she could hardly stand to see him leave. Watching him as an independent young man was unbelievable. Everyone that she had started life out with had now parted from her. At least Trey's parting would result in something good so she thought.

With Trey parting, she now had more time to concentrate on caring for Ray. He had been somewhat feeble at Trey's graduation. That worried Tina, so she kept vigilant watch on him. Ms. Miller saw how much she loved Ray and stepped in again to help her. Still Ray was becoming weaker by the day. Tina put him in a wheelchair after he fell and cut his head on the sink. She and Ms. Miller did his shopping and cooked his meals and bought them to him. He was the most gracious old man Tina had ever met. Oh you didn't have to go to all this trouble for me baby. You know I can still make a mean bologna sammich. They still laughed together regularly, but Tina was very concerned.

She had just left Ray's house Saturday morning. She was slightly concerned because he was a bit lethargic and feverish. His blood pressure, heart and lungs sounded fine when Tina examined him. She read him a bible verse and kissed him on his forehead. He mustered a smile. She promised to check back on him when she got off work. He lingered on her mind throughout the day however. She called Ms. Miller and asked her to stop in and check on him. Ms. Miller went by with some dinner and found him on the floor in convulsions. She called the ambulance and had him rushed to the hospital. Tina was just about at the end of her shift, when she was paged on a code blue in the emergency room. She was on Neurology rotation. She was ending a twenty hour shift, but she responded to the page. This is what she studied and worked for all this time she told herself and ran to the emergency room.

When she arrived at the table the resident was pronouncing the patient dead on arrival (DOA). Tina took a look at the patient. It was Ray. Ray she called to him. She immediately started CPR then pleaded for the staff to resuscitate the patient. I want this man resuscitated by all means. The nurse promptly said yes doctor. Tina paused involuntarily. She tilted her head and let out a long breath. It was as if the words yes doctor had caught her by surprise. Then she immediately returned to work. Ray she called him. Don't leave. She persisted working and calling him determined to bring him back. Everything she had worked for, her long years of medical school, her grueling schedule had all come down to this moment. If she couldn't save Ray it would have all been worthless, she felt. Tina felt her energy draining from her. She was at the point of exhaustion, but refused to give up. Death was a combative opponent, but her determination was the greater in this case. Ray was revived, but in critical condition.

Ray recovered minimally. He was not the same man. Actually he was no longer a man at all. He was confined to his wheelchair. The aftermath of his stroke had left him paralyzed on his right side. He had no bladder or bowel control. During his hospital stay Ray drifted in and out of consciousness with little short term memory. Tina regretfully conceded that Ray would not be going home. She put him in a nursing home that she hand picked. She wasn't content to leave him at that. She took a part-time position on staff at the nursing home working her days off. She felt that it was the least she could do. Besides lately there was never anyone to go home to.

She knew that this would leave little if no time for Greg. It didn't seem to matter to him anymore. Greg still occupied many of her thoughts however. She didn't know whether to give up or what. Greg was always on one of his weekend business ventures or seminars. At least that's what he called them. These kept him away often. When they did see each other arguing and yelling or complete cold silence would fill their time. To her bitter disappointment it felt more relaxing to stay away. She had to minimize her stress as much as possible.

Even though Ray was now terminally ill, Tina still enjoyed visiting with him. On his lucid days he remembered her and his apartment. He always felt the need to go home and do some nagging chore like his laundry or wash the breakfast dishes. There were many lucid enjoyable visits, but Tina could still see Ray's deterioration. She was careful to keep her official examining visits, and her friendly visits separate. More and more often Ray was not lucid. He rambled on about his memories of his childhood or young manhood.

The hard part about being a doctor was knowing the inevitable. Ray was becoming more confused. Tina regretted the visits when Ray didn't recognize her at all or worse yet confused her with of all people, her mother. Some days he was convinced that she was his long lost love Gloria Johnson. He was sure she had agreed to marry him and it was their wedding day. He sometimes had his male prowess on his mind. Tina still found it strange that men never forgot that. He made illicit offers which sometimes shocked Tina. C'mon here sweet honey. Sit right here on papa's lap and wiggle yo sweet lil bottom, right chair. Then he'd giggle merrily. Never were these antics pulled on Ms. Miller. He always referred to Ms. Miller as the supervisor that always smells so good. For some reason he behaved himself around her. Ms. Miller had that affect on most people. The two of them were Ray's only regular visitors.

Tina hadn't thought much about Ray's family of survivors until now. She realized she needed to get his affairs in order. She had no legal jurisdiction, and needed to find out who did. She began the long search that would stretch out past his natural life.

Her life was still such a juggling act, even with Trey gone and Ray in the nursing home. She had parted paths with so many of her loved ones, but she still kept tabs on each of them. She hadn't seen Greg for three weeks, but they had spoken briefly over the telephone. They agreed to meet at home that weekend. Their schedules were the only thing that allowed them to stay married, never seeing one another long enough to break up. This arrangement seemed to suit Greg well. He was quite content, which signaled to Tina he was satisfying his manhood elsewhere. Everytime she thought of that she wanted to cry to her breaking point. Somehow she'd always manage to pull herself back from the edge. Usually she called Ms. Miller for a quick talk or visit. Sometimes even a visit with Ray did the trick.

She hadn't taken time to realize before now that this was the first time she wasn't going to live in the projects or on the streets. Greg however had been insistent and anxious to get out of the Whittenhall Projects. She had vetoed every home he found. The ones he had picked were far to plush and big. Greg wanted a flashy display for his boys. He wanted to be the high roller that everyone looked up to. He didn't count the cost. He just rolled the dice. Tina was making some money but she was also in a lot of debt. Yet, as he told it, living in the Whittenhall impeded his drive and creativity. He therefore couldn't find a way to make enough money to take care of his family. Tina tried but couldn't make him grasp the reality of their financial situation. Greg argued that being around the filth and drugs there in the Whittenhall depressed him and pulled him down. When he played his big card, everything exploded into a fierce war. He threatened to move on his own without her. They fought back and forth over and over again. There was no conversation when they were together unless it was an argument. The pressure was actually infringing on Tina's work. She finally could no longer stand it. She conceded.

Greg conceded slightly as well. Greg conceded on the size of the house they were going to buy but not the location. He had to have something impressive. He finally chose a relatively small place, but the neighborhood was quite upscale. The house was quaint and cute. Tina also had to admit the cleanliness and quietness of the area was refreshing. It did relieve the pressure at some level to simply walk up to the door without stepping over broken glass, cigarette butts and drunken bodies. The silence was truly relaxing as well. She looked around and was filled with instant pride. These were the reasons she hated to doubt Greg. As impractical as it all was it sure felt dammed good.

They had barely unlocked the front door when Greg's new preoccupation became furnishing the place and making it really nice. He swore he'd keep his bank job and pay off everything he bought. Greg's job bought in comparatively little income for the size of his taste. Between medical school bills, malpractice insurance and Greg's expensive taste, Tina struggled constantly to keep the household going including their relationship. She had hoped that moving into the new house would give their marriage a boost. It did in some ways for a while.

Greg had the place completely furnished within a couple of months. It was outstandingly attractive. It looked like a layout for a real estate magazine or showcase home. His taste was undeniably exquisite. Since he was home alone most of the time, it was designed for his taste. Tina loved seeing the pride in his eyes. His contentment bought a level of peace back to their relationship.

Greg was a very social person. He had friends and family over day and night. Tina knew she might come in any time day or night and find people there, some familiar and some strangers. Tina thought her requests that Greg curve the parties, would be approved. Instead Greg became irritated and told her in a seething rage, she should appreciate him being home and not running the streets. She decided to relent. She didn't want to start a whole new war.

Late one afternoon Tina came home. She was waiting on Greg. She thought she'd do some light cleaning and make a nice dinner. She looked forward to sleeping next to him for the rest of the evening. They needed to talk, but she wanted to make it as pleasant as possible. They had finally found a place suitable for Greg's taste but barely suitable for their pocket books. She hadn't been able to spend much time there as it were. She was always too busy at the hospital or taking care of Ray. Now for the first time it seemed she had time to really examine and enjoy it. She walked from room to room scanning it slowly with her eyes.

It was a small carpenter style house, in the lower end of the pricy Blue Rock neighborhood. She was cleaning up the place a little and hoping Greg would be home shortly. She didn't have much to do. Greg was, if nothing else, very neat. A pillow out of place here or there, a little vaccuming is generally all that was needed. That's why it was a shock to her when she went upstairs to the bedroom to find a terrible mess. It appeared that Greg had left suddenly. There were towels and clothes everywhere. The dresser where his cologne usually sat orderly inside their boxes, were thrown about. Some of the bottles were even outside the boxes. More strangely, some of the tops were off of the bottles. It almost looked as if a kid had climbed on the dresser and played dress up. Greg never made this kind of mess Tina thought. She felt a nagging uneasiness, but she shrugged it off. His stacked shoe boxes, which were normally color coordinated and stacked neatly under the suites that he wore them with, were thrown about the floor. It looked as if he couldn't find the shoes he wanted and had thrown a temper tantrum. Maybe he was really late this morning, and made a mess of the bedroom and bathroom getting ready, Tina heard herself speak. She started picking them up and putting them back in the boxes. Two mix matched shoes were left once she'd stacked the boxes back in the closet. Tina scratched her head.

She couldn't figure it out. It was so unlike Greg to lose or scatter his shoes. She searched the bedroom and the adjoining bathroom and the closet shelves all to no avail. She found herself looking in silly places. Why am I looking in the dresser drawers for a shoe she said to herself. She decided to call off the search.

All of the moving and stirring had made her thirsty. She went downstairs to the kitchen for a glass of cold water. She wasn't surprised to open the refrigerator and find an empty water pitcher. Humph men, she snickered. She went to the faucet and filled her glass with luke cool water. She moved about the kitchen slowly as she sipped it down. She gravitated toward the kitchen door casually thinking she'd better check it for locked. As she approached she realized that a large object was protruding through the glass window of the door. Her heart jumped and pounded. Her first question was had someone tried to break in? Fear started to slowly drizzle over her as she cautiously approached closer. Had someone actually broken in? When she got to the door she refocused her eyes, then pulled her brows down. It was one of the shoes she been searching for upstairs. Tina checked the door to see if it was locked. It was. She pulled the shoe out of its lodged place and the glass fell to the floor around her feet. She stared out the window and about the back entrance. Everything looked perfectly still and quiet. She was completely baffled, as she backed away with the shoe still in her hand. She wandered into the breakfast room, a small nook in the corner of the kitchen. Her eyes were still examining the shoe when she realized there was glass all over the floor and the table in the nook. She gasped. She recognized the broken pieces. They were her dinner plates from out of the cabinet. Tina ran out of the kitchen screaming. She was panicked. Maybe someone had abducted Greg or beaten him up and locked him in the basement. She ran back to the bedroom. She was acting on sheer impulse at this point. She snatched the phone form the nightstand and dialed the police. She ran into the bathroom with the shoe still in her hand. The phone was ringing and her heart was pounding hard. She felt she should hide in case someone was in the house. She snatched back the shower curtain, and jumped in the bathtub. Something curious grazed her periphal vision. The window was open and an aqua blue bra was dangling over the edge of the window. It looked like someone tried to throw it outside in a hurry and simply missed. It was plain to see there had been a fight here but still too many pieces of the puzzle were missing. Tina was still analyzing the scenario, when a voice came over the receiver which was now hanging from the coil over her shoulder. Tina was sure Greg hadn't thrown the bra in the window. He was a better shot than that she thought. She'd seen him play basketball. She lifted the bra up in the air toward the light of the window. She examined it closely. She was startled by a voice yelling twelvth precinct. Never mind she screamed back at the receiver and threw it down not bothering to hang it back up. She wondered now where was the other shoe. She needed it to finish piecing together her crime scene.

She began to search again. By now she had developed the prowess of a detective, and nothing escaped her notice. The bedroom window curtain was torn. The mirror was smeared like someone had thrown something and tried to wipe it off quickly with a piece of toilet paper. A handle was broken on one of the dresser drawers. She moved over to the bed, and snatched the messy covers completely off of the bed and threw them in the middle of the floor. There were two pairs of panties. Two pairs Tina screamed out puzzled. Two pairs, a beige pair and an aqua pair which obviously matched the bra from the window. Tina ran out of the bedroom and grabbed the phone on the first floor. She started leaving messages all over town for Greg. She waited the entire night, but Greg never called or returned home.

The next morning Greg called her at the hospital. Too busy to talk at the time she asked him to meet her at the nursing home while she visited Ray later that evening.

When Greg entered the room he looked extra fine and polished. She could hardly stop herself from jumping into his arms and smothering him with kisses. Greg nodded his head acknowledging Tina, then bent to eye level with Ray in the wheelchair. He took Ray's hand and spoke to him gently. Tina remembered why she fell I love with him. His voice was calm, deep and strong. It washed over Tina like a cool shower. The baritone in his voice excited both her and Ray. Ray turned his head slowly toward the voice and his mouth fell open in utter surprise. Ray's eyes were wide and tearful. Aaaawh, ooooh, boy where you been Sammie boy? Now here you is. Ray squeezed Greg's hand and pulled it up to his eyes. Then he bowed his head and sobbed like a baby. I dun told mama I was gon brang you home boy. Now here you is Ray moaned. Tina stepped between them and lifted Ray's face. Ray Ray she called, trying to jolt him. He looked at her slightly annoyed. Ray this is Greg not Sammie boy, she commanded. This is Greg my husband. This is not Sammie boy, she talked slow as if that would help the words penetrate the senility. Who is Sammie boy Ray she asked patiently. My baby brother, Mama's boy he answered still somewhat annoyed with her. But Ray this is Greg Walton. Say something, she nudged Greg. Ray how you doing, I'm Greg. Again Ray turned to the voice and called Sammie boy more convinced than ever. C'mon boy let's gone on home. Mama nem all waiting for us. He sobbed again. Tina told Greg to leave, and she'd meet him at home. She stayed with Ray for the next couple of hours and tried to calm him down. Finally Tina gave him a mild sedative to sleep.

Ray died in his sleep that night. Tina called her mother and even Rayshaun and informed them. She rearranged her schedule at the hospital, and made arrangements to spend the next week cleaning out his apartment. She could ill afford the time, but it was necessary.

Tina realized you don't know someone until you clean out their apartment. Going through Ray's things she found tons of letters addressed to her mother, Gloria Johnson. She found pictures from down south with Ray and his siblings all labeled by name and date. He had tons of books on Alcoholism and Drug Addiction. Ray was far more organized and intelligent than she had ever imagined. She found his legal affairs in order, and well maintained. She found a complete, signed and notorized will. The only surprise was that he had named her executor of his estate. How'd you know Ray she heard her own voice speak aloud. More surprisingly she found legal papers regarding her and her brothers. Apparently Ray had tried to adopt her and her two brothers when they were young. The court had denied him adoption and guardianship in favor of her mother. Tina felt her anger rising. They don't give a lovely fig about little black kids she said out loud, still staring at the papers. We could have been saved all that pain and suffering she mumbled on. We could have had a roof over our heads day and night she continued shaking her head from side to side. She felt she was about to cry. She placed the letter back in the envelope. Thank you Ray. Thank you for trying she said out loud again.

It took the next few days before she finished going through all of the letters Ray had left behind. She had a much clearer picture of his realationship with her mother and what drove them apart. The last straw between them was Ray's attempt to adopt them. Even though they were wedged apart Ray had repeatedly asked Gloria for her hand in marriage. Instead Gloria took off with them and didn't allow them to stay in Ray's company for long afraid that he'd try to abduct them. Tina wondered if that was why they never settled in one place. Tina hated her mother now.

The next box of Ray's was a cigar box wrapped in a plastic bag, and placed inside a brown paper bag. Tina had expected it to be filled with sentimental whatnots. Instead Ray had stashed his important financial papers there. Tina just always assumed that Ray never had much money. She blinked and squeezed her eyes tightly over and over when she read his bank statement. Ray had saved nearly thirty thousand dollars. Twenty seven thousand eight hundred and ninety two dollars, Tina said out loud in disbelief. Oh yeah and sixty three cents she mumbled non chalantly. All this time they all thought Ray was living meagerly out of necessity. There were a few personal letters mixed in with the business. They actually seemed to be more like diary letters. Some letters in the same bag confirmed that Ray had made a considerable amount of money when he owned the corner bar where they used to wait for her mother to pick up her next trick. She hated calling her mother a whore, but she finally accepted that she conducted herself as one.

Ray had also lost a lot of money in bad investments and loans he'd tried to extend to family and friends. All in all he had managed a successful business at one time. It seems that when he lost the love of his life, he lost his drive and ambition. He had just managed to hold on to the last thirty thousand dollars.

There was another small envelope. It contained a stack of small certificates. Tina inspected them carefully. They looked quite important and to Tina's suspicion somewhat familiar. She read the small note wrapped around it written in Ray's own script. It read: this is the envelope Gloria gave to Tina that day. Tina couldn't believe her eyes. It all flooded back at once. She could see her mother's panicked face as she jumped into the car and screamed go! That turquoise blue dress and shoes to match she had on running down the street was a blur. Tina remembered the trust she'd sealed in her heart when she shoved the envelope in her hand and said keep this. Tina tasted the saltiness of her tears. I must have left this in Ray's car she said aloud wiping her eyes and nose with her forearm. These are mature bank bonds Tina said reading the fine print on the certificate. She must have stolen them from the angry store owner that chased her down the street. Tina slammed the cigar box shut and huffed. She headed immediately to see her mother. Gloria's gonna have to tell the whole truth for once in her life Tina yelled into the air.

Chapter Six

Eventuality

Tina still felt the frustration of not getting through to Greg. He partied harder than ever with his friends in the new house. He missed work often. Some days he was quite late and others he simply just didn't make it to work at all the following morning. Either way was fine with him. Needless to say he lost job number six.

He was ignoring the bills and creditors that called constantly. He decided he needed seed money for a fool proof investment now that would save them from all of their credit worries. He began to complain to Tina constantly. He pleaded for her trust in his business venture. He accused her of not having faith in him and his goals. He assured her with this one last venture they'd hit the big time and be able to live the "good life" as he put it.

Tina tried over and over again to reason with him about their debt. When Tina refused to go along with his plan, Greg was furious. The long battles and inflating debt, left her depressed and exhausted. Her concentration was poor and her drive was gone. She was in jeopardy of being expelled from her residency program. The chief resident had already informed her that she would have to make immediate arrangements to resolve her personal problems or leave the residency program.

The choices were bitter. She could easily work as a nurse practitioner, or with certification as a physician's assistant. Either would allow her to make a comfortable living. That would allow Greg to focus on his venture. But medicine was now more than a means of making a living. She was no longer in it for the money or title. She had the unbelievable opportunity to save lives, and it meant the world to her. Losing her place in the residency program was nearly unthinkable. The other option was for her to give up on her marriage. It was the staple and pillar of her life. With her rocky unstable beginning she had no greater fantasy than a solid family life, with a loving man.

As much as she loved Greg, their relationship had deteriorated into a slew of daily arguments, and seething grunts and groans. It had taken its toll on them both. Finally Greg packed his clothes and left. Greg like most men didn't understand that loss of love in your life was also loss of power. Love is the most powerful thing in a person's life. The players, the macs, and the pimps didn't seem to realize that. The lesson love teaches most frequently is that love is forgiving but the more you push it out or throw it away the longer it takes to return to you. Yet they destroyed love like it was poison. In essence, they destroyed their own power as if it was useless to them.

Despite their battles Tina couldn't be happy without Greg in her life. She wanted to share her life with him and more than anything she wanted to have his baby. Begging had supplied her with her survival in her early years. She thought she had broken free of that life when she left her mother, but she couldn't stand to lose Greg especially at this point in her life. She had recently lost Ray. Trey had claimed his independence. Rayshaun, she hung her head for a moment, was probably lost to the streets forever. She felt the tears well up in her eyes. Losing Greg or anyone else right now would be overwhelming for her. Greg was the last of her immediate family and she couldn't bear to lose him. She had to do what she had to do-beg. It was her life's lesson from her mother. Begging seemed her only resort. She begged relentlessly.

Finally she lured Greg home with only the clothes on his back. He still refused to commit to a permanent return. Instead Greg was still angry, and hammered her about her lack of faith in him. He continued to argue that he needed a woman who would fully trust in him. That to him was the epitome of love. Tina laid next to him in bed listening silently. He hit her with the hardest words she'd ever heard him say. You don't love me he groaned over and over. There was no way he could believe what he just said Tina thought. The sting from his words lingered and swelled inside her. The words rose from her feet to her ears as if she was being submerged in a pool of water, and drowned in the words. Everything went black before her eyes.

She resisted drowning. She gasped and caught a large breath of air. Greg was still commanding her obedience, but she could only see his sexiness. She lunged forward and knocked him over in the bed, pulling the covers over them both. He was yelling some fool hardy words which she ignored. She ripped his clothes off and smothered his mouth with hers. She just wanted him to make love to her. She closed her eyes and pretended that all their problems had disappeared. She cupped his thin firm buttocks and guided him into her coochie. For one more night their relationship had transcended the routine rut and misery. For the moment that was enough for Tina.

Greg moved back home, but he didn't bring everything back with him. Tina could feel the distance in his heart. She focused her free time at home with him. Still she could detect the division in his heart. It was not all there with her. Tina wondered who was holding the other half of his heart. Still they agreed to start a family, and making it was all the fun.

Greg still bitterly complained that he needed investment money. Tina had taken the thirty thousand dollars from Ray and paid back some school loans and bills and it was exhausted. But Greg was more and more insistent that if they were to have a family he would need to have his own business.

When he seduced Tina over dinner she listened to his whole foolproof, five year plan. His eyes were sparkling in the dusk light. Sounding like a Wall Street genius he explained that he only needed fifty thousand dollars and it would all work out. Tina had to admit Greg was a brilliant businessman. He impressed her thoroughly. Afraid more of losing him again, Tina conceded.

They went the following morning and filled out the loan papers using the new house as collateral. The loan officer promised it would only take one week for the processing and Greg could pick up the check. Tina started her new rotation with a fresh bundle of energy and excitement. Greg's smile was like fuel in her veins.

The hospital was very busy as she suspected. She thought of Greg often throughout her day. She'd sneak off and call him every chance she got, which wasn't often. She felt like a school girl hiding in the girls room to smoke or do some other bad deed. It was refreshing.

Over the first few days she called the house several times, but got no answer. A few wicked thoughts crossed her mind but she dismissed them. She reassured herself that Greg was busy setting up his business venture. She knew how devoted Greg was when he set his mind to something.

The next weekend she was off work. She still hadn't spoken to Greg, but decided they would celebrate tonight. She stopped by the store and brought cake and champagne. She opened the door and dropped the champagne bottle on the floor. The house was stripped bare including the pictures on the wall. The living room furniture was gone. Tina ran from room to room screaming for Greg. There was dead silence. She grabbed the phone to call the police. It was dead silent too. Tina ran through the house searching the closets and bathroom cabinets until the picture came into focus. Tina collapsed on the bare floor and sobbed uncontrollably.

The next morning she felt numb all over. The silence in her house screamed out to her, calling her stupid and foolish. It filled her heart and head with dread and confirmed her loss. The tears flooded her eyes effortlessly. She dragged herself to the bathroom and looked in the mirror. She didn't care how horrid she looked. It was ironic at this point, she had no medicine for what she felt. She heard a barrage of questions in her head. One question kept recurring. Why did he leave me? That question hung around her neck like a noose. She had given him everything she had to give and then some. The song of the Kings and Judges was viciously turned up in her head, and she cowered on the floor.

Tina was stuck in her house ravaged with her pains and fears. It had all caught up to her. Like a street brat that had overstepped her boundaries, she had been caught in a trap like any common rodent. She lost track of time and reality. She lay sprawled across her floor for what she wanted to be forever, hoping time would end. She stared straight ahead in a daze. The light outside her window rose and fell over and over, but she never made a sound.

The sounds of the traffic passing by and occasional car horns shattered her bridge and she had to start all over again. She spiraled into her dense darkness, with the torn off noose still hanging around her neck. She could see herself in a deeply wooded forest. She had to get across the water since the edge of the earth she stood on was crumbling. There were tiny slivers of wood everywhere. She realized quickly that each sliver fitted another in a particular way. She had to build a bridge across the never ending water to the other side of the earth. She had to move quickly and quietly. Heavy weights and loud noises loosened the ground underneath her much more rapidly. She started over again and again because of the noises. She pushed them back further and further, the noise makers, until there was total silence again. She opted for total silence. It was the only way she could build her bridge. There was total silence for forty days and forty nights.

Suddenly, the loudest sound exploded through her ear. Her eyes widened. She realized she had never shut them as they moved quickly about the room. It was very bright, and she could barely see. The sound exploded once again. She felt a jolt to her body. It was Ms. Miller. She asked Ms. Miller if she had finished her bridge and made it across the water.

Ms. Miller found Tina on the floor in her own filth. She called an ambulance and had Tina rushed to the hospital. Seven days of rest in the hospital and therapy bought reality rushing back on it's evil course. Greg had cashed the check and disappeared forfeiting the collateral, their house. With her credit and her career severely damaged, she moved back to the Whittenhall. It was the natural law of nature. When all else fails you resort back to what you know best. For Tina she figured that was ghetto life. She figured the irony was fitting. She'd be the only medical doctor living in the projects. What was more appropriate for a street brat that tried to move beyond her station in life.

Her short respite from Whittenhall had spoiled her. She stood watching out the window of her fifth floor apartment. The sounds and voices jolted her. Bitter contentions, words shot back and forth like guns between the residents saddened her. Hell was her home and a safety net that had caught her from hitting the ground.

The stench of piss, and fried swine furrowing through her window actually made her nauseous. Whittenhall looked and seemed so familiar to her, but it felt totally different. It wasn't as easy to go back as she had thought it would be. She knew she had to turn back to her career in medicine if she was going to save her own life. She wrote a letter to her hospital board and chief resident officer. She pleaded with them to return to her residency. She visited the hospital regularly and tried to keep in touch with her training. Two weeks later she got a letter from the hospital review board stating that she could start her residency over the following year.

Tina wanted to be close to medicine until she could get back into her training. She went to the neighborhood clinic and took a position as a physician's assistant (P.A.). She felt satisfied to be able to practice medicine and help her community. There she treated several of the Kings and Judges and neighborhood high rollers that had mistreated her in her childhood. When she'd ask if they remembered her most of them didn't. More irony she thought. Their words and song was vivid in her ears and they didn't even remember her. She still found it interesting to treat them and see where their lives had led them. Often Tina found their lives had led them essentially nowhere.

One morning she was treating a crack addicted mother. Tina wasn't startled or surprised. She treated several drug addicted people in the community. She still tried with all her might to convince them to break the addiction. Most cases were useless though. She still presented the mother with a pamphlet and instructions on how to begin to break free of drug addictions. She thought just maybe this mother would try to save herself and her child. But when the mother called her little baby girl a black sambo for touching the doctor's stethoscope, Tina lost control.

How dare you speak to her like this Tina barked. She is a little person in need of love and attention. How dare you provide such a miserable existence for her, simply because you can't accept your own failures. How dare you put her in such danger and blame her for the hell you're in. She is a beautiful little girl. How dare you ruin her mind with your own self hatred and self destruction. You're self medicating with drugs to hide your own vulnerability. You better pull yourself together or you'll be dead in a year, and you'll have given her nothing but a bad example to remember.

Tina was livid. She immediately called Child Welfare Services and had the little girl removed from her home. Tina petitioned the court for custody and was granted full custody of three year old Natasha Cummings. Tina was over joyed and proud. It had been a while since she had had to care for anyone else. She had longed to start a family with Greg, and now motherhood was calling her. She felt like she was strong enough to protect and nurture her new little girl. She adorned her and felt she had a lot to offer her. Tina knew she could change the course of Natasha's life for the better.

When Natasha arrived Tina could tell that ghetto life and Kings and Judges had effected her. Natasha was afraid to trust her. She was afraid to show affection. She was afraid of abandonment. Tina cuddled her and took Natasha to the mirror daily and held her finger to her face. She outlined her eyes with her finger and told Natasha to repeat after her. I am beautiful because God made me beautiful just like I am. Natasha's little voice cracked as she tried to bravely repeated the words, but self hatred had already been bred within her. Tina was determined to remove it.

It took months of loving, nurturing and affection before Natasha could trust Tina. She constantly assured Natasha she would never leave her or hurt her. Finally after tons of toys and candy, Tina felt they had sealed their bond.

It was time for Tina to start her residency again. She helped Natasha understand what she was going to do and why. She introduced her to Linda. Needless to say Linda fell in love with Natasha immediately. Natasha trusted Linda immediately. Tina left her baby at Linda's daycare where she knew Natasha would be loved and nurtured. She bought her home as often as she could, but felt guilty about leaving her. She knew that in the end it would all be to Natasha's benefit. Natasha responded well to the love and devotion as most children do. Linda's environment was good for her.

Time flew by and Tina excelled throughout her residency. She completed her hours and training, but not without growing stronger and more determined still. Ms. Miller made it a point to be her first official patient at the clinic. Tina thanked her with a complete physical and plan of care. She knew she couldn't have made it without Ms. Miller. She never let Ms. Miller forget her appreciation.

It was another two years before Tina had straightened out her credit and paid off many of her bills. After a total of six years since she lost her house and Greg she was able to move out of the Whittenhall again. She bought a small house in Wellesly Township, just big enough for her and Natasha. Finally the work had begun to pay off.

One morning while she was fixing breakfast Natasha ran into the kitchen with her wedding veil on. Tina laughed histerically at the sight of it. She hadn't seen the veil since her wedding day. She took the veil off Natasha's head and placed it on her own. She went to the mirror to look at herself. She smiled wide and started to remember her journey. Before she knew it there was a well garbed African queen staring back at her in the mirror. The queen stood erect and confident. Her eyes were glowing like white diamonds. She stared directly into Tina's eyes, piercing her heart. She invited Tina to sit on the throne in front of her. Behind her stood a myriad of proud warrior queens of all different colors and tribes. They were a fierce, loyal sisterhood. Tina obliged. The queen added a row of tall pillars to Tina's veil. Tina instantly knew she had been assigned to royalty. A new song started to play in her head. It was a song of love and wealth. She straightened her posture. Tina took a long deep breath. She stared at herself until her eyes sparkled like the diamonds of the queen's. She knew she had to wear the veil everyday in a sense of protecting her community. It was only right. Through her veil she had seen the self medicating choices made by her community. Their continual purchase of fancy clothes, cars and jewelry, was their attempt to validate themeselves. Yet it was as fleeting as grains of sand in their hands.

Tina decided to volunteer at the neighborhood clinic indefinitely. She also started a "drug and alcohol free" program in the Whittenhall projects.

Tina felt her journey had finally led her to self-love and security. She shook her head and realized she had won over all the Kings and Judges, over all the sins and failures of her mother, over her fight to get out of the ghetto, over all her own demons, over everyone's expectations of her. She had finally prevailed.